Visions of the New World in the Drama of Lope de Vega

American University Studies

Series II
Romance Languages and Literature
Vol. 67

PETER LANG
New York • Bern • Frankfurt am Main • Paris

Robert M. Shannon

Visions of the New World in the Drama of Lope de Vega

PETER LANG
New York • Bern • Frankfurt am Main • Paris

Library of Congress Cataloging-in-Publication Data

Shannon, Robert M.
Visions of the New World in the drama of Lope de Vega.

(American university studies. Series II, Romance languages and literature ; vol. 67)
Bibliography: p.
1. Vega, Lope de, 1562-1635 – Criticism and interpretation. 2. Vega, Lope de, 1562-1635 – Political and social views. 3. Explorers in literature. 4. Indians of South America in literature. I. Title. II. Series.
PQ6490.H5S53 1989 862'.3 87-29319
ISBN 0-8204-0574-4
ISSN 0740-9257

CIP-Titelaufnahme der Deutschen Bibliothek

Shannon, Robert M.:
Visions of the new world in the drama of Lope de Vega / Robert M. Shannon. – New York; Bern; Frankfurt am Main; Paris: Lang, 1989.
(American University Studies: Ser. 2, Romance Languages and Literature; Vol. 67)
ISBN 0-8204-0574-4

NE: American University Studies / 02

Printed by Weihert-Druck GmbH, Darmstadt, West Germany

I am very grateful to SAINT JOSEPH'S UNIVERSITY for its support of my research.

*I dedicate this, my first re-creation, to my mom, JESSIE SHANNON, and to my friend, colleague, teacher, and fellow-*lopista*, WILLARD KING.*

Contents

Contents

Introduction

It is a curious fact that Golden Age drama remained relatively silent about the conquest of America until the end of the 16th century. Marcos Morínigo, author of *América en el teatro de Lope de Vega,* discusses, however, one obscure 16th century play entitled *Auto de las cortes de la muerte,* composed by Micael de Carvajal and Luis Hurtado ca. 1552–57. This play, according to Morínigo, was published in Toledo in 1557 and was performed frequently. The uniqueness of the play rests principally on its clear support of Las Casas. Morínigo states, " . . . el auto nace bajo la sugestión directa de la *Destruyción* del P. Las Casas y repite muchos de sus argumentos . . . "[1]

Because *Las cortes de la muerte* reflects some of the controversies surrounding the Conquest which will be explored in Lope de Vega's plays, a brief sampling of relevant scenes is useful. A clear reminiscence of Las Casas is found in scene 19 when an Indian cacique and his retinue appear before the Court of Death to lament their ill treatment at the hands of ruthless Spaniards. The cacique says,

> Los indios occidentales
> y estos caciques venimos
> a tus cortes triunfales
> a quejarnos de los males
> y agravios que recibimos.[2]

The Indians express their gratitude for the salvation of their souls through their conversion to Christianity; however, they complain of the cruelty of the conquistadores and their exclusive interest in American wealth:

Por sacarles los anillos
¿qué dedos no se cortaron?
¿Qué orejas para zarcillos
no rompieron con cuchillos?
¿Qué vientre no traspasaron
las espadas con gran lloro?
Destos males, ¿qué pensaron?
¿Qué en sus cuerpos sepultaron
nuestros indios sus tesoros? (321)

"La Muerte" sympathizes with the plight of the Indians and attempts to comfort them by telling them that just as God rescued them from idolatry, so He shall free them from the "lobos robadores."

This play also introduces three saints—Saint Augustine, Saint Dominic, and Saint Francis—all of whom beg the Indians to be patient. Scene 19 ends with the saints' interpretation of the significance of the discovery of America to Spain:

San Francisco: ¡Oh, Indias, pluquiera a Dios
que vuestra tierra cocida
y oro no diérades vos;
pues por ella hay entre nos
tanta multitud perdida!
Porque cuanto allá se afana
con trabajos, con pendencias
no hay médico que lo sana
que, al fin, cuanto se gana
va con muy malas conciencias. (44)

. . . .

Santo Domingo: Di, India, ¿por qué mostraste
a Europa esos tus metales
falsos con que la llevaste,
y después nos la enviaste
cargada de tantos males?
¿No le bastaban las minas
de pecados que tenía
tan profundas y continas
sino cargarla de espinas
con que mata cada día?
¡Oh, India, que diste puertas
a los míseros mortales

para males y reyertas!
Indias que tienes abiertas
las gargantas infernales!
¡India, abismo de pecados!
¡India, rica de maldades!
¡India de desventurados!
¡India, que con tus ducados
entraron las torpedades! (33)

While the saints exhort the Indians to bear their sorrows with patience, the spirits of earthly pleasure—the Devil, the Flesh, and the World—rejoice in their triumph over the forces of good.

Satanás: ¡Como! ¿Y piensan de estorbar
que las gentes no pasasen
a las Indias a robar?
¿No saben que es el caudal
y la mejor granjería
de la región infernal?
Mas, en fin, el oro es tal,
qu es piedra-imán que traía.

Carne: Hermano, ¿no ves las galas
del mundo fuera de ley;
cuántos palacios y salas,
y a cada ruin nacen alas
de vestirse como el rey?
Pues, ¿cómo puede sufrirse
si no van allá a buscar
para el comer y vestirse
y si no dejan morirse,
que acá no hay do lo ganar?
Las mujeres bastan solas
a echar allá a sus maridos,
que como unas amapolas
andan ya con largas colas
en sus trajes y vestidos;
sustendaldas por ahí
si la India no provee;
que no hay un maravedí,
si no van por ello allí
y allá los quiero: (me cree).

Mundo: ¡Gran cosa es la libertad

y estar libres de mujeres
y de hijos, en verdad!
La India gran calidad
tiene para los placeres.
Carne: El vivir allá es vivir
que acá no puede valerse;
lo que yo te sé decir
que pocos verás venir
que no mueran para volverse. (33)

The depiction of the role of the Spaniards in America is, of course, highly unfavorable. The quest for gold propels men of low birth to abandon all Christian principles for worldly pleasures. Spanish women are no less guilty; they encourage their husbands to cross the Atlantic in order to satisfy their own greed. Spanish moralists like Carvajal and Hurtado considered America to be the seat of sin and religious ignorance. The natives are ignorant of religious truth and continue their idolatry, and the Spanish settlers abandon their faith for secular pleasures. Morínigo concludes, " . . . ya desde mediados del siglo XVI estaba bastante difundido, por lo menos en ciertos círculos, el pensamiento de que el oro de las Indias contribuía a relajar la moral."[3]

The *Auto de las cortes de la muerte* offers only one scene showing the ill-treatment of the American Indians by the Spaniards. It has been suggested, however, that ca. 1585 in Cervantes' heroic drama *La Numancia* there are implied criticisms of Spanish conduct in the New World. In an article entitled "Cervantes' *Numancia* and Imperial Spain" Willard King argues that there exists in the play a parallel between the oppressive Roman armies and the Spanish Imperial armies which strove to incorporate the native Americans into the Empire. She writes:

> It requires little effort of imagination on our part, and surely it required none on Cervantes', to see the similarities between those brave Numantine "bárbaros" of the second century B.C., who fought for their liberty against "los fieros romanos," and the equally brave Araucans of the sixteenth century of the Christian era fighting for their land and liberty against "los fieros españoles."[4]

> The Numantine-Roman strife, safely remote from contemporary problems, provided a classic, emblematic, epic story which could and does serve as a vehicle for much profound meditation about the trajectory, legitimacy, power, burden, and mistakes of empire. If Cervantes' purpose had been solely to glorify imperial Spain, the story of Numancia, supreme example of resistance to imperial aggression, would not have been appropriate. *Numancia* is no simple exaltation of a tribe of noble savages representing "eternal" Spain, as the critical commonplace repeated unreflectively over the years would have it; for Scipio represents what Cervantes' contemporary Spain had become, and Cervantes was both *proud of,* and *troubled by,* the mutation. Thus his play is a complex interweaving of multiple themes and preoccupations, many of them contradictory- prudence vs. daring, sophistication vs. simplicity, human enterprise vs. fate and fortune, the rights of peoples vs. the demands of empire—and to that complexity, tension and condensation, this heroic poem owes its compelling power.[5]

Perhaps we might attribute the silence of Golden Age dramatists concerning the Spanish enterprise in America to the opposing adjectives King mentions—"proud" yet "troubled"; indeed, the problems of empire were vexing to monarch and vassal alike. Spaniards were troubled by reports from abroad of the atrocities perpetrated by fellow citizens, yet they felt much pride in the heroic feats of their countrymen who risked their lives on the high seas, found lands and islands unknown to Europe, and attempted to implant the gospel of Christ in the New World. Yet there was, I repeat, silence in the *corrales* of Madrid on the subject of America until the end of the 16th century. Marcelino Menéndez Pelayo informs us that Lope de Vega was the first Spanish dramatist to treat America in his play *El nuevo mundo descubierto por Cristóbal Colón*; the critic writes, "Lope . . . fue el primer dramaturgo que se embarcó en este ingrato argumento, de tan seductora apariencia."[6]

Although Lope probably wrote the drama *El nuevo mundo . . .* between 1598–1603,[7] the desire to exalt Spain's American enterprise appears earlier in his epic poem *La Dragontea,* which, according to Federico Carlos Sainz de Robles, was probably written in 1597 and no later than April, 1598.[8] In this narrative poem, which reveals a passionate hatred for England,

Lope decries his compatriots' lack of praise for the overseas enterprise:

> ¡Oh, patria!, cuántos hechos, cuántos nombres,
> Cuántos sucesos y victorias grandes,
> Cuántos ilustres y temidos hombres
> De mar y tierra, en Indias, Francia y Flandes!
> No sabes cómo digas, cómo nombres
> Sus altas obras, ni sus vidas mandes
> A los archivos inmortales fuertes
> Después de sus hazañas y sus muertes!
> No es falta de escritores, patria mía;
> Que el Tajo, el Betis claro en sus arenas,
> El Pisuerga, el Genil, y el Turia cría
> Cisnes que mueren, por faltar Mecenas,
> Con esto se adormecen cada día
> En la contemplación de las Sirenas.
> Pues tienes quién haga, y quien te obliga,
> ¿Por qué te falta, España, quien lo diga?[9]

In addition to *El nuevo mundo*, there are two other extant plays about America by the "Fénix de los ingenios": *Arauco domado* (1598–1603)[10] and *El Brasil restituido* (1625),[11] and other dramatists followed Lope's lead. Tirso de Molina, who travelled to Santo Domingo between 1615 and 1618,[12] composed a trilogy about the Pizarro brothers: *Todo es dar en una cosa* (1626–30), *Amazonas en las Indias* (1629 or 1632), and *La lealtad contra la envidia* (1626–30).[13] Pedro Calderón de la Barca published in the *Cuarta parte de sus comedias* (1672),[14] *La aurora en Copacabana*. A collaborative work about America entitled *Algunas hazañas . . .* was undertaken by no fewer than nine authors: Antonio Mira de Amescua, the Count of Bastos (son of the Marquis of Belmonte), Luis de Belmonte Bermúdez (resident in America between 1602 and 1613),[15] Juan Ruiz de Alarcón (born in Mexico City ca. 1581),[16] Fernando de Ludeña, Luis Vélez de Guevara, Jacinto de Herrera, Diego de Villegas, and Guillén de Castro, and published in 1622.[17] Pedro Rejaule y Toledo (pseudonym Ricardo de Turia) published *La bellígera española* in 1616.[18] From Gaspar de Avila came *El gobernador prudente* (pub. 1663).[19] In

1665, *Los españoles en Chile* was published by Francisco González de Bustos.[20]

From the above list of plays one can conclude that many of the most renowned and distinguished playwrights of Golden Age theater did concern themselves with the Spanish-American empire. The total number of plays devoted to the New World experience is very small, however, when compared to the social and historical importance of the discovery.[21]

As the Spanish stage had long exercised the task of presenting its national heroes before the public (e.g., *Los siete infantes de Lara* by Juan de la Cueva, *Los hechos de Garcilaso de la Vega* by Lope de Vega), the above-cited plays lay the problems of empire before the public and attempt to inform and illuminate 16th- and 17th-century audiences about the problems of discovery, conquest, and colonization. In these plays there are heroes and heroines, villains and ruffians representing and portraying varied visions of America.

Spanish Golden Age theater has long been viewed as a reflection of the collective moral, philosophical and aesthetic values of the Spanish people. It has occasionally addressed, albeit at times in veiled fashion, such controversial issues as the limitations of the rights of the monarch, *La estrella de Sevilla*, (anon., ca. 1617), or the tyranny of a village *comendador* in Lope's *Fuenteovejuna*, (ca. 1614) or the role of the stars in the determination of one's fate, Alarcón's *El dueño de las estrellas* (ca. 1620), or Lope's *El caballero de Olmedo* (ca. 1622).

The purpose of this study is to examine Lope de Vega's three extant American plays in order to determine if the controversies outlined here concerning the conquest and colonization of the New World are addressed in them, that is, to what extent they show awareness of the arguments advanced by theologians such as Las Casas, Sepúlveda and Vitoria.

All these plays make use of chronicle-histories or epic poetry, and I have examined *El nuevo mundo descubierto por Cristóbal Colón* (1598–1603), *Arauco domado* (1604–6), and *El Brasil restituido* (1625) in relation to these sources. I hope to identify in each play the sources which Lope has followed in the process of artistic creation and where he has departed from their lead in order to reveal, perhaps, his own personal observations. Francisco López de Gómara's *Historia de las Indias y conquista de México* and Gonzalo Fernández de Oviedo's *Historia general y natural de las Indias* are the two suggested sources of *El nuevo mundo*. *La Araucana* by Alonso de Ercilla and *Arauco domado* by Pedro de Oña are the possible sources of Lope's *Arauco domado*. At least four writers are possible sources of *El Brasil restituido*: Fadrique de Toledo y Osorio, Francisco de Avendaño y Vilela, João de Madeiros Correia, and Bartolomeu Guerreiro.

Notes

[1] Marcos A. Morínigo, *América en el teatro de Lope de Vega* (Buenos Aires: Instituto de Filología, 1946), 43. My discussion of this play follows Morínigo's outline 42–49.

[2] Micael Carvajal and Luis Hurtado de Toledo, *Las cortes de la muerte . . . BAE 35*. Ed. Justo de Sancha, (Madrid: Atlas, 1950), 31. All quotes are from this edition. Page numbers follow subsequent quotes.

[3] Morínigo 47.

[4] Willard F. King, "Cervantes' *Numancia* and Imperial Spain," *MLN* 94 (1979): 208.

[5] King 217. We must bear in mind that Cervantes' *Numancia* does not overtly deal with America. Cervantes uses the Roman-Numantine strife to covertly parallel the Spanish-Araucanian conflict. It is for this reason that one designates Lope's *El nuevo mundo* . . . as the first extant Spanish drama which deals openly with the problem of America.

[6] Marcelino Menéndez Pelayo, "El nuevo mundo descubierto por Cristóbal Colón," *Estudios sobre el teatro de Lope de Vega*, 65 Vols. (Santander: Aldus, 1949) 34: 312.

[7] S. Griswold Morley and Courtney Bruerton, *Cronología de las comedias de Lope de Vega* (Madrid: Gredos, S.A., 1968) 370.

[8] Lope de Vega, *La Dragontea*, Ed. Federico Carlos Sainz de Robles, *Obras escogidas: Lope de Vega*, 3 Vols. (Madrid: Aguilar, S.A., 1964) 2: 299.

[9] Lope, *La Dragontea* 322–323.

[10] Morley and Bruerton, 285. See Chapter 3 for my proposed date of composition of the play.

[11] Morley and Bruerton 70. *El Brasil restituido* is an autograph manuscript, dated by Lope himself, on October 23, 1625. The manuscript is located at the

New York Public Library. The lost plays of Lope de Vega which treat the theme of the New World are *La conquista de Cortés* and *El Marqués del Valle*. Concerning *El Marqués del Valle* Stephen Gilman writes, "It is possible that a good portion of it . . . may have dealt with the hero after his return to Spain." ("Lope de Vega and the 'Indias en su ingenio,'" *Spanische Literatur im Goldenen Zeitalter* [1973]: 103.). Of *El Arenal de Sevilla*, an extant play by Lope, C.M. Fernández Shaw writes, "Incluyo *El Arenal de Sevilla* entre las obras de Lope dedicadas al tema americano porque este es el principal de su trama, aunque su acción se desarrolle en una ciudad peninsular." ("América en Lope de Vega," *Cuadernos hispanoamericanos*, 54 [1963]: 681).

[12] Pedro Nolasco Pérez, "Tirso de Molina: Pasajero a Indias," *Estudios: Tirso de Molina: Ensayos sobre la biografía y la obra del Padre Maestro Fray Gabriel Téllez* (1949): 187 and 196.

[13] For dates of composition of the three plays see: Tirso de Molina (Gabriel Téllez), *Todo es dar en una cosa, Amazonas en las Indias, La lealtad contra la envidia*, Ed. Blanca de los Ríos, *Obras dramáticas completas: Tirso de Molina*, 3 Vols. (Madrid: Aguilar, 1969) 2: 645, 697, and 735.

[14] For date of publication see: Angel Valbuena Briones, *Perspectiva crítica de los dramas de Calderón* (Madrid: Rialpa, 1965) 312.

[15] Luis de Belmonte Bermúdez writes in the prologue to the play that he was in Lima, Peru in 1605. See Guillén de Castro y Bellvis, *Algunas hazañas de las muchas de don García Hurtado de Mendoza*, In *Obras de Guillén de Castro y Bellvis*, 3 Vols. (Madrid: Tipografía de "Revista de Archivos," 1925) 3: 595.

[16] Julio Jiménez Rueda, *Juan Ruiz de Alarcón y su tiempo* (Mexico: José Porrua e Hijos, 1939) 15.

[17] For date of first publication see: Forrest Eugene Spencer and Rudolph Schevill, *The Dramatic Works of Luis Vélez de Guevara: Their Plots, Sources, and Bibliography* (Berkeley: University of California P, 1937) 317.

[18] For date of publication see: Ramón de Mesonero Romanos, Ed., *BAE Dramáticos contemporáneos a Lope de Vega* (Madrid: Atlas, 1951) xxiii–xxiv.

[19] For date of first publication see: José Toribio Medina, Ed., *Dos comedias famosas y un auto sacramental* (Santiago de Chile: Litografía Barcelona) 7.

[20] *Parte Veinte y dos de Comedias Nuevas, Escogidas de los mejores ingenios de España*, (Madrid: Andrés García de la Iglesia, 1665). This play may be read at the University of Pennsylvania, Van Pelt Library, Rare Book Collection.

[21] Glen F. Dille, "El descubrimiento y la conquista de América en la *comedia*," *Hispania* 71 (1988): 493. This recent article discloses three additional plays: *Hernán Cortés triunfante en Tlaxcala* (lost) by Jacinto Cordero; *Las palabras a los reyes y gloria de los Pizarros* by Luis Vélez de Guevara; and *La conquista de México* by Antonio Enríquez Gómez (pseud. Fernando de Zárate).

1

The Discovery of the New World and Its Intellectual Consequences

The birth of Imperial Spain occurs in the year 1492 with the discovery of a chain of small islands in the Antilles. The commander of the expedition, Christopher Columbus, believed he had reached the rich shores of the Orient and had found for the Catholic Monarchs a new and more rapid route to the wealth of the Indies. In a letter to Ferdinand and Isabel, Columbus states the crown's position on the purpose of the voyage:

> Vuestras Altezas, como católicos cristianos y Príncipes amadores de la santa fe cristiana y acrecentadores della, y enemigos de la secta de Mahoma y de todas las idolatrías y heregías, pensaron de enviarme a mí Cristóbal Colón a las dichas partidas de India para ver los dichos príncipes, y los pueblos y tierras, y la disposición dellas y de todo, y la manera que se pudiera tener para la conversion dellas a nuestra santa fe.[1]

In 1493 Pope Alexander VI formally entrusted the Catholic Monarchs with the task of evangelizing the natives of the Indies in his bull *Inter Caetera*. One can conclude, therefore, that the vision of the Spanish crown of America was intimately united to the propagation of the teachings of Christ. The justification of the Conquest resided precisely in the supremely important goal of saving the souls of the Indians.

The Crown's desire to extend its religious beliefs to the Indians is highly understandable from an historical point of view. Indeed, Spain was, perhaps, the only European power capable of such a task. As Columbus states, Spain was the enemy of

Islam. For nearly eight centuries prior to the discovery of the New World, the Christian kings of Spain had waged war against the Moorish invaders of the peninsula with the purpose of re-establishing Christian rule throughout the land as one of its goals.

The struggle to recapture Spain from the Moors began in the hills of Asturias ca. 722, in Covadonga, and ended on January 2, 1492, with the surrender of the last Islamic stronghold, the city of Granada. In this moment of victory the Jewish population of Spain, which for centuries had been the target of attack, ridicule, and torture by Christians, were formally expelled from the country; only those Jews who were willing to embrace the teachings of Christ and be baptized were to remain on Spanish soil. The Spanish crown also looked with fear and suspicion upon its newly conquered Moorish population. The fear of revolt and the proximity of Granada to Moorish Africa caused the monarchs to induce a large number of this non-Christian segment of Spain to leave the kingdom. In the autumn of 1493 some six thousand Moors departed Spain for Africa. It was not, however, until 1502 that the Crown, urged by Archbishop Cisneros of Toledo, required the Moors of Granada to convert to Christianity or leave the country. As of this date, 1502, Spain became a country of at least nominal Christians (but virtually all the newly baptized *moriscos* continued for decades to follow their old faith quite openly).

One can easily see in this scenario of religious orthodoxy the motivation and the historical pressures behind the Spanish Crown's zeal to bring the natives of its newly-discovered territory into the fold of Christ. Spain, indeed, was to play the role of the defender and champion of Catholic ideals throughout the 16th and 17th centuries: the expulsion of the Jews and Moors from Spain, the struggle against the spread of Protestantism in Northern Europe, the resistance to the extension of the Ottoman empire in the Mediterranean, the conversion of the Indians in America are all parts of the same enterprise.

The long struggle to create a religiously unified peninsula is transplanted to the New World as a drive to convert and save the souls of the native American population. There exists, however, another important parallel between the Reconquest and the Conquest. Derek W. Lomax is one of many historians who points to booty as an important motivation for the Christians who reconquered Spain from the Moors. He states, "Booty was an important motive for fighting, and as well as slaves, gold, silver, precious stones, and cloths, it normally included sheep and cattle."[2] He writes further:

> By 922 the Asturian kings had conquered about one-fifth of Spain. No doubt they did so primarily because in early medieval Europe any king's first duty was to be a successful warrior, conquering his neighbors and rewarding his followers with booty, and Asturian warriors, like Franks, Lombards, or Murcians, would not tolerate a king who failed in this duty.[3]

The extraction of gold and silver and other precious metals from the mines and temples of the New World is a fact well known and documented by friend and foe of Spain. Christopher Columbus himself enticed the Catholic Monarchs with the prospect of riches from the Indies. In his diary of his first voyage to the Indies Columbus writes on Saturday, October 13:

> Traían (i.e. the Indians) ovillos de algodón filado, y papagayos, y azagayas, y otras cositas que sería tedio de escribir, y todo daban por cualquiera cosa que se los diese. Y yo estaba atento y trabajaba de saber si había oro, y vide que algunos dellos traían un pedazuelo colgado en un agujero que tienen a la nariz, y por señas que pude entender que yendo al Sur ó volviendo la isla por el Sur que estaba allí un rey que tenía grandes vasos dello; y tenía muy mucho. Trabajé que fuesen allá, y después vide que no entendían en la ida. Determiné de aguardar fasta mañana en la tarde, y después partir para Sudueste, que para según muchos dellos me enseñaron decían que había tierra al Sur y al Sudueste y al Norueste, y questas del Norueste les venían a combatir muchas veces, y así, ir al Sudueste a buscar el oro y piedras preciosas.[4]

Lewis Hanke writes in *The Spanish Struggle for Justice in the Conquest of America* that the Spanish character has a "tendency toward polarization; a native passion for extremes."[5] The following anecdote quoted by Hanke underlines the author's statement concerning the polarity of the Spanish national character and certainly points to a problem of grave concern to both crown and colonizers. Hanke notes:

> The conquistador Francisco Pizarro once replied to an ecclesiastic in his company who was protesting the despoilment of Indians in Peru and urging upon him that God and the faith ought rather to be made known to them: "I have not come for any such reasons. I have come to take away from them their gold."[6]

Hanke states that Spaniards responded to both secular and sacred motives in the Conquest of America. The historian quotes the conquistador Bernal Diaz: "We came here to serve God and also to get rich."[7] Charles Gibson writes in his history, *Spain in America,* "For the early friars the propagation of the faith was an objective as compelling as gold to the conquistadores or tribute to the *encomenderos,* and no one who reads their record can seriously think that it was not."[8] Thus it is clear that there exist two polar motives in the Spanish psyche in regard to the Conquest of America: the propagation of the Catholic faith and the reward of material wealth. Furthermore, both impulses—spiritual and secular—have their historical antecedents in the Reconquest of Spain.

The infinitive "encomendar" in Spanish is translated into English as "to entrust"; the *encomienda* system established during the very early days of the colonization period[9] entrusted the Spanish landowner with the protection and religious instruction of the Indians who, in return, tilled his soil, planted and harvested his crops, and worked in his mines. Here, once again, the sacred and the secular intertwine—the landowner or *encomendero* supposedly provided religious instruction to the Indians; the Indians provided manual labor for the *encomendero.* While the crown seems to have taken seriously the need for religious instruction and conversion of the Indian, the *encomendero* put priority upon the manual labor provided by the natives; for these men, perhaps, the *encomienda* system was regarded as the just recompense for their efforts in risking the perils of the high seas and settling a new frontier.

Concerning the royal attitude toward the *encomienda* system, which many moralists and theologians in Spain and the New World considered as a form of slavery, Gibson states:

> The problem for Queen Isabella lay in reconciling economic needs with the professed Christian purposes of Spanish imperialism. There can be no question that the obligation to Christianize the Indians, as originally enunciated by the papacy, was taken seriously by the Queen. On the other hand, her condemnation of Indian slavery . . . was neither uncompromising nor disinterested. On a number of occasions the Queen countenanced, and even demanded a share in, the Indian captives as slaves. It is true that formal enslavement, in the Queen's view, was not to affect the entire native population. It was rather a punishment meted out to resisting, rebellious or cannibalistic individuals and tribes. The Queen explicitly took the position that Indians innocent of punishable crimes were "free" crown subjects. But like other such subjects, they were liable to tribute exaction and in the conditions of the West Indies colony they might be compelled to work. Thus "free" Indians became available for *encomienda* assignments. The monarchy, notably inconsistent in many aspects of its imperial administration, never deviated from its position that the indigenous population was technically free.[10]

As Gibson states, we have before us a royal policy which is inconsistent; indeed, one might say that it is a policy of contradictions which could only favor the *encomendero*. In brief, all nonrebellious or noncannibalistic Indians were free, but as subjects of the crown, they were bound to pay tribute just as the free citizens on the peninsula did. But since the Indians had no money, tribute came in the form of manual labor rendered to the *encomendero*. Manual labor was not left to the prerogative of the Indian; it was his duty, his payment for Christianization and acculturation to Spain's mode of life. Thus, the technically free Indian became virtually a man of bondage.

Royal proclamations on the freedom of the Indians had little effect on the manner in which the natives were treated. Gibson writes:

> In Hispaniola, natives were formally distributed to Spanish colonists who used them in placer mining, agriculture, and stock raising, and

> who reduced their Christianization to baptism *en masse*. *Encomienda* Indians were overworked, abused, bought and sold, and otherwise treated in ways that did not distinguish them from non-*encomienda* Indians. And even in law those who escaped might be recaptured and condemned to outright slavery, as punishment for neglecting their obligation to work.[11]

The question of Indian rights to freedom heavily burdened the conscience of the crown and many Spanish scholars. Two divergent interpretations of justice and how to achieve it emerged. Hanke states:

> One group regarded Indian conversion as important, but secondary, and its members devoted themselves to justifying to the royal conscience the virtual enslavement of the Indians as a means to develop the resources of the New World for the benefit of the crown and for the glory of the Spaniards and Spain. The other group placed primary emphasis on Indian conversion and the welfare of the Indians, relegating to an inferior place the material development of the continent. Both groups sought political power as the indispensable force required to make their views prevail, the ecclesiastics just as energetically as the conquistadores.[12]

It is certainly a credit to the Spanish Crown that it not only permitted but encouraged freedom of speech in Spain and in the colonies. Hanke indicates that King Ferdinand commanded on August 14, 1509, that "no official should prevent anyone from sending to the King or anyone else letters and other information which concerns the welfare of the Indies."[13] The crown prohibited the censorship of mail from the Indies to Spain and encouraged scholarly debate on American problems before tribunals established on both sides of the Atlantic. Spanish universities became seats of heated debate on the rights of the Indian and on his nature, that is, whether he was a rational human being or a species of the irrational animal kingdom. The islands and small mainland settlement of the New World also became embroiled in the issue of the Indian's right to freedom versus his obligation, as a subject to the Crown, to render the monarchy such goods and services as were deemed necessary:

manual labor to the *encomendero* and precious metals to the Catholic Monarchs.

One of the first men to voice his objection to the manner in which the Indians were being treated in the New World was Friar Antonio de Montesinos. Lewis Hanke gives a detailed description of the cleric's sermons and of the settlers' reaction to them:

> On the Sunday before Christmas in 1511 a Dominican friar named Antonio de Montesinos preached a revolutionary sermon in a straw-thatched church on the island of Hispaniola . . . Montesinos delivered the first important and deliberate public protest against the kind of treatment being accorded to the Indians by his Spanish countrymen.[14]

Hanke states that the vicar of the order relayed to the governor's delegation that Montesinos had spoken for the entire Dominican order. On the following Sunday Montesinos once again mounted the pulpit and inveighed against his countrymen. He announced to his congregation that all those who held slaves were in mortal sin and would not receive absolution. King Ferdinand, realizing the explosive nature of such sermons, ordered Governor Diego Columbus to reason with Montesinos. The Crown threatened to punish the Dominican order of Hispaniola if they persisted in disseminating ideas which might endanger the lives and livelihood of the settlers, inspire revolt among the natives, and threaten the Crown's hold over its new lands. With the tacit protection of the Crown the *encomenderos* continued to exact manual labor from the native population. Hanke states that the first two decades of Spanish rule were periods of almost unchanged exploitation of Indians. A royal letter dated August 14, 1509, stated that the Indians were to serve for only one or two years, and not for life. As might be expected, the order was not strictly enforced; indeed, a hereditary *encomienda* was the de facto system until the end of the 16th century.

Friar Bernardo de Mesa, one of the king's religious advisors, prepared a thesis in which he stated that although the Indians were free men, they suffered from the sin of idleness. He concluded that it was the obligation of the monarchy to aid the native population in overcoming this vice. The natives' tendency to be idle made absolute freedom injurious to their spiritual needs. Friar Bernardo therefore insisted that some kind of servitude was necessary to purge the Indians of the perilous sin of sloth and encourage them to a more industrious way of life.

Two friars—the Franciscan Alonso de Espinel and the Dominican Antonio de Montesinos—presented their points of view before the king and reached a compromise "which while recognizing the freedom of the Indians and their right to humane treatment, concluded that they must be subject to coercion to be kept close to the Spaniards in order that their conversion be effected."[15]

The Crown decided that the *encomienda* system was sound since it seemed to lend itself to the evangelistic mission which Pope Alexander VI, Ferdinand, and Isabel had established as their formal and singular duty in America. On this basis, the Laws of Burgos, the first comprehensive code of Indian legislation, were promulgated. The Crown issued these laws on December 27, 1512. Hanke remarks:

> These laws are the most complete statement that we have of the crown's conception at that time of the ideal relationship between Indians and their Spanish masters . . . The *encomenderos'* responsibilities are here spelled out in detail. They were to bring Indians together in villages near the Spaniards in new houses especially built for them, burn old dwellings. *Encomenderos* were obliged to provide religious instruction to Indians. One third of the Indians were to work in gold mines, but laws prohibited exploitation of pregnant Indian women and overworked Indians. The last item says that if Indians gave proof of being able to live under their own government, they were to be allowed to do so and pay only ordinary feudal dues to Spain.[16]

The 1512 Laws of Burgos were, from their conception, doomed to utter failure and eventual repeal. One obvious reason for the collapse of these laws was the immense distance between the king and his advisors and the colonists, some of whom deeply resented any intrusion upon their right to use

Indian labor as a means of insuring their survival in a distant and, at times, hostile land. These colonists were fully aware of their rights to exact labor from the Indians who resisted the authority of the Catholic Church, the See of Rome, and the Spanish monarchs, all seeking the spiritual conversion of the native populace. These rights to propagate the faith of Christ and to bring the natives under the protection of the Spanish crown were, for the *encomenderos,* well delineated in several papal bulls of donation and the legal document known as the "Requerimiento," written around 1512, probably by Juan López de Palacios Rubios. This document, which was read to all newly-discovered Indians, in essence required the Indians to recognize the authority of the Catholic Church, its pope and the Spanish monarchs. If the Indians refused to accept the Spanish proposition, the consequences, they were informed, would be grave: coercive subjugation, alienation of property and punishment as traitors to the Crown. As stated, the colonists believed that they were within their legal rights, as set forth by the pope and the monarchy. The small restrictions on these rights contained in the Laws of Burgos were therefore considered as an infringement upon their rights as loyal subjects of the crown and a reversal of existing laws, designed to alter their livelihood and seignorial mode of existence. The colonists, then, were prepared to argue their views before the king and his appointed council and, if necessary, undermine any royal proclamation which diminished or curtailed their privileges and rights as Spanish subjects.

Another important factor in the failure of the Laws of Burgos was the plethora of diverse and divergent opinions concerning the Indians. The quills of men of letters were actively penning their heterogeneous opinions on such matters as the most effective manner of incorporating the idolatrous natives into the fold of Christianity, the human or subhuman nature of the Indian, the right to enslave the Indian or require forced labor from him, and the nature of just war. As stated earlier, such a variety of opinions on such problematic issues for sixteenth-century men and the fervor of those men who wrote about and defended their particular persuasion on these issues speak highly of the Spanish people who struggled for justice for all in the New World. These divergent attitudes, however, often produced more confusion than clarity for the Spanish monarchs, who were, with the aid of their advisors, to arrive at a reasonable and justifiable solution to the Indian question. Although the Spanish crown struggled in laudable fashion in its willingness to lend ear to all who would speak and write on these questions, the end result was, perhaps, a state of royal paralysis: the inability to come to a conclusive and workable decision concerning the government of its overseas empire. The failure of the Laws of Burgos to bear fruit can then be attributed to the profusion of conflicting ideas on the Indian issue and the Crown's inability to derive from them a coherent, cohesive and convincing plan which would be both just and reasonable to all concerned.

In the period of emotional and intellectual fervor of the early sixteenth century, many scholars and settlers believed that a failure to resolve the issues surrounding the Indians, the *encomenderos*, and the conquistadores would lead to war. In his article "New Viewpoints on the Spanish Colonization of America" Silvio Zavala states:

> During the period when the validity of the proclamation (requerimiento) drawn up by Palacios Rubios was admitted, and even after the first statement of the problem of Spanish claims to the West Indies had been revised, systematic consideration was given to the possibility that relations between the Europeans and the Indians might take the form of war.[17]

In theory Christianity, as revealed through the gospels, is incompatible with war; Christ commanded his followers to love their neighbors as themselves and to turn the cheek for more punishment when struck by another. Christians are bound by the doctrine of peace; therefore, war, which is the ultimate embodiment of force, is, at least in theory, an unacceptable alternative.

In the above-cited article Zavala notes:

> In spite of Christianity, wars continued to be fought and new views were shaped to fit this fact. Christian thinkers did not condemn all war; they merely demanded that it be just and for sufficient and reasonable cause. From the time of Saint Augustine these thinkers also asked that the aim of war should be the re-establishment of peace. These basic ideas continued to develop during the medieval period, and by the time we reach the *Summa Theologica* of Saint Thomas Aquinas in the thirteenth century we find a mature Christian doctrine on the problem of war.[18]

Zavala states that "The Spanish conquest of America is situated historically at the meeting point of medieval and modern doctrines, when *just* war—not merely war without qualification—was still spoken of and the facts were interpreted in the light of Scholastic theory."[19]

One of the most important writers on the subject of just war was Friar Francisco de Vitoria, born around 1483 either in Vitoria, the provincial capital of Alava, or in Burgos; in 1506 he enrolled in the Dominican Colegio de Santiago in Paris and remained in the French capital for more than sixteen years. He was, early in life, an enthusiast of the Dutch humanist Erasmus of Rotterdam. In 1522 Vitoria returned to Spain to teach theology at the Colegio de San Gregorio in Valladolid. In 1526 this teacher received "la cátedra de prima de teología" at the University of Salamanca; he taught there until his death in 1546. Thanks to the notes taken by his students during his lectures at the University of Salamanca, we have his thoughts on the Indian issue preserved in his *Relecciones sobre los indios y el derecho de guerra*, presented at the University in 1539, and divided in two parts: *De indis* and *De jure bello*.

It is important to note that Francisco de Vitoria very probably belonged to the often persecuted caste of "cristianos nuevos" of Spain.[20] Given the recent expulsion of Jews from Spain and the fear under which many *conversos* lived who remained in the country, the reader of his *Relecciones* is strongly tempted to judge that specific passages in Vitoria's lectures derive from the yearning of his caste for universal justice and peace and tolerance among men of different creeds and, therefore, explain in part, the theologian's position on Indians, colonists, and just war. Because Vitoria is considered to be the founder of modern international law, it is appropriate to outline his argumentation on the Indian issue set forth in his *Relecciones*. Although there is no direct connection between Vitoria's thought and Lope de Vega's theater, a detailed synopsis of Vitoria's lectures is useful also in order to appreciate Lope's courage in bringing the controversies surrounding the Indians and the Spaniards to the 17th-century stage. Certainly, many of the issues raised by Vitoria in the mid-16th century continued to weigh upon the consciences of Spanish intellectuals at the end of the century.

Vitoria begins by stating that the Indian question is a point on which there is much doubt; lawmakers, he states, cannot adjudicate the Indian problem; it is a matter to be resolved by the Church.

Vitoria asks his students, "si estos bárbaros, antes de la llegada de los españoles, eran verdaderos dueños pública y privadamente . . . si eran verdaderos dueños de las cosas y posesiones privadas, y si había entre ellos algunos hombres que fueran verdaderos príncipes y señores de los demás."[21] After presenting the Aristotelian argument espoused by some that the serf (the American Indian, in this case) owns nothing and acquires all for his lord (the Spaniard), the professor states,

> Contra esto diremos que ellos (i.e. the Indians) estaban pública y privadamente en pacífica posesión de sus cosas, y por lo tanto, mientras no se demuestre lo contrario, deben ser tenidos por verdaderos señores y no puede despojarles de su posesión, sin justa causa. (48–9)

Arguing against those who believe that the sins of the Indians deprive them of dominion, Vitoria says that sin does not impede the sinner from government. "El dominio se funda en ser el hombre imagen de Dios, pero el hombre es imagen de Dios por su naturaliza, esto es por las potencias racionales, luego no se pierde por el pecado mortal" (51–2).[22]

Vitoria now directs his attention to the question of the Indian's faculty of reason and its bearing upon the right to dominion. He asks, "si para que alguien sea capaz de dominio, se requiere que tenga uso de razón" (58). Vitoria concludes that the capacity to suffer injury and insult is the determining factor in who has dominion. A child who has not yet reached the age of reason can suffer "injuria" and, therefore, has just title to dominion. Moreover, the crux of dominion is founded upon the fact that man is made in God's image. Therefore, children have dominion; the child exists for himself and not for the benefit of others and is, for this reason, not categorized as irrational. He states further that madness, or the allegation thereof, does not preclude the right to dominion.

The First Part of *De indis* ends with an emotional pronouncement which certainly must have stirred the consciences of his students:

> Y grave cosa sería negarles a ellos [i.e. the Indians], que nunca nos infligieron injuria alguna, lo que no negamos a los sarracenos y los judíos, perpetuos enemigos de la religión cristiana, a quienes reconocemos verdadero dominio sobre sus cosas que no sean de las arrebatadas a los cristianos. (62)

The Indians have brought neither harm nor injury to the Spaniards and should not be denied the liberty of possession of their land and goods.

The professor goes further to clarify misinterpretations of Aristotle's position on slaves; to those learned men of Spain who wished to apply Aristotle's idea that some men are by nature slaves due to their lack of reason in governing themselves, Vitoria retorts that the Spaniards cannot deprive the Indians of their possessions because they are, in the judgment of some, intellectually inferior; nor can the Indian be sold as a slave on these grounds. A clear reading of Aristotle, says Vitoria, informs us only that those who are of "corto ingenio" need the guidance of those who demonstrate higher capacity for reason and, therefore, government.

In the Second Part of *De indis* Vitoria sets forth and refutes the Titles upon which the Spanish crown lays just and legal claim to the Indies. The first alleged title states that the emperor is the lord of the world. Vitoria states that this idea is presumed to be supported by both Aristotle and Saint Thomas Aquinas, but he responds, ". . . esta opinión carece de todo fundamento. Y, por tanto, nuestra primara conclusión será la siguiente: El emperador no es señor de todo el orbe" (68).[23] Vitoria states that dominion can only exist in virtue of natural, divine, or human law, but none of these rights entitles the Emperor to be the lord of the earth. The professor substantiates his argument by citing Saint Thomas Aquinas and Aristotle and concludes that an emperor cannot justly lay claim to the title of the earth's ruler through the assertion of a natural right.

Concerning the donation of empire through divide right Vitoria says that the emperor of Spain has no legal claim which justly makes him lord of the world, and since this title is invalid, he cannot usurp the possessions of the native Americans or implant his own governors and laws in the New World without the consent of the Indians, who are in legal possession of their land, property, and government.

The second title alleged to justify the possession of the provinces of the New World is that of the authority of the See of Rome. Vitoria states that some argue that the pope is the temporal lord of the earth and has the right, through Christ, to donate the government and administration of the Indies to the Catholic Monarchs. Their conclusion is that the pope is Christ's vicar on earth and, therefore, through the spiritual powers invested in him through Christ, is the temporal lord of the earth. The pope, therefore, has the divine power to distribute the earth's people and possessions for the benefit of Christ, his Church, and the propagation of the faith. Those Indians who deny the authority of the pope as their supreme spiritual leader on earth and the mission of the Spaniards to bring them the blessings of Christ relinquish their right to peace, and the Spaniards may justly wage war upon these infidels. Vitoria denies the legality of this title: "El Papa no es señor civil o temporal de todo el orbe, hablando de dominio y potestad civil en sentido propio" (76). The pope's temporal powers are restricted to those matters of spiritual concern; both the temporal and spiritual powers of the pope are to be directed toward happiness, that is, the welfare of his flock.

In sum, if the Indians do not wish to accept the authority of the pope as their spiritual leader, the Spaniards cannot use this refusal as a justification for waging war; one cannot confiscate the unbeliever's goods.

The third title, which for some men of Vitoria's day proved the Spaniards' legitimate right to the Indies, is called "el derecho de descubrimiento." Vitoria says that it will take few words to show the error of such a line of argumentation; he says that the Indians owned the land long before they had set eyes on the bearded men from the sea and are the only ones who can legally distribute it. Vitoria's opponents argue, however, that since the Indians do not accept Christ, it is wholly legal to distribute their lands; they argue further that blasphemy against Christ or mockery of Christian symbols are also just motives for war against the Indians and the confiscation of their lands. In their view infidelity justifies war. To these charges the friar argues, "Los bárbaros, antes de tener noticia alguna de la fe de Cristo, no cometían pecado de infidelidad por no creer en Cristo" (84). Vitoria charges that man's attempt to understand, through human diligence, the mystery of the faith is sufficient for invincible ignorance, i.e., that such a person who is unaware of the teachings of Christ bears no guilt for his ignorance since he has used all available means known to him to understand the mysteries of God. He concedes that the "bárbaros" may be condemned for such sins as idolatry or other mortal sins but not for infidelity to the teachings of the Church.

Vitoria goes on to condemn the "requerimiento," the legal document read to the Indians by the Spaniards which, after summarizing the creation of the earth and the sins of the first parents of man and of the advent, death, and resurrection of the Redeemer, and the establishment of the successors of Christ upon the throne of Rome and the benevolence of the Catholic Monarchs, exhorts the natives to accept the faith of Jesus Christ or suffer the pangs of enslavement, confiscation of goods and property and/or death:

> Los bárbaros no están obligados a creer en la fe de Cristo, al primer anuncio que se les haga de ella, de modo que pequen mortalmente por no creer lo que simplemente se les anuncie y proponga diciéndoles que la verdadera fe es la cristiana y que Cristo es Salvador y Redentor del mundo, sin que acompañen milagros o cualquiera otra prueba o medio de convencimiento (89).[24]

Vitoria believed that the true faith was not to be accepted blindly. It had to be nurtured by convincing arguments and fortified with the good example of those who preached these doctrines. The "bárbaro," he says, must believe that the preacher is worthy of his faith and trust; however, the "bárbaro" is wholly ignorant of the intentions of these friars who bring news of Jesus and the need for conversion and salvation.

What recourse do the monarchy and the Church have if predication is undertaken in a bland and understanding fashion and the Indians remain obdurate in their traditional beliefs? The friar states, "si la fe se ha propuesto a los bárbaros del dicho modo y no la aceptan, los españoles no pueden hacerles la guerra por tal razón, ni obrar contra ellos por derecho de guerra" (90). Therefore, Vitoria concludes that since the Indians have caused the Spaniards no harm, there are no grounds to justify war against them.

The professor interjects a personal note into his lecture, a feeling, a repugnance which certainly was shared by many scholars of his day concerning the activities of many of the conquistadores and colonizers of the New World. Here Vitoria laments the state of affairs of his country's imperial enterprise:

> . . . Tengo noticias de muchos escándalos, de hechos inhumanos y de actos de impiedad perpetrados en esas regiones. No se ve, en consecuencia, que les haya sido predicada la religión de Cristo lo bastante piadosa y convenientemente para que estén obligados a asistir. Pues si bien es cierto que muchos religiosos y eclesiásticos varones, con su vida y ejemplos y diligente predicación hubieran consagrado a esta tarea el trabajo e industria necesarios, no pudieron hacerlo, estorbados por otros cuyos intereses son muy ajenos a eso. (92)

The evangelical mission of friars seeking the conversion of the native population to the doctrine of Christ is thwarted by those Spaniards who wish to exploit the Indian for personal gain.

The fifth title upon which the monarchy laid claim to America and its inhabitants was based upon the sins of the "bárbaros." It was argued that war could be justly waged against the native population for their mortal sins: cannibalism, incest, homosexuality—all sins against God's natural laws. Vitoria argues against this title; neither pope nor Christian prince have jurisdiction over the Indians and, therefore, cannot punish them for sins against nature.

The sixth title is "el de la elección voluntaria," i.e. the natives' acceptance of the Spanish king as their lord after his messengers speak about him (Requerimiento). Vitoria strikes down this title for the following reasons:

1. Fear and ignorance are present among the Indians when they are confronted with armed soldiers who exhort them to accept an unknown man as their earthly leader. Furthermore, the Indians may be ignorant of what is being demanded of them due to the language barrier.
2. Fear and ignorance vitiate the possibility of "elección voluntaria."
3. The native population already has its leaders, princes, and lords, and it would be wholly unreasonable for them to accept a new and foreign lord without the consent of the people.

"A special donation of God" is the seventh title invoked by the crown. Vitoria presents the argumentation of those who support this title: ". . . Dios, en sus singulares juicios, condenó a todos estos bárbaros a la perdición como motivo de sus abominaciones y que los entregó al poder de los españoles . . . " (98). Vitoria makes two points:

1. Even if God decreed the perdition of the Indians, one would not conclude from this fact that those who might destroy them would be free from guilt.

2. There are Christians who have greater sins in their customs than the Indians.

The Second Book of the *Relecciones, De jure bello,* presents Vitoria's views of legitimate rights which the monarchy could invoke as just cause for settlement in the New World or war against the Indians. Vitoria calls the first title "the right of natural society and communication"—"la sociedad natural y comunicación." Under this title the Spaniards may live in the New World as long as no harm is done to the Indians. Vitoria indicates that it is man's natural right to live and settle where he wishes; furthermore, it is inhumane to treat guests of a country in an inhospitable manner. Visitors to a country cannot be exiled if they are guilty of no crime; this means, for the theologian, that the Spaniards cannot be forced into exile by the Indians if they have not caused harm or injury.The lecturer hastens to add, however, that the Indians do have the legal right to expel the enemy from their land.

Vitoria tells his students that friendship among men is a natural right; it is unnatural to prohibit commerce and communication among men of good will. He adds that the rivers, the sea, and the mountains are all public property, and, therefore, any attempt to restrict the use and enjoyment of them constitutes a violation of man's natural rights. It would be a grave offense against the Spaniards, as guests in the New World, should the Indians limit or prohibit the use of, or access to, these common properties of man.

The professor believes that free commerce is a divine right. He states that it is permissible for the Spaniards to engage in commerce with the natives but not when such commerce would be to the detriment of the country. The Spaniards may export to the New World those products which the Indians lack and, in exchange, extract from the natives "oro o plata u otras cosas en que ellos abundan" (104). Neither Indian nor Spanish prince may prohibit such commerce since it is a divine right. The communality of mankind makes the fruits of creation common to all men. Gold, silver, and other riches found in the rivers or in the seas are the property of the finder. Vitoria logically does not restrict commerce in the New World to a Spanish monopoly, though that indeed was the Crown's policy.

Should the Indians refuse the Spaniards cohabitation in the New World, the Spaniards must show that their intentions are honorable, peaceful. If the Indians refuse peaceful cohabitation, the Spaniards may defend themselves and their natural right to peaceful cohabitation. One should note that this is the first time in the *Relecciones* that the professor has given legal justification to his countrymen to arm themselves against the Indian and defend what is naturally and divinely theirs: a free society in which all may live peacefully and the right to barter and to offer to another people goods that they lack in exchange for goods needed by the other trading party.

If the Spaniards, says the friar, do not achieve peaceful coexistence with the natives and have exhausted all means to this end, the imperial armies can legally occupy their cities and subjugate the Indians. In such a war in which one party has been denied its right to peacefully cohabit the New World, the victor has full claim to the spoils. Should the Spaniards defeat the Indians, the former, as victor, has the right to enslave the vanquished. The prince of the victors becomes the judge of the vanquished. The vanquished must follow the command of the prince. The conquering prince may condemn the natives according to the gravity of their misconduct.

Friar Francisco de Vitoria offers his students another title by which the Spanish monarchy might justify its presence in the New World and under which it might declare just war against the Americans. This title is "the propagation of the Christian religion." The Spaniards, he notes, have the right to preach to the Indians. The professor goes on to state that if the Spanish missionaries were prohibited from preaching the good news, the Indians would never enjoy eternal salvation. Fraternal correction is a natural right, as is love. "Y dado que ellos (i.e. the Indians) están no solo en pecado mortal, sino también fuera del estado de salvación, a los españoles les compete el corregirlos y dirigirlos, y aún más, parece que están en la obligación de verificarlo" (111). Vitoria would grant to the Spanish clergy not only the task of evangelization and conversion of the Indian population but also the charge of verification of the adherence to Christianity after baptism.

The Dominican friar turns his attention once again to the role of the pontiff in the propagation of the faith. He asserts that the pope can legally grant the evangelical mission to one nation and that the pope has temporal power in spiritual matters. James Brown Scott writes: "It will be recalled that, in denying to the Pope jurisdiction in matters material and temporal in the New World, Vitoria was careful to reserve from the denial the spiritual domain."[25] Since the pontiff can make temporal decisions which involve spiritual matters, he can prohibit other Christian nations from commerce with the Indians if, in his belief, such commerce would impede the evangelistic mission of the Spaniards. Vitoria believed that such prohibition was necessary to avoid possible conflicts between Christian nations, which could hinder the conversion of the natives. Moreover, he states, "puesto que los príncipes de España fueron los primeros que, bajo sus auspicios y a sus expensas hicieron realizar aquella navegación, y descubrieron tan dichosamente el nuevo mundo, justo es que la tal peregrinación se prohiba a los demás y que solo ellos disfruten en lo descubierto" (112). It would seem that the "fruits of discovery" to be enjoyed solely by the Spaniards are those of the spirit. The Spaniards are to reap the spiritual rewards derived from the salvation of the American Indian. As Vitoria states, the pope has the temporal power to entrust the missionary efforts to the Spaniards and to exclude all other European powers from such spiritual involvement. The pontiff may not, however, restrict European nations from commerce with the Indians or extraction of gold and other precious metals from rivers, mountains, etc. if these activities do not interfere with the propagation of the faith.

The Dominican states that war cannot be waged upon those Indians who hear the gospel and reject it. He hastens to add, however, that should the natives prohibit the promulgation of the gospel or punish converted Indians, Spain could justly wage war. The Spaniards have the legal right to preach the gospel; the Indians have the legal right to reject Christian doctrines but not to obstruct the teaching or practice of them. Should the Indians attempt to impede the teachings of Christ among their people, the war waged by Spaniards must be carried out in moderation, keeping present the interests of the Indians, their conversion and salvation. Other methods of evangelization must be brought forth, if possible, to minimize the possibility of war and the failure of the apostolic mission. Vitoria tells his students that he has no doubt that the Spaniards found it necessary to take up arms in order to remain in America; however, he laments, "temo que las cosas hayan ido mas allá de lo que el derecho permitía" (114). Like many of his countrymen, Vitoria was acutely aware that laws and human rights were, indeed, being violated by ruthless conquistadores who seemed little concerned with the welfare or conversion of America's Indians.

In his fourth title Vitoria supposes that "una gran parte de los bárbaros se han convertido a Cristo" and asks what steps could be taken in their behalf: " . . . el Papa puede, habiendo causa razonable y pídanlo ellos [i.e. the Indians] o no, darles un príncipe cristiano, arrancándolos a sus anteriores señores infieles" (115).

The fifth title authorizes the Spaniards to dethrone tyrannical princes for the practice of nefarious acts such as human sacrifice or cannibalism. Vitoria gives the Christian prince full authority to depose such a tyrant in order to protect the lives of the innocent natives.

The sixth lawful title is called "True and Voluntary Choice"—"verdadera y voluntaria elección." Vitoria hypothesizes that the Indians, comprehending "la huminidad y sabia administración de los españoles," might freely and of their own accord accept the prince of Spain as their supreme earthly ruler and thereby, as subjects of the monarchy, be governed by Spanish law. Vitoria did not believe that such a transition of power necessitated the consent of the entire populace—only the majority.

The friar's zeal for the establishment of a Christian America annexed to the Spanish Empire leads him to assert that the Christian majority of one province can "elegir príncipes no solo para ellos, sino para toda la república . . . " (117). Concerning this title Scott states, "The sixth lawful title is one which needs only to be stated in order to be queried."[26] This, indeed, seems to be the case since, if the Christian majority can implant their chosen form of government not only in those provinces where they are most populous but also in the entire country, it is clear that the title of "verdadera y voluntaria elección" is vitiated by the obvious fact that the Indians' choice of government has no political validity since they are, in the first place, outnumbered by Spaniards who, no doubt, would freely and voluntarily choose the Spanish monarchy as their head of state and, secondly, by the fact that such a Christian majority could extend its choice of government not only to those regions in which they are the clear majority but also to the entire country, where, no doubt, the Indian population would exceed the Christian.

The seventh title is brief; it is named "razones de amistad y alianza." The friar states that an Indian tribe engaged in war with another Indian tribe can ally itself with the Christian armies in order to defeat a common foe and reap the spoils of victory.

Vitoria approaches the eighth title with caution and no little reservation. "Otro título," he announces, "podría no ciertamente afirmarse, pero sí discutirse, considerando lo que puede tener de legítimo. Yo no me atrevo a sostenerlo, ni tampoco a condenerlo de lleno" (118). Vitoria refers to the question of the Indians' capacity for reason and government, previously discussed at the end of his first *Relección*. The professor is now prepared to address the question of the Indian's ability to reason and govern effectively and to outline recourses the Spanish crown might have should it be proven that the natives were, as many strongly contended, devoid of reason and, therefore, inept in governmental matters.

As usual Vitoria begins with the opposing argument—the belief that the Indians are irrational and, therefore, cannot adequately govern themselves. Vitoria asserts that there seems to be some truth in this argument, and if so, the Spaniards should govern them. The word used to describe the Indians' intellectual inferiority is "amente" (a-mente) i.e. the lacking or privation of the mind. The word carries the connotation of childlike. The Indian, it was asserted, bore the characteristics of a child, of a being not at the age of reason. Vitoria offers the following hypothesis: if all adult Indians should perish, leaving only their children, the Spanish prince could legally take charge of these children until they reached the age of reason. In like manner, if one can prove that the native adults lack reason, the prince can also govern them.The theologian suggests that the assignment of the native population to the trust, care, and government of the Spaniards, in view of their paucity of reason, would be an act of charity and mercy.

Vitoria is not totally persuaded by this line of argumentation although he finds some grounds for its support. Note how carefully the theologian treads the uncertain paths of Aristotle and serfdom in the following passage. The friar refers to those who contend that the Indians are natural serfs:

> Hay que apuntar también que en esta argumentación *puede* aprovecharse lo antes afirmado: de que hay quienes son siervos por naturaleza, y como tales *parecen* ser estos bárbaros, *podrían* por lo tanto ser gobernados como siervos. (120, emphasis added)

Certainly, here as in other portions of the *Relecciones*, the professor runs dangerously close to contradiction. Note, however, that Vitoria carefully states that the argumentation that the Indians are unsuited for government due to their puerile faculties *can* ("puede") or *may be* used to substantiate the notion that the Indians are by nature serfs; furthermore, the theologian states that the Indians "parecen"—seem—to fit into the category of natural serfs in the accepted Aristotelian definition of the term. The careful measuring and weighing of each word concerning this matter can only indicate that Vitoria was not to be easily persuaded by the "según dicen" reports from America. Therefore, when Vitoria announces to his class that there *may* be justification for the assertion that the Indians are in need of guidance in laws and customs, he states his personal reservations on this delicate subject. Unequivocal proof would be the only evidence Vitoria could accept. Verified reports and not hear-say would, in the mind's eye of Vitoria, resolve the matter and determine the course of action the monarchy could legally take.

Vitoria begins the second part of *De jure bello* by quoting several biblical passages from the New Testament which beseech the Christian community to spurn hatred, vengeance, aggression. He states, however, that these biblical references represent advice to the Christian but are not precepts of law. Basing his arguments upon the teachings of Saints Thomas and Augustine, the friar concludes that war is not opposed to the spirit of Christianity. Indeed, there is no ideological conflict between the evangelical laws and natural or societal laws. When a nation has been unjustly assaulted, it has the blessings of God, country, and international law to rise up against the aggressor and to punish him and to reclaim all things which the aggressor may have illegally taken. War is also justifiable when a nation wishes to avenge evil perpetrated against it, reclaim, or defend its possessions. A nation may wage a defensive war; one must repel force with force. Furthermore, a nation may engage in offensive warfare when there has been a previous injury.

The theologian accepts the definition of Saint Augustine of just war; it is one whose purpose is to redress wrongs—to avenge, to punish the aggressor. A just war is also one which attempts to punish a nation for failing to castigate the wrongs of its subjects who have been perpetrators of evil; just war may also be waged against the nation which refuses to return to the offended nation the plunder which it has unjustly captured. War is ultimately justified under these conditions because the final result of war is the restoration of peace.

Vitoria now addresses the second question: Who has the right to declare war? His answer is direct and clear: anyone can undertake a defensive war to protect himself or his possessions because it is legal to repel force with force.

What, asks the friar, is the reason or cause for a just war?

When is it licit to combat the enemy and when is it illicit to do so? Concerning the latter question, the professor offers three cases:

a. Differences in religion do not justify the right to wage war. Such war waged on these grounds is unjust.[27]
b. One cannot wage war to increase land area.
c. War cannot be waged for the glory of the prince or for his personal advantage.

The distinguishing factor between the tyrant and the legitimate prince is that the former wages war for his own personal benefit while the latter undertakes war for the benefit of the people. The prince receives his authority from the public. The prince who obliges his subjects to battle for his own gain and benefit converts his free subjects into serfs.

The prince, Vitoria states, has no greater power over foreigners than he does over his own subjects; since the prince cannot raise his sword against his subjects, it follows that he cannot raise his sword against foreigners unless they have offended the Republic. Natural law prohibits the use of force against the innocent. Therefore, the prince cannot wage war against those who do not endanger his Republic.

What acts are permissible in a just war? Is it legal to use any means of warfare for the preservation of the Republic and the welfare of its citizens? Vitoria responds that anything which is in the best interest of the public is permissible in war. Furthermore, one can recover all lost things in war or regain the price of them. The theologian obviously views booty as a legitimate means for the Republic to recuperate material goods which the enemy has unjustly taken or destroyed. Concerning booty, he states that one can take the goods of the enemy for the expenses incurred in war.

The prince who wages a just war has license to do all that is necessary to ensure peace after defending the Republic, "por ejemplo, domoliendo sus fortalezas y levantando fortificaciones en el territorio enemigo, si ello fuere indispensable para evitar peligros ocasionados por sus adversarios" (137). The legitimacy of this right lies in the fact that the purpose or end of war is the establishment of peace and security.

Vengeance is also permissible for the prince who wages a just war. The prince has jurisdiction over the vanquished to ensure that the enemy will abstain from further injurious actions. Vitoria gives the Republic the power to punish pernicious citizens. Peace cannot be achieved without castigation of the enemy.

With reference to the legality of killing the innocent (women, children, pilgrims, clergy) who may be entangled in the ravages of war, Vitoria declares that there is no justification for such action. Nor is it legal to attack a fortress in which the enemy is housed with the innocent. Vitoria's opinion seems to be based on a logical premise: to attack the innocent is to create another enemy of the State. Although Vitoria opposes the killing of the innocent in war, he favors and considers just the expropriation of arms, ships, artillery, money, crops, animals, etc. from the innocent in order to debilitate the enemy and ensure that weapons not be used against those who wage a just war. Should there be a prolonged war, it is legal to despoil the enemy soldiers as well as the innocent since their riches protract the war.

Concerning the rectitude of the captivity and enslavement of the innocent, Vitoria makes a distinction between war waged among Christians and pagans or Moors (sarracenos) and one waged among Christians. In the former case Vitoria has no doubt that it would be highly recommendable to enslave the innocent of the enemy since the injuries received by Christians from them have been enormous, although the war is not seen as a religious war. Vitoria had in mind the long struggle of the Reconquest of Spain when he formulated his position concerning the captivity and enslavement of the innocent of the Moorish enemy. The friar takes a different position concerning the enslavement of the Christian enemies' innocent: he states that enslavement is not a viable choice but the taking of captives for ransom is.

Vitoria tells his students that one must offer peace to the rebellious enemy, but if rebellion continues, the nation that is attacked has the right to kill the rebels. It is legal to kill the warriors who attack after the establishment of peace.

Concerning the expropriation of the enemy's land or the occupation of a city or fortress, Vitoria states that such an act can be done for the sake of peace, but restitution must be made when the hostilities have ceased. The conqueror may, however, retain property or goods as compensation for the damage and destruction committed by the enemy. Punishment must be proportionate to the guilt and must not be or seem unreasonable. The conqueror may also impose contributions upon the vanquished to compensate for the damages caused by the enemy. Such contributions are just punishment.

Concerning the dethronement of the enemy prince and the installation of new governors, Vitoria states that such action is generally impermissible. However, if it is undertaken with the intention of averting greater danger to the Republic, or to redress a multitude of atrocities perpetrated by the enemy, or if it is the only means to secure peace, such an action would be legal.

While the thoughts of Francisco de Vitoria had great impact in Spain, the writings of Bartolomé de las Casas exercised great influence not merely on the history of colonial America but also on the opinions of his countrymen about the Indians. His concept of justice and belief in the equality of all men led him to denounce what he perceived as inhumane treatment of the Indians; to the detriment of his country, many European intellectuals found in his works, the *Brevísima relación de la destrucción de las Indias* in particular, justification for the assertion that the Spaniards were brutal and savage people who had sought America's riches under the cloak of religion. Las Casas composed the *Brevísima* in 1542 while lobbying at the court of the Emperor for reforms for the Indians between 1540 to 1542. The tract helped to foment an atmosphere favorable to the king's New Laws of 1542. The *Brevísima* was published in 1552 and translated into six European tongues by 1626.

In the *Brevisima* Las Casas views the natives as innocent, loving and unpretentious people who are capable of indoctrination in the Christian faith. He sees some Christians as bloodthirsty, avaricious exploiters of the spiritual and physical welfare of the indigenous population. While opponents of Las Casas' assertions have rightly pointed out the wild exaggerations of the number of Indians killed by the Spaniards,[28] there is ample documentation to support the cruel treatment of the Indians at the hands of the Spaniards. Las Casas was one of the many friars in the New World who advocated the peaceful conversion of the Indians and who stressed this aim as the foremost objective of the Spaniards in America.

On the peninsula Las Casas certainly lacked no opposition to his view on the American Indian. Many scholars in Spain deemed the natives of America beasts of burden, a species of subhuman with no soul, in a word, a serf.

Juan Ginés de Sepúlveda was, perhaps, the chief spokesman in Spain for the position that the American Indians were, by nature, slaves. *Democrates alter, sive de justis belli causis apud Indos* (1544), deemed by the University of Alcalá as unsuitable for publication due to its "unsound" doctrines, sets forth, in dialogue form, Sepúlveda's view concerning the conquest of the natives in America. The work centers upon a conversation between Leopoldo, a German Lutheran, and Demócrates, through whom Sepúlveda speaks and convinces the former of the complete justice of the wars waged against the Indians; the king, states Demócrates, has the obligation to wage these wars in order to spread the Gospel and to wrench the Indians from their abominable sins and customs.

Demócrates declares that there are four principal reasons which justify the war against the Indians. These are: for the gravity of the Indians' sins—idolatry, sodomy, cannibalism; the rudeness of the Indians' nature, which obliges them to serve the more refined nature of the Spanish lords; in order to promulgate Christ's teachings, which would be speedily accomplished through the subjugation of the natives; and to protect the innocent natives from the cruelties of their own lords. Although the *Democrates . . .* was not published, the content of the work was well known to the king, his advisors, and Spanish intellectuals. Sepúlveda did publish in Rome in 1550 his further defense of *Democrates . . .*, entitled *Apologia pro libro de justis belli causis*.

The great debate took place in Valladolid from mid-August until mid-September of 1550. Doctor Sepúlveda and Las Casas were the principal debaters. Las Casas' position, as well as Sepúlveda's was, from the outset, clear to all. In his *Argumentum apologiae* Las Casas intended to rebut the theories of Sepúlveda as set forth in his *Democrates* by stating, as he had done on previous occasions, that the only means to attract the Indian population to Christianity was through peaceful predication. He accepted the notion that the Indians would, under these conditions, not only accept the faith but would also be willing to live harmoniously with the colonizers and accept the authority of the emperor and the pope.

Sepúlveda adhered to his argumentation presented in the *Democrates*. He stated at the debate that the Spaniards were wholly justified in the enslavement of the natives due to the superiority of Spanish weaponry and bodily strength, as well as superior prudence, genius, virtue and humanity. He declared that it was the duty of the monarch to spread the Gospel to the New World, and the most effective means of achieving this end was through force. Using Aristotle's *Politics* as his guide, the Doctor stated that the Indians were inferior to the Spaniards by natural law; it was, therefore, prudent for the king to place the Indians in the custody of their superiors in order to insure the welfare of both master and servant. If the Indians failed to recognize this fundamental difference between master and slave, the Spaniards would have the needed justification to wage war upon the insubordinate natives and to take away their property. The Indians must learn the good morals, the prudence, and wisdom of the Spanish in order to lead a better life.

Las Casas rebutted his opponent and used his *Apologética historia de las Indias* to this end. He stated that the Indians were not semi-animals to be used as property of the Spaniards. He affirmed that the Indians compared favorably to the peoples of ancient times, were rational beings, and fulfilled Aristotle's requisites for a good life. In many ways the Indians were superior to the ancients since the former exhibited greater religiosity. The tribes of Mexico were superior to the ancient Greeks and Romans in rearing and educating their children and in marital arrangements. The Indian women were hard workers. The temples of Yucatán were as worthy of admiration as those of Egypt. His conclusion: the Indians were in no manner less rational than the ancients, and certainly not to the Spaniards and that the Indians manifested to some degree, qualities superior to those of the Spaniards.

The great debate of 1550 ended without resolution. It would seem that Sepúlveda's opinions were not well received, since none of his treatises were published until the 18th century. Las Casas, to the contrary, continued to write and publish his thoughts on the subject; the *Confesionario . . .* and the *Brevísima* were published in Seville in 1552. Hanke states: "Even after his death in 1556 his books circulated everywhere."[29]

By the end of the 16th century, the noble intentions of the Spanish Crown to discover and colonize and convert the natives of the New World had led to many controversies within the country and abroad. Spanish friars decried the exploitation of the natives by the landowners. Landowners complained that their rights to extract manual labor from the Indians were being violated. Debates raged on the Peninsula with regard to the nature of the Indian; was he a sub-human species, a serf, inferior to the Spaniard, and, therefore, better governed and protected under the tutelage of his Castilian lord? Was the native capable of reason, and could he be Christianized through peaceful means, or was war the only solution to this end? Could the Spanish nation legally and morally conquer and subject the native Americans? Was the authority of the king and pope sufficient to overthrow native lords and institute Spanish government, customs, and allegiance to the papacy and Spanish monarchy? Under what conditions could the Spaniards legally wage war upon the natives? Amid these political, philosophical, ethical conflicts emerges the first of a small number of Golden Age plays dealing with the affairs of America, written, perhaps not surprisingly, by Spain's foremost dramatist, Lope de Vega. This play is *El nuevo mundo descubierto por Cristóbal Colón.*

Notes

[1] Cristóbal Colón, *El primer viaje de Cristóbal Colón* (Madrid: Instituto Histórico de Marina, 1943) 14–15.

[2] Derek W. Lomax, *The Reconquest of Spain* (New York: Longmans, 1978) 101.

[3] Lomax 25. See also John Huxtable Elliott, *Imperial Spain: 1469–1716* (New York: Saint Martin's P, 1967) 50, and Gabriel Jackson, *The Making of Medieval Spain* (London: Thames and Hudson, 1972) 54.

[4] Colón 54–5.

[5] Lewis Hanke, *The Spanish Struggle for Justice in the Conquest of America* (Boston: Little, Brown, 1965) 5–6.

[6] Hanke 6–7.

[7] Hanke 7.

[8] Charles Gibson, *Spain in America* (New York: Harper, 1966) 68.

[9] The *encomienda* system was institutionalized by Nicolás de Ovando in 1502. See Hanke 20.

[10] Gibson 51–2.

[11] Gibson 52.

[12] Hanke 7.

[13] Hanke 9.

[14] Hanke 17.

[15] Hanke 23.

[16] Hanke 23–4. For the text of the New Laws see: Lewis Hanke, Ed., *A History of Latin American Civilization: Sources and Interpretations* (Boston: Little, Brown, 1967) 135–144.

[17] Silvio Zavala, "New Viewpoints on the Spanish Colonization of America," *A History of Latin American Civilization: Sources and Interpretations* Ed. Lewis Hanke, (Boston: Little, Brown, 1967) 126.

[18] Zavala 126.

[19] Zavala 127.

[20] Américo Castro, *The Spaniards* Trans. Willard F. King and Selma Margaretten (Berkeley: University of California, 1971) 74.

[21] Francisco de Vitoria, *Relecciones sobre los indios y el derecho de guerra* Trans.

Armando D. Pirotto (Buenos Aires: Espasa-Calpe, 1946) 47. All further quotes are from this edition and have the page number at the end.

[22] Here, perhaps, is an indication of Vitoria's *converso* linage. When the Spanish Jews were expelled in 1492, their property, possessions, and lands were confiscated.

[23] ". . . The dream of a universal Empire, centered in Spain under Charles' rule, began to titillate the fertile imagination of Spaniards. At the Cortes of Santiago-Coruña (1520), the Bishop of Badajoz . . . proclaimed Charles as King of Kings; their heir to Trajan, Adrian and Theodosius; destined by God to inherit from Rome the vocation of the Empire. Charles' prime minister, Gattinara,recited into the Emperor's ear the visionary pages of Dante's *monarchia universalis*. Other humanists of Erasmian extraction—men like Juan and Alfonso de Valdés—were persuaded that Charles had been chosen by God to impose upon Europe a political solution guaranteed by Imperial power, and to resolve the religious schism with a general council where dogmatic differences could be transcended by an Erasmian formula for Conciliation." Carlos Noreña, "Francisco de Vitoria, America, and the Empire," *Revista de Estudios Hispánicos* 12 (1978): 73. Vitoria's pronouncement to his class that the emperor is not lord of the earth contradicts the prevalant notion that Charles V was destined by God to rule all mankind.

[24] It is likely that such arguments against forced mass conversions derive from Vitoria's caste history.

[25] James Brown Scott, *The Spanish Origin of International Law* (Washington, D.C.: School of Foreign Service, Georgetown University, 1928) 154.

[26] Scott 157.

[27] Again, one is tempted to view Vitoria's opinion in light of the mass forced conversion of the Spanish Jews in the 16th century. Vitoria seems to indicate that the forced conversion of the Jews was illegal.

[28] A prime example is Ramón Menéndez Pidal, *El Padre Las Casas: Su doble personalidad* (Madrid: Espasa-Calpe, 1963) 106–8 and 321–23.

[29] Hanke 130.

2

Visions of the New World in *El nuevo mundo descubierto por Cristóbal Colón*

The text of *El nuevo mundo descubierto por Cristóbal Colón* was first published in *Parte IV* of Lope's plays in 1614, as Marcelino Menéndez Pelayo indicates in his *Estudios sobre el teatro de Lope de Vega*.[1] As this critic observes, the title *El nuevo mundo* appears in the *Prólogo* of Lope's Byzantine novel, *El peregrino en su patria*, published in 1604[2]; the appearance of this title in *El peregrino* leads Menéndez Pelayo to the plausible conclusion that the abbreviated title refers to the play published in 1614 with the expanded title given above.[3] The list of *comedias* found in *El peregrino* has been of considerable value to scholars of Lope's theater in determining the probable dates of composition of the playwright's dramatic repertoire before 1604. Morley and Bruerton, using, in part, the list of *comedias* in the *Prólogo* of *El peregrino*, have concluded that the date of composition of *El nuevo mundo* lies between 1598 and 1603.[4] Since *Los hechos de Garcilaso de la Vega y el moro Tarfe* is, at present, the earliest extant play known to *lopistas* (composition ca. 1579–83),[5] it is clear that *El nuevo mundo* is among the playwright's earliest dramatic productions.[6]

By the time of composition of *El nuevo mundo* there were many chroniclers of the events of the discovery made by the conquistadores, friars, settlers, and natives of the Indies. Menéndez Pelayo affirms in the above-cited study that Lope's source for *El nuevo mundo* was one of two, perhaps both, chroniclers: Francisco López de Gómara (1511–1566), who published his *Historia de las Indias y conquista de México* in Zaragoza in 1552 and/or Gonzalo Fernández de Oviedo (1478–1557),[7] who published the First Part of his *Historia general y natural de las Indias* on September 30, 1535 in Seville; the Second and Third Parts were completed in 1548, according to Daymond Turner, but not published until the 19th century.[8] Lope had at his disposal, therefore, only the First Part of Oviedo's chronicle, while he had the complete text of Gómara's work to read while preparing his drama about the New World.

It is understandable that Menéndez Pelayo would have considerable reservations concerning which of the two chronicles Lope might have used in composing his *El nuevo mundo* since many of the details and anecdotes of the play can be found in Gómara and Oviedo alike. While asserting the possibility that Lope read both chronicles, Menéndez Pelayo concludes with reservations, no doubt, that Oviedo was the primary source for the composition of *El nuevo mundo*.[9] Other critics of the play affirm that Oviedo alone served as Lope's source.[10]

That Oviedo served as the primary source of Lope's play rather than Gómara is plausible, but Menéndez Pelayo offers no documentation for his assertion that such is the case. I intend to demonstrate in this chapter that Lope has used both Oviedo and Gómara as guides in his writing of the play but tends to rely more heavily upon Oviedo's account. Furthermore, it must be emphasized that Lope does not adhere to either Gómara or Oviedo in rigorous fashion, since such a course would restrict artistic creation. Lope expands upon, elaborates, or changes certain details of the chronicles, often to heighten dramatic impact; in some cases he avoids controversies presented in the chronicles which might have added to the dramatic effect of the play had they been more fully utilized. This is not to suggest that Lope has totally ignored conflict and controversy in *El nuevo mundo* but that they are subordinated to the portrayal of the messianic mission of the Spaniards in the New World. I shall explore here those passages of the play which best exemplify Lope's vision of America and attempt to show the source from which Lope has taken his information, how he has used it, how he departs from it, and where his own attitudes are most probably perceived.

In *El nuevo mundo descubierto por Cristóbal Colón* there are essentially two ruling themes reiterated throughout the play: religion and wealth. These concepts are not mutually exclusive; rather they form the basis of a type of debate related to the purposes, intentions, and motivations of the first conquerors of America. On one hand the idolatry of the Indians is contrasted with the religious fervor and the evangelical mission of the Spaniards. On the other hand the evangelic mission of the conquerors is contrasted with the mundane compulsion to secure gold and the Spaniards' desire to become rich from the booty of conquest. The debate between the temporal and religious drives is evident from the beginning of the play. In the twelfth scene of the first act, three allegorical figures—la Providencia, la Religión Cristiana, and la Idolatría—appear on stage to discuss their ideas concerning the purpose of the conquest. La Religión states, "De la Fe las Indias son;/Dios quiere gozar su fruto: vuélvele ¡infame! el tributo."[11] A little further on, La Providencia adds, "Esta conquista se intente/que para Cristo ha de ser." (10). To the argumentations of La Religión and La Providencia, La Idolatría rejoins:

> Pues los lleva [i.e. the Spaniards] la codicia
> a hacer esta diligencia.
> So color de religión
> van a buscar plata y oro
> del encubierto tesoro. (11)

La Providencia synthesizes these two opposite opinions concerning the purpose of the conquest by insisting that if the Spaniards come in search of gold, this desire is surpassed by the messianic intention; the lure of gold is only the bait used to accomplish the larger goal of destruction of idolatry:

> Dios juzga la intención:
> si El, por el oro que encierra,
> gana las almas que ves,
> en el cielo hay interés,
> no es mucho le haya en la tierra.

Y del cristiano Fernando,
que da principio a esta empresa,
toda la sospecha cesa. (11)

The allegorical figures in the play are obviously not to be found in the chronicles of Gómara or Oviedo; they spring from the fertile poetic imagination of Lope and serve to present various concepts about the Spanish mission in the New World. Through the allegorical figures, the dramatist presents contrasting visions of the intentions of conquest—the conversion and salvation of the Indians through Christian indoctrination versus the desire to exploit the riches of America and, at the same time, offers a synthesis of these polar views. Lope presents a view of the Spanish mission in America which, while not denying the historical truth of the quest for American riches, emphasizes the conversion of the natives as a superior motive for Spanish conquest. La Providencia's synthesis of two opposed views serves as the cornerstone of the entire play; Lope will not whitewash the disconcerting reports of Spanish greed for material wealth but will demonstrate through his characters the spiritual zeal (or the awakening to it) of the Spanish friars and explorers.

The debate over the purpose of the Spaniards in the conquest of American continues, as mentioned, throughout the *comedia*. Two of the most valuable opinions concerning this question are expressed by the commander of the expedition and the Spanish monarchs. When Columbus finally attains an audience with Ferdinand and Isabel, he attempts to persuade them to finance his expedition to the Indies with the following argument:

Yo iré si tú, señor, me das ayuda
a conquistar los indios, los idólatras;
que es justo que a la fe cristiana nuestra
reduzca un Rey que se llamó Católico
con la prudente y más dichosa Reina
que han visto las edades de oro antiguas. (13)

Neither Gómara nor Oviedo records the messianic desire of

Columbus while speaking to the Catholic Monarchs; both chroniclers write only of Columbus' promise of gold, silver and other riches to the monarchs to stimulate their enthusiasm for the proposed exploration. Unlike Gómara, Oviedo does reveal, however, the commander's wish to propagate the Christian faith when he arrives in America. Oviedo writes:

> Antes que Colom entrase en la mar algunos días, tuvo muy largas consultaciones con un religioso llamado fray Juan Pérez, de la orden de Sanct Francisco, su confesor, el cual estaba en el monasterio de la Rábida (que es media legua de Palos, hacia la mar) . . . Se fue Colom al mesmo monasterio y estuvo con el fraile comunicando su viaje e ordenando su alma e vida y apercibiéndose primeramente con Dios, y poniendo, como católico, en sus manos e misericordia su empresa, como fiel cristiano, y como negocio en que Dios esperaba ser tan servido por el acrescentamiento de su república cristiana. Y después de se haber confesado, rescibió el sanctísimo sacramento de la Eucaristía, el día mesmo que entró en la mar; y en el nombre de Jesús mandó desplegar las velas y salió del puerto de Palos por el río de Saltes a la mar Océana, con tres carabelas armadas, dando principio al primer viaje y descubrimiento destas Indias, viernes tres días de agosto, año del nascimiento de nuestro Salvador de mill y cuatrocientos y noventa e dos años, con la buena ventura, efectuando este memorable hecho movido por Dios, el cual quiso hacer a este hombre arbitrario e ministro para tan grande e señalada cosa.[12]

Oviedo reveals the religiosity of Columbus as well as his desire to extend the faith to the inhabitants of the New World. As Columbus was one of the prime movers in the discovery, Lope deemed it necessary to record in his play the religious zeal and evangelical commitment of the commander. That these superior attributes are not recorded by the chroniclers during Columbus' audience with the monarchs does not indicate that Lope has not been inspired by Oviedo's account cited above. As previously stated, Lope does not follow the chronicles slavishly. Lope thought as a dramatist and not as an historian; in paralleling Columbus' messianic vision with that of the monarchs (as we shall see) during the royal audience, the dramatist portrays unanimity of opinion between monarchs and commander at the moment the proposal for exploration is formally presented. Thus in the *comedia* Columbus offers religious reasons to justify his expedition: the desire to convert the idolaters to the holy faith of Spain.

During his interview with Columbus, the King offers his reasons for wanting to facilitate the voyage. Lope writes:

> Pues dádselo [i.e., the money] a Colón, y el cielo guíe
> sus altos pensamientos y deseos
> porque a la fe vuelvan los idólatras
> y se ensanche de España el señorío.[13] (13)

King Ferdinand expresses here two motives for his desire to undertake the American enterprise: the conversion of the Indians (religious motive) and the augmentation of Spain's power (political and patriotic motive). The above quote is important for the mere fact that the declaration comes from the king, and, therefore, represents the official policy of the State on the conquest.

Both chronicles record the crown's desire to sponsor the voyage to the Indies to redeem the natives. Gómara writes of the royal couple who listened to Columbus' narration of his first trip:

> Estuvieron los reyes muy atentos a la relación que de palabra hizo Cristóbal Colón, y maravillándose de oír que los indios no tenían vestidos, ni letras, ni moneda, ni hierro, ni trigo, ni vino, ni animal ninguno mayor que perro; ni navíos grandes, sino canoas, que son como artesas, hechas de una pieza. No pudieron sufrirse cuando oyeron que allá, en aquellas islas y tierra nuevas, se comían unos hombres a otros, y que todos eran idólatras; y prometieron, si Dios les daba vida, de quitar aquella abominable inhumanidad, y desarraigar la idolatría en todas las tierras de Indias que a su mando viniesen: voto de cristianísimos reyes, y que cumplieron su palabra.[14]

Oviedo records the following concerning the matter:

> No contentándose aquellos sanctos príncipes con sola su empresa e conquista sanctísima que entre las manos tenían, con que dieron fin a la subjeción de todos los moros de las Españas . . . pero, demás de reducir a España toda a nuestra católica religión, propusieron de enviar

> a buscar este otro Nuevo Mundo, a plantarla en él, por no vacar ninguna hora en el servicio de Dios. Y con este sancto propósito mandaron despachar a Colom . . . (22)

Examination of the above passages from the chronicles reveals an important fact: while Gómara reports Ferdinand's and Isabel's desire to convert the "idolators" after Columbus' return to Spain from his first voyage, Oviedo records the Monarchs' messianic inclination before the commander has set sail on the first voyage. As stated, royal pronouncements concerning the American enterprise were extremely important since they set forth the official attitude of the State. Lope de Vega, clearly aware of the weight of the crown's position and attitude in shaping the course of historical events, and attentive to the dramatic impact, perceived the advantages of Oviedo's account. By establishing the crown's wish to extend Christianity to the natives before, rather than after, the discovery, the dramatist demonstrates to his audience that the crown's principal concern is the salvation of native souls; the crown's evangelic quest is formulated in Oviedo and Lope as an initial motive for the voyage to America and not as a mere afterthought.

In *El nuevo mundo*, Christopher Columbus, after hearing the King's official declaration, concludes:

> Dadme licencia, porque pienso luego
> en Palos de Moguer hacer mi flota,
> y en el nombre de Dios ir, y hallar la tierra
> que os ha de dar riqueza, y a mí fama. (13)

The three key words in these lines are "Dios," "riqueza," and "fama." Here at the end of the first act Columbus summarizes all the motives of the conquest mentioned thus far. It will be an enterprise that will magnify the glory of God through the conversion of the natives, of Spain through the acquisition of wealth from the unknown world, and of the commander through the heroic deeds which he will achieve for Creator and country.

Both Gómara and Oviedo record, as does Lope, the historical

fact concerning the place of departure of Columbus' first voyage. Gómara writes, "Armó Cristóbal Colón tres carabelas en Palos de Moguer a costa de los Reyes Católicos . . . " (166) Oviedo states:

> E fuele [i.e. Columbus], confirmada la dicha capitulación por un real privilegio que le fue dado desde a trece días, que se contaron treinta de abril, en la cibdad de Granada, del dicho año de noventa y dos. E con este despacho partió Colom donde es dicho [i.e., from the "villa de Sancta Fe"], y fuese a la villa de Palos de Moguer, donde puso en orden su viaje. (23)

Furthermore, there are passages in both chronicles which view the voyage to the Indies as a divinely inspired mission. There are, likewise, passages in the chronicles which extol the glory of the Spanish nation and people. In the "Epístola Dedicatoria" of the first part of Oviedo's *Historia general y natural*, addressed to the "reverendísimo e ilustrísimo señor, el cardenal de España don Fray García Jofre de Loaysa . . . " (3), one reads,

> Nuestro Señor ha acrescentado las victorias de la Cesárea Majestad y se aumentan más cada día; y aún las cosas de las Indias e sus riquezas paresce que crescen a vuestra sombra; el servicio de Dios en ellas floresce; las repúblicas de cristianos que allí hay se ennoblecen; los reinos de España se enriquescen, y todo va de bien en mejor. (5)

In this passage one finds the essence of Columbus' pronouncement: God, wealth, fame; God has granted Spain great victories in the Indies; He has given the country great wealth to better serve Him, and He has established in the Americas communities of Christians which grow in nobility and virtue.

A similar laudatory passage about the blessings of God on the Spanish nation and people is found in Gómara's dedicatory epistle to King Charles; referring to the Indians Gómara writes:

> Y como no conoscen al verdadero Dios y Señor, están en grandísimos pecados . . . Aunque todos los indios, que son vuestros subjectos, son ya cristianos por la misericordia y bondad de Dios, y por la vuestra merced y de vuestros padres y abuelos, que habéis procurado su con-

> versión y cristianidad. El trabajo y peligro vuestros españoles lo toman alegremente, así en predicar y en convertir como en descubrir y conquistar. Nunca nación extendió tanto como la española sus costumbres, su lenguaje y armas, ni caminó tan lejos por mar y tierra, las armas acuestas. (156)

Lope's thoughts concerning the mission of Spain in the New World do not vary from those presented by the chronicles. The exploration undertaken by Christopher Columbus will magnify the glory of God, bring wealth to the Spanish nation and fame to the explorers. The remarkable aspect in Lope's play is the conversion of lengthy narrative statements into dramatic debate or speeches which serve to delineate Columbus' character. The result is more vivid and memorable in the play than in the chronicles. In the two remaining acts, which take place on the high seas or in America, Lope exemplifies through the actions of the characters the religious fervor and the monetary impulse as motives for the overseas expedition.

The Propagation of Christianity as a Motive for the Conquest

The two remaining acts provide many examples of the evangelic impulse of Columbus' journey to America. In the sixth scene of the second act Columbus and his sailors disembark for the first time in the New World on the island of La Deseada. The first act of the commander is to implant a cross in the sand at the seashore. He says to Friar Buyl:

> Padre, dame aquesa cruz,
> que aquí la quiero poner;
> que éste el farol ha de ser
> que dé al mundo nueva luz. (22)

In Gómara's chronicle there is no mention of the implantation of the cross on the shores of any of the islands Columbus discovered during his voyages to America. Referring to the Indians of Guanahaní during the first encounter between men of the Old World and the New, Gómara writes, "Andaban tan humildes, tan bien criados y serviciales como si fueran esclavos de los españoles. Adoraban la cruz, dábanse en el pecho, e hincábanse de rodillas al Ave María, como los cristianos." (167)

In Oviedo's chronicle there is no mention of the implantation of the cross during the first voyage; however, during the second voyage Oviedo records:

> Cuando llegaron a la sancta Vera Cruz de la cibdad de la Concepción de La Vega, es de saber que el segundo viaje que el almirante don Cristóbal vino a esta isla, mandó a veinte e tantos hombres que fuesen a cortar un buen palo derecho y alto e bien hecho. E los más de aquellos a quien mandó, eran hombres de la mar; e fue con ellos Alonso de Valencia . . . , e cortaron un árbol grueso e redondo, e de lo más alto dél, cortaron un tronco que atravesaron, haciéndolo cruz, la cual será de diez e ocho o viente palmos de alto. Afirman muchos e tienen por cosa pública e cierta que ha hecho miraglos después acá, y que el palo desta cruz ha sanado a muchos enfermos; y es tanta la devoción que los cristianos en ella tienen, que hurtan muchos pedazos e astillas della así para llevar a España como a otras partes. (64–65)

There can be no doubt that Lope has availed himself of Oviedo's account of the miraculous cross which Columbus ordered to be erected. Gómara's information does not express the adoration by the Christians of the cross, rather that of the Indians. In a subsequent scene which will be discussed shortly, Lope reveals the devotion of the Indians to the cross. Lope may have derived his scene depicting the Indian devotion to the cross from the above-cited passages in Gómara; however, the devotion of the natives is also described in Oviedo following the paragraph cited above.

One is tempted to suggest that the "Fénix" was quite impressed by the visible signs of Spanish devotion to Christian principles when he read Oviedo's account. For him such a report might serve as confirmation of the adherence of the crown and its subjects to the noble challenge of propagation of Christianity among the natives of America. At any rate, Lope did perceive the value of Oviedo's account, which lends credence to the sincerity of the evangelic mission of the exploration. As a playwright interested primarily in the portrayal of Spain's holy mission in America and conscious of dramatic impact, Lope perceived the advantages of Columbus' order to implant the cross on the shores of La Deseada; as this is the first action taken upon disembarkation, stress falls upon the religious nature of the voyage. Thus Lope heightens and underscores the religiosity of the commander by using Oviedo's anecdote, which occurred during the second voyage and is the first action taken by the commander in America.

Lope then develops Oviedo's declaration that the Spaniards showed great devotion to the cross erected at Concepción de la Vega: the protagonist Columbus orders everyone to kneel before the cross which has just been fixed on the shores of La Deseada. Friar Buyl asks that "cada cual hable con ella [la cruz]." (22) Each principal sailor—Columbus, his brother Bartolomé, Arana, Terrazas and Friar Buyl—proclaim their devotion to the cross:

Colón: Cama ilustre, donde Dios-
Hombre murió echado en ella. (22)

....

Fray Buyl: Arbol de la nave hermosa
de la Iglesia, tú que igualas
con jarcias y con escalas
la que Jacob vió gloriosa . . . (22)

....

Bartolomé: Vara de Moisés divina
que dividió el mar Bermejo; (22)

....

Arana: Verde laurel de victoria
de la cabeza de Cristo,
ya en el otro mundo visto
para vuestro honor y gloria. (22)

....

Terrazas: Arpa de David, templada
donde estuvo, en tres clavijas

fijo, aquel que tuvo fijas
las cosas que hizo de nada. (22)

Interspersed with these lines are allusions by Bartolomé, Arana and Terrazas to the Indians' practice of idolatry and the Spaniards' desire to convert the natives to the Catholic faith. Bartolomé states: "Vara de Moisén divina/que dividió el mar Bermejo;/farol, norte, luz, espejo/por donde el hombre camina,/ en esta tierra, aunque indina,/por no conocer al cielo." Arana proclaims; "Oro en medio de la escoria/desta falsa idolatría . . . " Terrazas declares: "Convertid a vuestro celo/todo este bárbaro polo." This scene, depicting Spanish piety and evangelism, and native idolatry, is, as previously stated, an elaboration of Oviedo's account of the implantation of the cross during the Second Voyage. Through the litany of praise to God for safe arrival Lope exemplifies and illustrates Oviedo's statement—"es tanta la devoción que los cristianos en ella [la cruz] tienen"—and underscores the necessity of conversion of pagan souls.

An important fact about Lope's use of his sources emerges. The dramatist is historically inaccurate in stating that La Deseada was discovered on Columbus' first voyage. According to Gómara (168) this island was discovered during the second voyage. Oviedo states the same (35). Lope combines details from the first and second voyages with little regard to the historical accuracy. Realizing the hardships of such a voyage, Lope probably chose this island because of the idea of rest, sanctuary, comfort, and joy which the name "La Deseada" implies. The change of name from "Guanahaní" to "La Deseada" certainly is a poetic untruth, quite willful on Lope's part.

Furthermore, the inclusion of Friar Buyl is another historical inaccuracy, as he accompanied Columbus on his second crossing according to Gómara (176) and Oviedo (35). The inclusion of Buyl in a play dealing with the first transatlantic voyage and the declaration that La Deseada was discovered during the initial voyage are clear indications of the liberty Lope takes with history in order to meet his ideological and poetic requirements.

In the third scene of the last act Pinzón informs the audience that he has written a letter to Friar Buyl, who has carried the Good News to the Indians of Haiti and Barucoa. Pinzón requests the friar to return to La Deseada to offer mass to the Indians and the Spaniards:

> Ya le escribo que no tiene
> razón de no darse prisa,
> que aquí se espera su misa
> con regocijo solene
> y los indios y los cristianos
> ya al cielo alzamos las manos
> por ver aquel día franco
> que baje Dios al pan blanco
> de los cielos soberanos. (32)

In the next scene the Indian woman Tacuana speaks of the virtues of Friar Buyl and adds that all the Indians wish to hear mass:

> Y la cruz nos predica
> aquel bendito monje,
> que le trujo en sus espaldas
> por la redención del orbe,
> desde Haití a la hermosa Chile
> generalmente se adore
> y la misa que esperamos
> mueva nuestros corazones.[15] (33)

The above-cited passages are quite obviously important because they reveal the sincere devotion of the friar and Pinzón, but they are also significant since they indicate the promulgation of the Gospel to other regions, which underscores once again the sincere convictions of the Spaniards to extend the word of Christ to the "bárbaros." Of equal importance is the fact that here one perceives the growing devotion of the Indians to the Christian faith and to its ministers. Here explorer and Indian together express the desire to participate in Christian rites.

In these passages one notes the constant supplication by the

Indians that Friar Buyl offer mass to the inhabitants of La Deseada. It seems that here is an example of deliberate suppression of historical facts by Lope de Vega, perhaps to avoid controversy, but most probably to avoid deviation from the central thrust of the drama: the depiction of Spanish devotion to God and their evangelization to the natives. The chronicles actually record an acrimonious dispute between Christopher Columbus and Buyl. When the Admiral returned to America on his second crossing, he was accompanied by Buyl and other clerics of the order of St. Benedict. Upon arrival, Columbus learned of the ill treatment of the Indians by some of the Spaniards who had remained in La Española. Gómara declares:

> Cuando volvió [Christopher Columbus] halló muchos españoles muertos de hambre y dolencias, y otros muchos muy enfermos y descoloridos. Usó de rigor con algunos que habían sido desacatados a sus hermanos Bartolomé y Diego Colón, y hecho mal a los indios. Ahorcó a Gaspar Férriz, aragonés, y a otros. Azotó a tantos, que blasfemaban dél los demás; y como parecía recio y malo, aunque fuese justicia ponía entredicho el vicario fray Buil para estorbar afrentas de españoles. El Cristóbal Colón quitábale su ración y la de los clérigos. Y ansí anduvo la cosa muy revuelta mucho tiempo, y el uno y el otro escribieron sobre ello a los Reyes. (170)

Oviedo offers more detail concerning the disagreement between the commander and the cleric. Like Gómara, Oviedo states that Columbus ordered the hanging of the Aragonese sailor Gaspar Férriz, but he adds:

> El Almirante era culpado de crudo en la opinión de aquel religioso, el cual, como tenía las veces del Papa, íbale a la mano; e así como Colom hacía alguna cosa que al fraile no paresciese justa, en la justicia criminal, luego ponía entredicho y hacía cesar las horas e oficio divino, y el Almirante también tornaba a poner su estanco y entredicho en los bastimentos, e no consentía que le fuesen dados al fraile ni a los clérigos, ni a los que servían. (51)

None of the rivalry between Buyl and Columbus (all second voyage) is evident in the play. Lope, wishing to portray sincere

Spanish faith, merely states that the natives and sailors yearn for mass and holy communion. That Buyl had halted religious services is not mentioned since such discord would be counterproductive to the aims of the dramatist. One sees in this case the freedom with which Lope employs his sources; he has ignored for his purposes the controversy, but he has built upon it at the same time. The denial to the community of the sacrament (history) is transformed artistically into the petition by the community for Friar Buyl to return to La Deseada and offer mass to devout Spaniards and Indians (poetry). As Oviedo offers a more detailed account of the enmity between Columbus and Buyl, it is probable that Lope formulated his poeticized version of the controversy from Oviedo rather than Gómara.

At the end of the play Columbus returns to Spain accompanied by "seis indios bozales medio desnudos, pintados; un paje con un plato de oro, y otro con papagayos y halcones" (43), and he is received with great jubilation by the Catholic Monarchs. Ferdinand propounds once again the religious and national purposes of Columbus' voyage: "Que a España habéis dado un mundo/y a Dios infinitas almas . . . " (43) "Y mirad que os digo en esto/de vuestros hombros y vos/que o se ha puesto en ellos Dios/o al menos su Iglesia ha puesto" (43). As mentioned, the words of the King are important merely because they are uttered by him; in Golden Age drama he generally represents the supreme font of justice and order. Moreover, this royal declaration appears at the end of the play, which, in itself, is significant, as if it were the definitive word concerning the Spanish mission in the Indies. As at the end of the first act, the King reiterates that the discovery has lent glory to God and Spain, and he perceives the commander's voyage as a divine mission. It is important to note also that the King offers to be godfather of the Indians—"Seré el padrino yo mismo." (43), which once again underscores the religious nature of the enterprise.

From Lope's stage directions we learn that Columbus brought bars of gold with him on his return to Spain; however, it is important to note the monarchs' proposed use of the metal. Queen Isabel declares:

> Y yo se lo [i.e. "el oro"] quiero dar
> a la Iglesia de Toledo;
> que una custodia famosa
> pueden, señor, de ello hacer. (43)

Again the dramatist emphasizes the religious character of the American expedition; the first gold brought from the Indies will be used in God's temple.

The departure of Christopher Columbus from the Indies with a small group of natives, gold and commodities unknown to Western Europe is historically factual and recorded by Gómara and Oviedo. The former chronicler states:

> Tomó diez indios, cuarenta papagayos, muchos gallipavos, conejos (que llaman hutias), batatas, ajíes, maíz, de que hacen pan, y otras cosas extrañas y diferentes de las nuestras, para testimonio de lo que había descubierto. Metió asimismo todo el oro que rescatado habían, en las carabelas y con todos los demás españoles de aquel puerto Real; y con próspero viento que tuvo llegó a Palos en cincuenta días, de la misma manera que dicho habemos halló las Indias. (167)

Gómara also commemorates the baptism of six Indians and the decision of the royal family to serve as godparents to the new converts:

> Los seis indios se baptizaron, que los otros no llegaron a la corte; y el Rey, la Reina, y el príncipe don Juan, su hijo, fueron los padrinos, por autorizar con sus personas el santo baptismo de Cristo en aquellos primeros cristianos de las Indias y Nuevo Mundo. (167)

Oviedo recounts the return to Spain in much the same manner:

> E llevó de este camino el Almirante nueve o diez indios consigo, para que, como testigos de la buena ventura, besasen las manos al Rey e a la Reina, e viesen la tierra de los cristianos e aprendiesen la lengua, para que cuando aquestos acá tornasen, ellos e los cristianos que quedaban encomendados a Goacangarí, y en el castillo que es dicho de

> Puerto Real, fuesen lenguas e intérpretes para la conquista e pacificación e conversión destas gentes. (28)
>
> . . . .
>
> Digo que después que Colom salió en Palos con los indios que llevaba destas islas (de los cuales uno se había muerto en la mar) tomó los seis que iban sanos, e dejó allí dos o tres que estaban dolientes, e fuese a la corte de los Católicos Reyes a darles cuenta de su prosperidad e de lo que Dios acrescentaba en los reinos e señoríos de Castilla. (29)
>
> . . . .
>
> Duespués que fue llegado Colom a Barcelona, con los primeros indios que destas partes a España fueron, o él llevó, e con algunas muestras de oro, e muchos papagayos e otras cosas de las que acá estas gentes usaban, fue muy benigna e graciosamente rescebido del Rey e de la Reina. (30)
>
> . . . .
>
> Seis indios llegaron con el primero Almirante a la corte, a Barcelona, cuando he dicho; y ellos, de su propria voluntad, e consejados, pidieron el baptismo; e los Católicos Reyes, por su clemencia, se lo mandaron dar; e juntamente con Sus Altezas, el serenísimo príncipe don Juan, su primogénito y heredero, fueron los padrinos. (31)

One quickly gathers from the above passages from Oviedo and Gómara that Lope de Vega has followed his sources rather closely: the arrival of six Indians at the court, the transport of gold, parrots, etc., the baptism of the natives, and the desire of the royal family to be their godparents. The dramatist's account departs from history most noticeably when the Queen states that the gold will be used to make a monstrance for the Cathedral of Toledo; neither Gómara nor Oviedo records such a desire. The Queen's statement concerning the use of gold for religious purposes is probably Lope de Vega's invention.[16] The purpose for the inclusion of this royal pronouncement is unquestionably united to the nucleus of the drama: the portrayal of the religious and heroic spirit of the Spanish nation in its discovery and conversion of the Indians. Indeed, Lope has organized his drama *El nuevo mundo* in such a fashion that the religious component of the exploration dominates all other interests. As suggested earlier, Act I can be viewed as a debate concerning the motives of the conquest: greed vs. the salvation of the idolatrous natives; the debate between the allegorical figures (Lope's invention) is resolved by the King at the end of the act by the announcement that the proposed voyage will be undertaken for the glory of God and his nation. The commander of the expedition expresses these same values to the Spanish monarchs: God, nation, fame. While Act I presents the theory or the ideology behind the exploration, Acts II and III exemplify the theory primarily through the depiction of the piety of the Spaniards.

Before one concludes that Lope has presented his public with a totally favorable vision of the Spaniards, it must be affirmed that he does reveal in *El nuevo mundo* the other component of conquest debated in the first act: the quest for gold, riches, wealth. As stated earlier, however, the issue of gold is overshadowed by the religious thrust of the play.

Gold as a Motive for the Conquest

Stephen Gilman says in his article "Lope de Vega and the 'Indias en su ingenio'" that, "Lope may have celebrated Spain but he was too good and honest a historian to whitewash it."[17] Gilman's statement seems valid in the context of Lope's portrayal of the sailors' thirst for gold; however, as argued earlier in this chapter, Lope seems to avoid some of the controversies presented in the chronicles which would diminish the religious nature of the overseas enterprise. As Gilman states concerning the play, "Columbus' discovery and Spain's conquest were ultimately to be justified (in spite of venal and carnal 'conquistadores') by the exportation of Christ to a world that had hitherto been abandoned to Satan."[18] The sentiments expressed by La Idolatría and El Demonio in the first act were common accusations and indictments against many of the conquerors and settlers of the New World, as has been shown in chapter one; so prevalent was the notion that the conquest ignored the spiritual well-being of the Indians and sought personal gain that Lope could not, had he so desired, avoid the issue in composing *El nuevo mundo*. Although gold is an important motive for the conquest, the dramatist has subordinated its importance to the propagation of Christianity.

Throughout *El nuevo mundo* there are passages which indicate that Columbus perceives the Indies in terms of monetary gain. To the king of Portugal, he states:

> Iré a darte un Nuevo Mundo
> que a Portugal rinda parias,
> Para tu gloria y aumento:
> piedras, perlas, oro, plata. (2)

To Pinzón and his brother Bartolomé he laments:

> ¡Ah, Dios que no hay rey que quiera
> un Mundo Nuevo, un tesoro
> que aquesta mano le diera! (9)

To the Head Accountant he comments,

> Creed que son las Indias que busco;
> creed que hay gentes, platas, perlas, y oro,
> animales diversos, varias aves,
> árboles nunca vistos y otras cosas. (13)

Lope has followed his sources closely; the promise of wealth as an inducement for exploration is found in both chronicles. Gómara records:

> Y viendo al rey de Portugal ocupado en la conquista de Africa y navegación de Oriente . . . y al de Castilla en la guerra de Granada, envió a su hermano Bartolomé Colón . . . a negociar con el rey de Inglaterra Enrique VII, que muy rico y sin guerras estaba, le diese navíos y favor para descobrir las Indias, prometiendo traerle dellas muy gran tesoro en poco tiempo. E como trajo mal despacho, comenzó a tratar del negocio con el rey de Portugal don Alonso el Quinto, en quien tampoco halló favor ni dineros para ir por las riquezas que prometía . . . mas no perdió por eso punto de ánimo ni de la esperanza de su bienaventura que después tuvo. Y así, se embarcó en Lisbona y vino a Palos de Moguer, donde habló con Martín Pinzón, piloto muy diestro, y que se le ofreció, y que había oído decir como navegando tras el sol por vía templada se hallarían grandes y ricas tierras . . . Solamente Alonso de

> Quintillana, contador mayor, le daba de comer en su dispensa, y le oía de buena gana las cosas que prometía de las tierras nunca vistas . . . (166)

Oviedo writes that Columbus . . .

> . . . trabajó por medio de Bartolomé Colom, su hermano, con el rey Enrique VII de Inglaterra . . . que le favoresciese e armase para descobrir estas mares occidentales, ofreciéndose a le dar muchos tesoros, en acrescentamiento de su corona y Estados, de muy grandes señoríos e reinos nuevos . . . Así como vido que allí no era acogido su servicio, comenzó a mover e tractar la misma negociación con el rey don Juan, segundo de tal nombre en Portugal . . . Pero . . . no se le dió más crédito, ni el rey de Portugal quiso favorescer ni ayudar al dicho Colom para lo que decía . . . Turóle cuasi siete años esta importunación, haciendo muchos ofrescimientos de grandes riquezas y Estados para la corona de Castilla . . . Por medio del cardenal y de Alonso de Quintillana, fue oído del Rey e de la Reina; e luego se principió a dar algún crédito a sus memoriales y peticiones . . . (21–22)

One notes an obvious discrepancy in the reports of the two chroniclers; Gómara states that Columbus attempted to persuade Alonso V of Portugal to finance his exploration, while Oviedo writes that it was John II with whom Columbus spoke. Oviedo, of course, is correct; Lope has most probably availed himself of Oviedo's account since Columbus says earlier to Pinzón, "¡Cosa extraña, que en mil gentes/que he dicho este mundo ignoto/solo tú, amigo piloto,/. . ./le conoces y consientes!/¡Que conquiste el rey don Juan la India, que es tan dudosa,/y a que tantos hombres van,/y juzgue dificultosa/la que mis manos le dan." (8)

The conquerors in Lope's play also view the Indies as a means to become rich:

(UN INDIO CON BARRAS)

Pinzón: Ya trae, pese a mi mal.
Colón: Tomad con menos codicia.
Pinzón: Esto es nuestro de justicia,
y a nuestro trabajo igual.
Arana: Bien haya cuanto pasé.

Terrazas: Bien haya cuanto sufrí.
F. Buyl: Qué, ¿Besas las barras?
Terrazas: Si
mientras les dices la fe. (29)

Pinzón, Arana and Terrazas believe that the gold they receive from the Indians is their just reward for conquest and tribulations suffered in a foreign land. As shown in Chapter One, the notion of reward for military service—booty—has its roots in the Reconquest of Spain. Warriors knew that their efforts would be compensated by gold and lands; Lope's depiction of the three conquistadores mirrors this medieval tradition.

Lope, like his contemporaries, was quite aware of the reports of Spanish avarice in the New World. Francisco de Vitoria had informed his students of the "noticias de muchos escándalos" which poured into Spain from the Americas; Bartolomé de las Casas never ceased to indict his countrymen for greed, and his vituperations were continued by other scholars of like persuasion long after Las Casas' death, as seen in Chapter One. Gómara, while clearly no friend of Las Casas' theories concerning the nature and humanity of the Indians,[20] does record the thirst of his countrymen for wealth. Gómara writes:

> Entendiendo cuan grandísimas tierras eran las que Cristóbal Colón descubría, fueron muchos a continuar el descubrimiento de todas, unos a su costa, otros a la del Rey, y todos pensando enriquecer, ganar fama y medrar con los reyes. (177)

Oviedo, as stated, was an eyewitness to the affairs of the Indies, and he sets down many virulent attacks against the greed of many conquerors and their disinterest in the religious indoctrination of the natives:

> Mas, en la verdad, hablando sin perjuicio de algunos marineros que hay, hombres de bien, e comedidos e virtuosos, soy de opinión que por la mayor parte, en los hombres que ejercitan el arte de la mar, hay mucha falta en sus personas y entendimiento para las cosas de la tierra; porque, demás de ser, por la mayor parte, gente baja y mal doctrinada,

> son cobdiciosos e inclinados a otros vicios, así como gula, e lujuria, e rapiña, e mal sufridos. (46)
>
> . . . .
>
> Ni tampoco fue de todo punto la final perdición de los indios lo que es dicho; sino permitirlo Dios por los pecados de los descomedidos cristianos que gozaban de sus sudores de aquestos indios, si no los ayudaron con su doctrina de manera que conosciesen a Dios. (67)

In brief, the opinion of both chroniclers in the above-cited passages is that many Spaniards exhibit an inordinate desire to harvest the wealth of America; Oviedo states, furthermore, that many Spaniards do not fulfill their obligation to indoctrinate the Indians in the Christian faith. Lope de Vega reveals through Arana, Pinzón and Terrazas those personal qualities which disturbed Oviedo and Gómara, and certainly many others: thirst for gold and disinterest in the spiritual needs of the natives—(F. Buyl: "Qué, ¿Besas las barras?/Terrazas: "Sí—/mientras les dices la fe.").

To be sure, Lope was not inspired solely by either chronicle concerning the matter of Spanish greed and disinterest in the conversion effort. It must be stressed that the works and thoughts of Bartolomé de las Casas and other writers of like mind were well known in the Peninsula during the second half of the 16th century. Although Menéndez Pelayo prefers to maintain that Lope "ni . . . tuvo acceso a los textos entonces inéditos . . . de Fray Bartolomé de las Casas," his statement seems to ignore the host of publications of the Dominican's works beginning in the 1550s. I do not affirm that Lope de Vega did, indeed, read Las Casas, and I know no book or article which catalogues the works in Lope's personal library, which might shed some light on the question. However, the inescapable fact remains that most reasonably intelligent and informed Spanish subjects could not avoid the bombardment of denunciations of the practices of many settlers and conquerors. Lope was certainly aware of these reports through his readings of Oviedo and Gómara if nothing else. However, as there is no direct link in wording between the play and the chronicles or apparent paraphrasing of them, one cannot declare that Lope has derived the cited passage from either Gómara or Oviedo. Certainly the ideas expressed in Lope—thirst for gold/disinterest in evangelism—are found in Oviedo, yet such opinions were far too prevalent to affirm that the dramatist derived his information solely from either chronicle.

Not all Spaniards in *El nuevo mundo* are avaricious. Friar Buyl never succumbs to cupidity, and Columbus has many reservations about the ultimate value of gold, as seen in the previous quote and in the following:

> Colón: Llevaré animales y aves,
> los que aquí extraños hubiere.
> Terrazas: Otra cosa España quiere
> ya presumo que lo sabes.
> Colón: (HACE SEÑAS QUE SI)
> ¿Dices oro?
> Pinzón: Eso no más.
> Colón: ¿Tenéis desto?
> Terrazas: Que sí digo.
> Colón: Pues ¿de qué es el regocijo?
> Arana: Del oro que hallando vas.
> Colón: La salvación desta gente
> es mi principal tesoro. (29)

While Columbus uses gold as a means to tantalize the monarchs of Europe and thereby obtain the needed financial support for his voyage to America, he seems to place less emphasis on gold as a motive for his expedition; his interests seem to revolve more around the evangelic mission than the acquisition of wealth.

Gómara's account of Christopher Columbus' actions leading to his imprisonment is far removed from Lope's portrait of the Admiral. The chronicler reveals a man who seeks power and wealth through deceit and cruelty. The reader is informed that:

> Roldán y sus compañeros escribieron también a sus altezas mil males de Cristóbal Colón y de sus hermanos, certificándoles que se querían alzar contra la tierra; que no dejaban saber las minas ni sacar el oro sino a sus criados y amigos; que maltrataban los españoles sin causa nin-

> guna, y que administraban justicia por antojo más que por derecho, y que había el Almirante callado y encubierto el descubrimiento de las perlas que halló en la isla de Cubagua e que se lo tomaban todo y a nadie daban nada, aunque muy enfermos y valientes fuesen. (171)

There are, indeed, several passages in Gómara's *Historia de las Indias* which reveal the chronicler's less than enthusiastic opinion of Christopher Columbus. In the section which narrates Columbus' death, one notes a style which is almost devoid of profound sentiment for the sailor who had given Spain a new world; sentences are brief and abrupt:

> Llevaron su cuerpo a depositar a las Cuevas de Sevilla, monasterio de Cartujos. Era hombre de buena estatura y membrudo, cariluengo, bermejo, pecoso, y enojadizo, y crudo que sufría muchos los trabajos. Fue cuatro veces a las Indias, y volvió otras tantas . . . (172)

It is clear that Lope's vision of Columbus is at variance with Gómara's. Lope informs his audience that the salvation of the Indians is Columbus' principal concern, not the acquisition of wealth. Gómara, to the contrary, reports that Columbus was not only interested in the wealth of the Americas but also attempted to conceal his pot of gold from other explorers.

Oviedo reports the incident in which Columbus was accused of concealing treasures from his retinue; however, the chronicler takes a dim view of those who believe such gossip. He writes:

> Y este Bobadilla envió muchas quejas e informaciones contra el Almirante e sus hermanos, significando las causas que le movieron a los prender; pero las más verdaderas quedábanse ocultas, porque siempre el Rey e la reina quisieron más verle enmendado que maltratado. Pero diré lo que entonces algunos le oponían para culparle. Decíase que había querido tener secreto el descubrimiento de las perlas, e que nunca lo escribió fasta que el sintió que en España se sabía; e habían ido a la isla de Cubagua ciertos marineros llamados los Niños; e que aquesto lo hacía a fin de capitular de nuevo. Decían, asimismo, que era muy soberbio e ultrajoso, e que tractaba mal a los servidores, e que no obedescía, de las cartas e mandamientos de sus reyes, sino aquello quél quería, e que con lo de demás disimulaba e hacía su voluntad. Todo esto cuentan

otros de otra manera, e dicen que la muestra de las primeras perlas que se hobieron la envió el Almirante a los Reyes Católicos, luego que las descubrió, con un hidalgo dicho Arroyal. Y lo más cierto de todo fue que nunca faltaron en el mundo murmuradores y envidiosos. (65–66)

Lope de Vega's characterization of Christopher Columbus is intimately united with his personal vision of the role of his country in the Americas. In the drama the quest for material wealth is not the driving force behind Columbus' expedition. Gómara, on the other hand, does not merely report the rumors about Columbus' alleged avarice but seems to believe that these reports are well-founded; and in many instances he mocks the Commander; note, for example, Gómara's satiric account of Columbus' explanations to the Monarchs of the reports on his cruelty and avarice:

Oyéronle [the Catholic Monarchs] piadosamente las disculpas que les dió Cristóbal Colón, revueltas con lágrimas; y en la pena de alguna culpa que debía tener, o por quitar semejante bullicio o porque no pensasen que se les debía de dar para siempre la governación de aquella tierra a ellos, le quitaron de gobernar, cosa que mucho sintió; y aun cuando le dejaron tornar allá, fue harto, según sus negocios estaban escondidos y desfavorecidos. (171)

If we assume that Lope de Vega did indeed read Gómara's account of the New World, it is clear that such passages as these from Gómara would be of little service to the vision which the dramatist wishes to present to his public. Columbus' pronouncement in the play, "La salvación desta gente . . . ", is not recorded in either Gómara or Oviedo; however, Oviedo's more favorable attitude toward the Admiral was more in accord with the dramatist's need for an exemplary hero. Oviedo's rejection of the reports concerning Columbus' supposed avarice was sufficient for Lope to affirm that his expressed vision of Columbus was based upon historical fact.

It is important to note the slow conversion of Columbus' sailors in the play from cupidity toward the revelation of the deceit of gold. Terrazas and Arana declare in the first scene of the final act:

Terrazas: Tengo más o busco más;
pero todo este tesoro
deja mi disgusto atrás.
pues que no estás en el oro,
o contento, ¿dónde estás?
Al cielo he sido importuno
por tener y más tener;
ya tengo sin gusto alguno;
de donde vengo a entender
que no te tiene ninguno.
Arana: Tenéis razón, y advertid
que está en fe este oro o quimera,
como las arcas del Cid. (32)

These conquerors conclude that gold, like all mundane pleasures, is a deceitful source of felicity and contentment. Eternal delight is derived from God and not from the world, as Arana says:

Arana: Y pues no hay hombre ninguno
siendo común patria el cielo,
que no esté de gusto ayuno,
mucho se engaña en el suelo
si piensa tenerte alguno. (32)

The conquerors who had thirsted for gold now see the deceit, the error of such interest. Pleasure, they conclude, does not reside in mundane goods but in the eternal gifts of God. At the end of the play all of the principal conquerors—Columbus, Friar Buyl, Terrazas and Arana—are presented by Lope as men who are aware of the needs of the spirit and of the deceit of American wealth.

There is no passage in either chronicle which states, suggests, or implies the radical change in attitude which Lope exhibits in his play. This is to say that there is no explorer in either chronicle who renounces material wealth for spiritual reward. Lope de Vega has offered to his public not an historical account of the explorers' reawakening to spiritual values but his personal poetic vision. In this instance life is portrayed as it should be (poetry) and not as it is (history).

In the fourteenth scene of the last act the Devil (el Demonio) appears to Dulcanquellín, the lord or *cacique* of the natives of La Deseada, to persuade him of the error of Christian beliefs. One of his arguments is the following:

> ¡Oh qué gracioso que estás
> con esta amistad fingida!
> estos [i.e., the Spaniards] codiciando oro
> de tus Indias, se hacen santos,
> fingen cristiano decoro,
> mientras llevan todo el tesoro;
> que ya el otro llega a España. (41)

I have already cited passages from Gómara and Oviedo which support the Devil's allegations that many Spaniards seek nothing more than the wealth of the Indies, and, indeed Lope exhibits the hunger for material wealth in the play, as demonstrated. Of interest here is the revelation to Lope's audience that there existed an intimate relation between the Indians and the forces of evil. This notion is not necessarily the product of Lope's "ingenio." Gómara records several instances in which the Indians converse with Satan. Referring to the religious practices on the island of Española, Gómara writes:

> El principal dios que los de aquesta isla tienen es el diablo, que lo pintan en cada cabo como se les aparesce, y aparésceles muchas veces, y aún les habla. Otros infinitos ídolos tienen, que adoran diferentemente, y a cada uno llaman por su nombre y le piden su cosa. A uno agua, a otro maíz, a otro salud y a otro victoria. Hácenlos de barro, palo, piedra y de algodón relleno; iban en romería a Loaboina, cueva donde honraban mucho dos estatuas de madera, dichas Marobo y Bintatel, y ofrescíanles cuánto podrían llevar a cuestas. Traíalos el diablo tan engañados, que le creían cuanto decía. (172–173)

Oviedo writes:

> Y grande fue el mérito que adquirió nuestra nación en ser por españoles buscadas estas provincias; e tantos reinos de gentes perdidas e idólatras, por la industria y en compañía y debajo de la guía del primero almirante don Cristóbal Colón, reedificando e tornando a cultivar en

> estas tierras, tan apartadas de Europa, la sagrada pasión e mandamientos de Dios y de su Iglesia católica, donde tantos millones de ánimas gozaba, o mejor diciendo, tragaba el infierno; y donde tantas idolatrías e diabólicos sacrificios y ritos, que en reverencia de Satanás se facían muchos siglos había, cesasen; y donde tan nefandos crímenes y pecados se ejercitaban, se olvidasen.[21] (30–31)

The above citations from the chronicles suggest that Lope has followed Gómara here. In the first place Gómara states that there were frequent apparitions of the devil to the Indians and dialogues between them; furthermore, he adds that the devil deceives the Indians, who believe him. In the play the Devil appears to the *cacique* Dulcanquellín. Moreover, Lope leaves no room for doubt that his public is to interpret the appearance of the Devil as an indication of the religious error, the "engaño," under which the Indians live. As in the case of the royal pronouncements concerning the purposes of the conquest, it is important to consider what is said in relation to who says it. When the Devil informs Dulcanquellín that the Spanish quest for gold is the principal design of this nation, the dramatist wishes to convey to his audience that such a characterization of Spain's work in the New World is false and must be rejected as the utterance of man's "eternal enemy." One notices, therefore, two clear parallels between Gómara and Lope: the appearance of the Devil to the Indians and the idea that the Devil maintains the Indians in a state of deceit, in the shadows of sin and damnation.

Oviedo makes no mention of the actual appearance of the devil to the Indians. His concern lies with the sacrifices and rites offered by the Indians to the devil, which, the chronicler believes, leave the natives without hope of salvation. The writer regards the presence of the Spaniards in America as a means to the elimination of the nefarious religious practices of the Indians. From an ideological viewpoint Oviedo, Gómara and Lope agree that the Indians' worship of the forces of evil severs them from a healthy and desired relationship wtih God and His Church. However, as Gómara writes of the actual appearance of the devil to the Indians, it seems reasonable to assert that Lope has most probably taken this notion from him rather than Oviedo. This assertion leads to the conclusion that Lope consulted, if not read entirely, Gómara's *Historia*. However, it is to Lope's *ingenio* only that we owe the clever insertion into the Devil's speech of the main accusation against Spaniards.

Lope's inclusion of the scene in which the Devil speaks to Dulcanquellín has at least two functions within the play, one purely theatrical, the other ideological. From the theatrical point of view, it seems clear that Lope, following the Senecan tradition, wishes to horrify his audience with the spectacular; there can be no doubt that, in a nation where religious orthodoxy had been so firmly planted and where memories of the tales of struggle between Christian Spaniards and non-Christian Spaniards were still fresh in the minds of many of the *peninsulares*, the viewing on stage of the Devil would arouse horror and recall those bitter struggles among the warring religions in Spain at the close of the 15th century and the beginning of the 16th. From the standpoint of ideological thrust, the apparition of the Devil to an Indian serves as absolute justification for the presence of Spain in America to convert and save the souls of the "devil worshipers." Through this scene the playwright stresses the religious mission of Spain—the salvation of peoples who are ignorant of the teachings of Christ and His Church.

Characterization of the Indians

Lope de Vega establishes from the outset of his play a most unfavorable portrait of the *cacique* Dulcanquellín. Before the Indian leader of La Deseada appears on stage an *areito* is sung by the Indians.[22] Through this festive song and dance scene in which the audience experiences one of the customs of the American Indian, Lope creates a moment of dramatic irony; in what superficially appears to be a moment of celebration for the impending marriage of Dulcanquellín and Tacuana the dramatist subtly fashions an important aspect of the *cacique's* personality:

> Hoy que sale el sol divino,[23]
> hoy que sale el sol,
> hoy que sale de mañana
> hoy que sale el sol,
> se juntan de buena gana,
> hoy que sale el sol,
> Dulcanquellín con Tacuana,
> hoy que sale el sol,
> él Febo y ella Diana,
> hoy que sale el sol.
> A cacique tan hermoso,
> hoy que sale el sol,
> y a esposa de tal esposo,
> hoy que sale el sol,
> nuestro areito glorioso,
> hoy que sale el sol,
> consagre el canto famoso
> hoy que sale el sol divino,
> hoy que sale el sol. (17)

Irony lies in the verse "Se juntan de buena gana"; as the audience soon learns, Tacuana, previously promised in marriage to Tapirazú, has been abducted by Dulcanquellín from her native island, Haiti, and is being forced to marry the *cacique*. The irony of the *areito* is clear when Tacuana states to Duncanquellín:

> Dulcán, yo tengo entendida
> tu tierra y tu voluntad;
> pero no es la libertad
> por ningún precio vendida.
> No digo que te aborrezco;
> pero que, en fin, me has traído
> de mi padre y mi marido
> donde tus brazos merezco.
> Esta noche había de ser
> su esposa, si en esta tierra
> no lo estorbara la guerra

que en ella sueles hacer.
Es tu enemigo mi esposo,
supiste aquí nuestro trato,
dístenos arma y rebato
y robásteme furioso.
Con esto no puede ser,
en tantas guerras y pleitos,
que de tus bodas y arietos
reciba el alma placer. (18)

Through Tacuana's supplication to her abductor one perceives not only the irony of the Indians' *areito* but also several other important characteristics of Dulcanquellín:

1. He is not a man of peace but of war. He has waged war constantly upon the Indians of Haiti—" . . . si en esta tierra/no lo estorbara la guerra/que en ella sueles hacer."
2. Not only is Dulcanquellín a man who subverts public order through wars waged upon the inhabitants of Haiti but also a man who destroys private order by abducting Tacuana from father and fiancé. Dulcán knew of Tacuana's engagement to his enemy Tapirazú and, in spite of this knowledge, he carries the young maiden from her home and loved ones. True love and the sanctity of marriage are ignored by the *cacique*, who seeks, instead, his own personal gratifications. ["Supiste aquí nuestro trato . . . "]
3. Dulcán assumes that his wealth will be sufficient enticement to win the hand (if not the heart) of Tacuana—"Pero no es la libertad/por ningún precio vendida."

Indeed, Dulcanquellín boasts to Tacuana that he can offer her riches. As he speaks to Tacuana, Dulcanquellín reveals much of his values and qualities: love of power and riches, paganism, egocentricity and narcissism. He declares to Tacuana:

¿Hay cacique en esta tierra
tan generoso y gallardo,
desde el occidente pardo

donde nuestro dios se encierra,
hasta la cuna en que nace?
¿Quién en tierra y mar pudiera,
fuera del sol en su esfera
que todo lo rige y hace,
ser como yo poderoso?
¿Naturaleza y fortuna
no se juntaron a uno
para hacerme venturoso?
Dióme la naturaleza
cuerpo, ingenio, brío, furor,
sangre, arrogancia, valor,
salud, fuerza, y ligereza.
Dióme la fortuna hacienda
hízome rey, sujeto
a lo que ordenase yo
cuanta voz humana entienda.
Dióme la paz y la guerra
a mi poner o quitar;
perla y coral en el mar,
el oro y plata en la tierra.
Sale el diamante en su escoria
de la mina, donde en vano
resiste al trabajo humano,
de su dureza victoria.
Sale el topacio de gualda
y la morada amatiste,
el jacinto que azul viste,
la continente esmeralda,
el colorado rubí,
con el vario girasol
y cuanto sustenta el sol
desde Guayra a Potosí.[24]
Y todo sirve a mis pies
y servirá a los de entrambos,
solo adornando los tambos
adonde conmigo estés. (17–18)

Lope's spectators were, perhaps at this point, aware of the ironic effect of the *areito* and were confronted with a *cacique* who was nothing short of a tyrant. As Tacuana declares in an aside, "Disimulad, corazón,/la fuerza de este tirano,/mientras que tiene en la mano/más ventura que razón." (17) The irony of the *areito* serves as a musical prelude to the presentation of a *cacique* whose personal characteristics are far removed from the idealized conceptualization of the Christian king expressed by Terrazas to Dulcanquellín (Act III, Scene viii: "Allá, en España, decimos/que son los reyes espejo/donde se mira el consejo/que los vasallos seguimos." (37) The mirror image which Dulcanquellín reflects to his subjects is one of social and domestic subversion of order, excessive pride and arrogance.[25]

Act II, scene ii develops a character delineation of Dulcanquellín which is wholly unfavorable. Lope has presented here an *areito* and dramatic action which are essentially his own invention. Dulcanquellín, however, was not an Indian whom Lope conjured from his imagination; he is mentioned briefly in Gómara, though not in Oviedo. In a chapter entitled "Río de Palmas," Gómara narrates Pánfilo de Narváez's attempt to conquer and colonize an area "que cae treinta leguas encima de Panuco hacia el norte y toda la costa de Florida" (181) in 1527. During his peregrinations Narváez meets the *cacique* whom Lope dramatizes. Gómara declares:

> Vió Narváez ora a unos indios, que preguntados donde lo sacaban, dijeron en Apalachén. Fue allá: en el camino topó un cacique llamado Dulcanchellín, que, a trueco de cascabeles y saralejos, le dió un cuero de venado muy pintado que traía cubierto, y venía a cuestas de otro indio y con mucha compañía, que los demás tañían caramillos de caña. (181)

From the above passage one might conjecture that Lope found the groundwork for the partial development of his *cacique*. The *cacique* described by Gómara travels with the pomp and elegance befitting a king; he is carried in a litter on the shoulders of an Indian as his retinue follows and musicians entertain him on their flutes. This brief description of Dulcanquellín is certainly not far from the luxuries which Lope's Dulcanquellín describes to Tacuana—"Perla y coral en el mar. . . "[26]

Dulcanquellín, like all his subjects, welcomes the arrival of the Spaniards to his island kingdom and wishes to demonstrate his hospitality by offering his guests what he considers his most sumptuous native delicacies. To Auté, the *gracioso*, he commands:

> Mata, Auté, cuatro criados
> de los más gordos que hallares
> y entre silvestres manjares
> los pon en la mesa asados.[27] (30)

Dulcanquellín's order to Auté is, of course, an example of cannibalism, a custom which, according to Gómara and Oviedo, was widespread throughout the Americas; however, the former chronicler states that in the Lucayos islands (or Lucayas) which "caen al norte de Cuba y Haiti" (178) meat was not part of the natives' diet: "En muchas destas islas chiquitas no tienen carne ni la comen." (178) One may presume from Gómara's statement that he includes the eating of human flesh; if Lope read this passage, it seems he has generalized about the Indian practice of cannibalism, since La Deseada and Guanahaní would be among those islands which did not indulge in cannibalism. Oviedo refers to several small islands near La Deseada—Santa Lucía, Sanct Cristóbal, los Barbados—which are inhabited by cannibalistic Indians called the *caribes*: "Estos flecheros destas islas que tiran con hierba, comen carne humana, excepto los de la isla de Borinquen" (34–35). Again, La Deseada and Guanahaní are not mentioned as islands where cannibalism is a practice. However, as both chroniclers offer numerous examples of cannibalistic tribes,[28] Lope would most probably feel it not a rupture of verisimilitude to state that the Indians Columbus met were indeed cannibals. Furthermore, the depiction of cannibalistic Indians certainly heightens dramatic effect and stresses once again the need for conversion of the natives.

In addition to being a cannibal, Dulcanquellín is, of course, a pagan. In the long speech to Tacuana (II, ii), Dulcanquellín indicates that the sun is his people's principal deity: "¿Quién en tierra y mar pudiera,/fuera del sol en su esfera/que todo lo rige y hace,/ser como yo poderoso?" (18) Neither chronicler reports that the natives of the Caribbean Islands are worshipers of the sun. It is likely that Lope has again generalized about Indian worship based upon popular concepts of Indians, especially the Incas, who did worship the sun as supreme god. Again the dramatist strengthens dramatic impact upon his audience by informing them (or misinforming them) that the Indians whom Columbus met were worshipers of the sun. What the chronicles do make clear concerning the islanders is their worship of many idols.

The principal idol of the inhabitants of Lope's La Deseada is Ongol; neither chronicler mentions this god. The name is, perhaps, as Lemartinel and Minguet suggest, Lope's re-creation of the name of an Araucanian Indian named Ongolmo in Ercilla's *La Araucana* (Pt. I—1569; Pt. II—1578; Pt. III—1589).[29] In III, viii, Dulcanquellín tells Terrazas that for his conversion to Christianity he has incurred Ongol's ire: "Sin duda se enoja Ongol,/que le dejé y desprecié/por el Cristo que decís." (36) Throughout this act the Indians have been drawn gently to the Cross and the doctrines of Christianity, and one of the most intense moments of struggle occurs when Dulcanquellín agonizes between the faith of his forefathers and the new teachings of the Spaniards. Here is a moment of true passion and struggle between tradition and innovation, between the gods of the natives and the God of the foreigners. Bartolomé Colón wants all idols destroyed before Friar Buyl returns to La Deseada to offer mass to the natives and Spaniards; Dulcanquellín responds to Bartolomé:

> Temo tu Dios y tus razones temo;
> pero esta ley y fe que profesamos,
> como la recibimos la tenemos.
> Nuestros padres, que aquí nos la enseñaron,
> ya de nuestros abuelos la aprendieron,
> ellos de sus mayores, de tal suerte
> que tiene innumerables sus principios. (39)

It is highly probable that Lope de Vega was sensitive to the spiritual and emotional trauma experienced when one begins to perceive life or an interpretation of life, its values and significance, in a new light, if we are to judge from Dulcanquellín's above-cited pronouncement and from the following in which this pathos reaches its zenith; the *cacique* in a soliloquy (III, xiii) queries:

> ¿Qué haré? ¿Dejaré mi Ongol
> por este Cristo extranjero,
> Dios—hombre y Dios español?
> ¿Dejaré luna y lucero,
> noche, día, cielo, sol? (40)

Lope de Vega, from the vantage point of a 16th-century Spaniard, understood and accepted the value and importance of the Christian faith for all mankind; however, the above passages (which have no parallel in his sources) demonstrate the dramatist's understanding of the inner struggle which must occur for those who are confronted with a perception of life which is at variance with an accepted tradition.

Dulcanquellín's conversion to Christian dogma is a slow process. Initially he and all the Indians fall to their knees at the sight of the Cross when Christopher Columbus orders it to be implanted on the shores of the island, and the Indians sense that it is some new and strange god. This experience on the shores is, however, insufficient to persuade Dulcanquellín that the God of the Christians is supreme. What does seem to be a deciding moment for the *cacique* occurs when Ongol flees from the cross which Dulcanquellín possesses; in III, xi he confesses to Bartolomé, Pinzón and Terrazas:

> Pues os juro que anoche, oídme todos,
> Ongol me diera muerte, reposando
> en mi tambo real, si no tuviera
> esta cruz que me ha dado vuestro padre, [i.e., Buyl]
> que me rogó que la arrojase luego;
> mas yo no quise, y fuese dando gritos
> que despertaron mi dormida gente:
> llaméle y no volvió, y esta mañana
> me dijo que jamás verme podría
> si esta cruz de mi pecho no arrojaba. (40)

The above passage from Lope may be derived from Gómara. In a chapter entitled "Milagros de la conversión," the chronicler writes:

> Otros muchos clérigos y frailes mendicantes entendieron también en el convertir; y así baptizaron a todos los de la isla [i.e., Sto. Domingo] que no se murieron al principio. Quitarles por fuerza los ídolos y ritos cerimoniales que tenían fue causa que escuchasen y creyesen a los predicadores. Escuchados, luego creyeron en Jesu cristo y se cristianaron. Hizo muy gran efecto el santísimo cuerpo sacramental de Cristo, que se puso en muchas iglesias, porque con él *y con cruces desaparecieron los diablos,* y no hablaban como antes a los indios, de que modo se admiraban ellos. (176, emphasis added)

Beginning in Act III, scene viii, one notices the constant fluctuation of Dulcanquellín's religious faith—now pagan, now Christian. In this scene the *cacique* repents having abandoned Ongol: "Sin duda se enoja Ongol . . . " Terrazas, who has enjoyed the intimate company of Tacuana, tells Dulcanquellín that he saw her with her fiancé, Tapirazú, hiding in the woods.

> Terrazas: Por tu miedo se emboscaron.
> Dulcanquellín: Qué, ¿en el bosque se quedaron?
> Terrazas: Dentro del bosque los vi.
> Dulcanquellín: Di, ¿sabréme yo tener
> En uno des tus caballos?
> Terrazas: ¿Para qué?
> Duncanquellín: Para alcanzallos. (36)

As Terrazas promises to bring Tacuana to Dulcanquellín, the *cacique's* desire for revenge against the fleeing couple appears to diminish. Terrazas informs the *cacique* that Buyl will return to La Deseada the following morning to offer mass, and this event also seems to strengthen Dulcanquellín's faltering faith and soften his vengeful heart:

> Dulcanquellín: ¿Cuándo el padre viene?
> Terrazas: Creo
> que estará mañana aquí.
> Dulcanquellín: ¿Y dirá la misa?
> Terrazas: Sí.

Dulcanquellín: Verla y oirla deseo.
Ven y darás la instrucción
del altar del sacrificio.
Terrazas: Harás a Dios gran servicio.
Dulcanquellín: *No es poco en esta ocasión.* (37—emphasis added)

While there is no reason to doubt Dulcanquellín's sincerity in wishing to see Friar Buyl and celebrate mass, Dulcanquellín does not yet understand "sacrifice" within the Christian concept of the offering of bread and wine at the altar, the sacrifice of the body and blood of Christ for the sins of mankind.[30] His understanding of "sacrifice" is that of the slaughtering of a human being for the appeasement of the gods. Dulcanquellín has minimal understanding of the teachings of the Church or at least of the meaning of the sacrificial mass which he desires to hear. One clearly sees in scene viii the fluctuation of Dulcanquellín's beliefs from fear of reprisal by Ongol to the desire to hear mass, as well as his lack of full understanding of Christianity. The anticipation of the celebration of mass and the promise of reunion with Tacuana appear to moderate the *cacique's* desire to take revenge upon Tapirazú; however, Dulcanquellín's last statement to Terrazas may have an ironic twist. "No es poco en esta ocasión" may superficially mean that the opportunity to participate in the sacrifice of mass will be of great joy and consolation to him. However, as Dulcanquellín does not understand the Christian sacrifice, his words may be interpreted to mean that the mass will afford him the opportunity to offer his enemy Tapirazú as sacrifice to the Christian God.

Dulcanquellín seems resolved to accept Christianity by scene xiii, in part out of fear of death at the hands of the Spaniards should he refuse, in part because he understands that Ongol was a rebellious angel against Christ:

Dulcanquellín:
Pero sí lo dejaré [i.e., Ongol];
aunque la causa no sé
de que aventure su luz
por esto que llaman cruz,

en que su martirio fue.
Mas no los puedo faltar, [i.e., the Spaniards]
que si de su gusto excedo,
temo que me han de matar;
mas ¿quién busca a Dios por miedo
si por amor se ha de hallar?
No hay cosa más imposible
que dejar la antigua fe
y a la costumbre terrible.
Pero si Ongol ángel fue,
y Cristo Dios invencible;
aquél soberbio impaciente
que castigó su hacedor
por rebelde e imprudente,
seguir a Cristo es mejor. (40)

In the following scene of the final act, scene xiv, the Devil appears to Dulcanquellín and informs him of Terrazas' *rendezvous* with Tacuana. This news incites Dulcanquellín to rise up against the false Spaniards and their Christian God: "¡Oh gente vil, inhumana,/fieras de piedad desnudas/con pieles de ley cristiana!" (41) In scene xvi the *cacique* kills Terrazas and declares to the Spaniards: "Con falsa relación y falsos dioses/nos venís a robar oro y mujeres," and Auté announces: "Muertos son los más de ellos" [i.e., the Spaniards]. Dulcanquellín and Tacuana agree that the cross implanted on the shores should be removed; (Dulcanquellín): " . . . Pues al punto/se quite aquesta cruz de donde estaba./(Tacuana): Bien dices, tirad todos; ya está fuera." (42) Because Terrazas and other Spaniards have enjoyed the intimacy of Indian women, Dulcanquellín concludes that the Devil's pronouncements about the Spaniards' intentions in the New World are well-founded. Dulcanquellín rejects the Spaniards and their God.

This brutal scene in which the natives rise up against the conquerors for the abuse of their women is found in Oviedo and Gómara. This historical incident occurred after Columbus' departure from America for Spain (first voyage). Oviedo declares:

Luego se supo de los indios como aquellos cristianos les hacían muchos

> males, e les tomaban las mujeres e las hijas e todo lo que tenían, segund lo querían hacer. Y con todo esto, vivieron en tanto que estuvieron quedos e acuchillados [i.e., the Spaniards]; mas, así como se descomidieron con el capitán [i.e., Arana] que les quedó y se entraron en tierra adentro, pocos a pocos y desviados los unos de los otros, todos los mataron sin que alguno quedase.[31] (46)

Gómara writes:

> Gastaron mucho los Reyes en estas cosas y en el sueldo de cerca de mil y quinientos hombres que fueron a esta armada, que sacó de Cáliz Cristóbal Colón a 25 de septiembre de 1493; el cual, llevando su derrota más cerca del Equinocial que la primera vez, fue a reconocer tierra en la isla que nombró la Deseada; y sin parar llegó al puerto de Plata de la isla Española, y luego a puerto Real, donde quedaron los treinta y ocho españoles; y como supo que los habían muerto todos los indios, porque les forzaban a sus mujeres y les hacían otras muchas demasías, o porque no se iban ni se habían de ir, se tornó a poblar en la Isabela . . . (170)

Due to the similarity of each account, it would be difficult to ascertain which chronicle Lope might have used; however, three facts are important: (1) As Stephen Gilman states, Lope does not whitewash those events which left his countrymen in an unfavorable light; (2) the ill treatment of the Indian women causes Dulcanquellín to reject Christianity (at least momentarily); and (3) Lope has once again fused events from the first and second voyages. This Indian uprising against the Spanish soldiers occurred after the completion of Columbus' first voyage and before his second. During the uprising Columbus was in Spain.

The final scene of the play that takes place in America (III, xvii) reveals a miracle of the cross which finally convinces Dulcanquellín and his subjects that Christianity—in spite of those who may be poor representatives of it—is the true faith. I have already quoted a passage from Oviedo in which the chronicler speaks of the miraculous cross at Concepción de la Vega. It is likely that the miracle about which Lope speaks in the eighteenth scene of the final act is based upon this passage in

Oviedo. Lope's stage directions read: "Salga una cruz, con música, de donde la otra estaba, muy semejante a ella; suba poco a poco." (42) The replacement of an identical cross like the one the Indians have just cast into the sea indicates the eternal nature of Christianity and the fact that God intends His faith to be everlastingly implanted in the Americas for the salvation of the Indians. The scene ends with the conversion of the Indians to Christianity by their own volition. Dulcanquellín, whom Lope has depicted as a perverter of social and domestic order and who has fluctuated between belief and disbelief in Christianity, becomes, with Tacuana and Tapirazú, a member of the Church of Christ:

Dulcanquellín: ¡Mas escuchad, que reverdece el tronco!
¿Qué es esto, sol divino?
Tacuana: Que se aumenta
y va creciendo el arbol.
Tapirazú: Tened cuenta.
Dulcanquellín: Mal hemos hecho en matallos
Vámonos al padre a ver.
Tacuana: Desde hoy comienzo a temblallos.
Tapirazú: Hoy palo, el cetro has de ser
del rey de aquestos vasallos.
Danos otra vez perdón.
Dulcanquellín: Sin duda que es verdadera
la cristiana religión;
quien dijere que no, muera.
Tapirazú: Haz que lo diga un pregón. (42)

The moment of *anagnorisis*, of recognition, has come for Dulcanquellín, his enemy, and Tacuana. They have recognized the eternal truth of the Cross and are prepared to accept the teaching of Christ.

One of the more comical displays of Indian paganism occurs in the tenth scene of the second act when the muskets the Spaniards have placed at the foot of the cross (which they have erected on the shores of La Deseada) begin to fire. The Indians, full of terror and ignorant of the musket, believe that the shots emanate from the cross, and they fall to their knees in adoration of it as if it were another pagan god:

> Tacuana: Palo santo, palo hermoso,
> Dios en ti no conocido,
> si acaso de Dios has sido
> instrumento poderoso,
> no nos mates por tu ofensa,
> que ya todos te adoramos. (26)

The humor of this passage derives from the fact that the Indians fear the Christian symbol of man's salvation. The passage is ironic because this time the Indians do not adore a false god but the symbol of Christian faith. The act of kneeling before the cross indicates, perhaps, the innate instinct of man toward Christianity. This assertion—which one might term "the call of faith"—can be further supported by the following passage in which the Indians prepare to remove the cross from their shore:

> Tapirazú: ¡Por mi vida que he pensado
> que nos hemos engañado,
> y en quitarla [i.e., the cross] yerro hacemos!
> Dulcanquellín: ¿Cómo?
> Tacuana: Que debe de ser
> alguna sagrada cosa. (25)

Gómara makes brief reference to the Indians' devotion to the cross. Commenting on the natives of Haiti during Columbus' first encounter with them, Gómara writes: "Adoraban la cruz, dábanse en los pechos, e hincábanse de rodillas al Ave María, como los cristianos." (167) Referring to the second voyage, Gómara writes: "Sanaron muchos enfermos con el palo y devoción de una cruz que puso Cristóbal Colón la segunda vez que pasó, en la vega que llamaron por eso de la Veracruz, cuyo palo tomaban por reliquias. Los indios de guerra probaron de arrancarla, y no pudieron, aunque cavaron mucho." (176)

One might have reason to believe that Lope derived his information concerning the Indians' devotion to the cross from the above citations from Gómara. However, as indicated, Oviedo also describes the erection of the cross as well as Spanish and Indian devotion to it, the Indians' attempt to remove it, and the miraculous properties of it in the same paragraph and with far more detail:

> Y es tenida en mucha veneración [i.e., the cross], así por sus miraglos como porque, en tanto tiempo como estuvo descubierta, jamás se pudrió, ni cayó por ninguna tormenta de agua ni viento, ni jamás la pudieron mover de aquel lugar los indios, aunque la quisieron arrancar, tirando della con cuerdas de bejucos mucha cantidad de indios; de lo cual espantados ellos, la dejaron estar donde agora está, como avisados de arriba, o del cielo, de su deidad. Y como cosa sancta y a ellos de mucha admiración, no osaron porfiar en la arrancar de donde estaba; antes viendo como los cristianos tienen en la cruz mucha reverencia, e acordándose que aquella, allí hincada, no eran bastantes tantos hombres a la menear ni quitar de aquel lugar, la miraban con acatamiento y respecto, y se humillaban a ella de ahí adelante. (65)

It is clear that Tacuana's pronouncements concerning the sanctity of the cross, the fear and adoration of it, are to be found in Oviedo and not Gómara, if indeed they are not simply Lope's invention.

One facet of the conquest which reveals much about the character and customs of Indian women is the question of mixture of blood. In the fourth scene of the final act, Tacuana, who is quite attracted by Spanish men ("Esos endiosados talles,/lengua hermosa, y rostros nobles,/amoroso acogimiento,/ingenio y ciencia conformes . . . "), implores Pinzón to bring more Spaniards to the New World to marry Indian women:

> O los traigáis [i.e., your sons] a casar
> con nuestras hijas, adonde,
> mezclándose nuestra sangre,
> seamos todos españoles. (33)

In the following scene Arana attempts to seduce Palca, and when she succumbs with no resistance, the seducer realizes a difference between Indian and Spanish customs of perceiving sexuality:

Arana: Palca, ¿cómo va de pechos,
a ver?
Palca: Que no tengo oro.
Arana: De eso estarán satisfechos.
Solo estos vuestros adoro,
que de oro mejor son hechos.
No busco aquel oro aquí,
de que ya tengo un tesoro.
Palca: Pues, ¿cuál oro?
Arana: El tuyo.
Palca: Ansí,
pues, serás crisol del oro
y tendrásme toda en ti.
Arana: No vi tal facilidad.
Por deshonra tienen estas
el negar la voluntad;
que del no vestirse honestas
les nace esta enfermedad.
Soy tuyo, en fin . . . (34–35)

In contrast with Christianity, which preaches the submission of human will to the divine will, and unlike the tendency of Spanish society, which values the chastity of woman (*marianismo*), the Indian woman, according to Arana, considers the denial of the personal will to be wrong, even when it is a question of sexual intimacy. It is important to add that Arana condemns this attitude of Indian women, calling such submission to individual will an infirmity caused by the scant attire of the native women. However, as the last line of the above quote indicates, he takes advantage happily of the Indian woman's lack of inhibition.

One needs to recall the pronouncements of Gómara and Oviedo concerning the Indian uprising and killing of the Spaniards for the abuse of their women. However, Lope's Palca could never accuse Arana of abuse. Gómara does speak of Indian sexual practices, and in particular of their willingness to engage with men. Referring to the Indians of la Española, the chronicler states:

> Dicho he como se andan desnudos con el calor y buena templanza de la tierra, aunque hace frío en las sierras . . . Poca confianza y castidad debe haber en las mujeres, pues esto dicen y hacen. Fácilmente se juntan [los hombres] con las mujeres, y aun como cuervos o víboras, y peor. (173)

The seed of Lope's thought concerning the native women's lack of chastity lies in this passage from Gómara; no similar passage is found in Oviedo.

One of the most humorous scenes of the play occurs when the Spaniards arrive on the shores of La Deseada. Lope exposes here the lack of knowledge by the indigenous society concerning some of the most common aspects of European society: the horse, the mirror, writing. The dramatist also shows the logical lack of instruction of the Indians in Christian beliefs and their adoration of pagan gods. Lope utilizes the scene to create humor and astonishment and to stress again the need to propagate the doctrines of the Church to the "bárbaros." The fifth scene of the second act reveals all these aspects—the Indians' ignorance of both the common commodities of European life and Christianity. Auté, the *gracioso,* says to Dulcanquellín:

> ¡Oh valeroso cacique,
> de esta isla amparo y guarda!
> Vuelve los ojos al mar
> y verás en él tres casas,
> casas en el parecer
> y personas en la traza,
> que, envueltos en unos lienzos
> caminan sobre las aguas.
> Dentro vienen unos hombres
> que traen sobre las caras,
> como en la misma cabeza,
> espeso cabello y barba;
> unos asiendo unas cuerdas,
> con que los lienzos se alzan,
> y otros dando muchos gritos

porque los oigan las tablas.
Es gente alegre y discreta,
que unos a otros se abrazan
y quieren salir a tierra
a hacer areitos y danzas.
Las carnes son de colores,
a partes angostas y anchas,
que solamente les vi
blanco rostro y manos blancas,
de donde a veces salían
de unos palos unas llamas
envueltas en trueno y humo
que me dejaron sin habla.
No pude entender la suya,
aunque en todas sus palabras
Dios, tierra, y Virgen decían,
que deben de ser sus casas,
si no es que Dios y la Virgen
su padre y madre se llaman,
y la tierra algún amigo
que anda ausente de su patria. (21)

It is not difficult to decipher Auté's comical confusion. "Las tres casas" ("The three houses") are obviously Columbus' three ships: La Niña, La Pinta, and La Santa María, and the "lienzos" are, of course, the ships' sails. The *gracioso* is surprised to see bearded men since facial hair is not common among Indian men. The shouts of the Spaniards who raise the sails are not, as Auté supposes, directed to the boards ("las tablas") of the ship but to the men who are at the top of the mast to tie the sails in order to facilitate disembarkation. The references to the skin of many colors ("Las carnes son de colores . . . ") and the variation in corporal size ("a partes angostas y anchas . . . ") are explained by the armor in which the conquistadores are clad; the shoulder and waist of the armor, of course, are wider than other parts of the suit and only expose hands and face when the gauntlets are removed and the visor raised. The sticks which emit fire ("de donde a veces salían/de unos palos unas llamas . . . ") are the muskets which the Spaniards carry; the spectator was thereby made aware of the absence of firearms among the natives. The fact that Auté does not speak Spanish (Lope was obviously and understandably forced to stretch verisimilitude by making the *gracioso* speak a language which he declares he does not understand)—"no pude entender la suya"—creates another confusion which underscores the natives' lack of knowledge of Christianity. Auté believes that the exclamations "Dios, tierra y Virgen" (God, land and Virgin) refer to the ships in which the Spaniards sail, or to their parents, or to a friend. Auté's belief that God and the Virgin is a reference to the Spaniards' father and mother is somewhat ironic since, according to the traditions of the Western Church, God is the Father of Christ and the Virgin Mary is the Mother of Christ.[32]

Lope has elaborated greatly upon what the chroniclers report principally to create a moment of levity but also to remind his public that the Indians are wholly ignorant of Christianity. Furthermore, the dramatist has omitted the controversy about the sailor from Lepe which stems from the uncertainty about which sailor had the honor of seeing the land first.[33] What Lope has preserved is the moment when the sailors joyously exclaim "Dios, tierra, y Virgen." Oviedo writes:

> Así como el almirante vido la tierra, hincando de rodillas e saltándosele las lágrimas de los ojos del extremado placer que sentía, comenzó a decir con Ambrosi y Augustino: Te Deum laudamus, Te Dominum confitemur, etc.; y así dando gracias a Nuestro Señor con todos los que con él iban, fue inestimable el gozo que los unos y los otros hacían. (26)

Gómara declares:

> A otro día siguiente, que fue 11 de octubre del año 1492, dijo Rodrigo de Triana; 'Tierra, Tierra' a cuya tan dulce palabra acudieron todos a ver si decía verdad; y como la vieron, comenzaron el 'Te Deum laudamus', hincados de rodillas, y llorando de placer. Hicieron señal a los otros compañeros para que se alegrasen y diesen gracias a Dios, que les había mostrado lo que deseaban, allí viérades los extremos de regocijo que suelen hacer los marineros: unos besaban las manos a Colón, otros se le ofrecían por criados, y otros le pedían mercedes. (166)

It would be difficult to declare Lope's source in this case, given the similarity of Oviedo's and Gómara's reports. Auté's confusion over the meaning of "Dios, tierra y Virgen" is not to be found in either chronicle; however, each does offer amusing anecdotes of linguistic confusions between Indians and Spaniards which might have given Lope the idea of inventing a comic scene based upon language barriers.[34]

Conclusions

One of the objectives of this chapter has been to determine whom Lope has used as a source for the composition of *El nuevo mundo descubierto por Cristóbal Colón*. It is evident at this point that the dramatist has availed himself of both chroniclers. It appears, however, that Oviedo rather than Gómara was the writer upon whom Lope most heavily relied. Lope's use of Oviedo is most perceptible when he indicates the Catholic Monarchs' messianic intentions in supporting the expedition: while Gómara writes that the Monarchs decided upon the need to extend the Gospel to the Indians after Columbus' first voyage, Oviedo and Lope both emphasize that the evangelic mission was planned before Columbus departed Spain on his first voyage. The dramatist's preference for Oviedo's chronicle is also seen in Act II, scene vi, in which Columbus orders his sailors to erect a cross on the shores of the newly-discovered island, La Deseada. Although there is some alteration of the historical facts reported by Oviedo, Lope has clearly followed this chronicler's lead in the depiction of the erection of the Cross, the Spaniards' and the Indians' devotion to it, the natives' attempt to remove it, and its miraculous properties. The most compelling evidence pointing to Oviedo rather than Gómara in this instance is the fact that all the information Lope needed is centrally located in the former chronicle and far more detailed than in Gómara.

It appears that Lope has relied upon Gómara in the incident in which the Devil speaks to Dulcanquellín. Both Gómara and

Lope demonstrate that the devil makes frequent appearances to the Indians and that such intimacy reveals the spiritual blindness of the natives who worship him. Oviedo, by contrast, never indicates in his *Historia* that the devil appeared to the Indians. And surely Lope found the name of his Indian and some of his traits in Gómara's depiction of the *cacique* Dulcanchellín whom Pánfilo de Narváez met. Gómara narrates that the *cacique* was carried upon a litter and serenaded by flutists who accompanied him on foot. Lope greatly expands the general outline of the *cacique* provided by Gómara in his *areito* and elsewhere. The island king of Lope becomes a symbol of tyranny, egotism, and moral and social corruption.

Lope seems to rely upon Gómara for the depiction of the native women's lustfulness. Palca's submission to Arana in the play is clearly derived from Gómara who, unlike Oviedo, addresses the issue of the sensuality of the native women.

Lope tends to avoid controversies surrounding the conquest of the New World. The most noticeable example is the suppression of the dispute which erupted between Columbus and Buyl following his second crossing of the Atlantic concerning the Commander's treatment of the Spaniards. As stated, the purpose of the suppression is not merely to avoid the controversy which led to the cessation of the divine rites in the island, but to emphasize the predication of the Gospel to the Indians. When Lope does make a brief reference to a controversy (e.g., the rebellion of the Indians due to the abuse of their women), the significance of the event might pass almost unnoticed without examination of Gómara and Oviedo. Lope's principal purpose in the *comedia* is not to raise controversy but to demonstrate the need for evangelization and conversion and to show, when possible, the basically good and moral intentions of the conquest and conquerors.

One does perceive, however, a response to the charge made by Las Casas with regard to Spanish greed and thirst for material gain. While the dramatist has by no means masked his countrymen's thirst for gold, he has emphasized throughout the play that the spiritual direction of the Conquest is of far greater importance and will, in the end, triumph and stand as Spain's overwhelming achievement in America.

Finally, there are important differences between Lope and his sources. As demonstrated, Lope takes great liberty with chronology in this play. Over and over again he mixes episodes from the chroniclers' accounts of the first and second voyages in a play having to do only with the first voyage: La Deseada, Friar Buyl and the *cessatio a divinis*, the massacre of Spanish men for violating Indian women. In addition to the chronology issue is the question of the title of the play. Here again there is distortion of history since in the play Columbus says he is going to discover a "new world"; Columbus died in 1506 believing that "his discoveries had been in the Far Eastern waters."[35] Furthermore, Lope begins his play at the moment when the Catholic Monarchs recapture the Moorish stronghold of Granada in 1492, thereby linking two monumental events in Spanish history: the Reconquest of Spain and the discovery and Conquest of America.

Notes

[1] Marcelino Menéndez Pelayo, *Obras completas: Estudios sobre el teatro de Lope de Vega*, 65 Vols. (Santander: Aldus, 1949) 33: 306.

[2] Menéndez Pelayo 306. See Lope de Vega, *El peregrino en su patria*, Ed. Myron A. Peyton (Chapel Hill: U of North Carolina P, 1971) 119.

[3] Menéndez Pelayo 306.

[4] S. Griswold Morley and Courtney Bruerton, *Cronología de las comedias de Lope de Vega* (Madrid: Gredos, 1968) 178.

[5] Morley and Brueton 42.

[6] Menéndez Pelayo 227.

[7] Germán Bleiberg, Ed., *Diccionario de historia de España* 2 Vols. (Chapel Hill: U of North Carolina P, 1967) 2: 784.

[8] Daymond Turner, *Gonzalo Fernández de Oviedo y Valdés: An Annotated Bibliography* (Chapel Hill: U of North Carolina P, 1967) xv–xvi.

[9] Menéndez Pelayo 314.

[10] For example, Stephen Gilman, "Lope de Vega and the 'Indias en su ingenio,'" *Spanische Literatur im Goldenen Zeitalter* (1973): 112.

[11] Lope de Vega, *El nuevo mundo descubierto por Cristóbal Colón*, Eds. J. Le-

martinel and C. Minguet (Paris: Presses Universitaires de Lille, 1980) 10. I have used this edition of the play, adding all references to scenes. All further quotes are from this edition with the page number following.

[12] Gonzalo Fernández de Oviedo, *Historia general y natural de las Indias*, Ed. Juan Pérez de Tudela Bueso, *BAE* 117 (Madrid: Atlas, 1959) 23. All further quotes are from this edition with the page number following.

[13] Note the inaccuracy. No one could have known before the voyage that idolaters inhabited the New World.

[14] Francisco López de Gómara, *Historia de las Indias*, Ed. Enrique de Vedia, *BAE* 22 (Madrid: M. Rivadeneyra, 1852) 167. All further quotes are from this edition with the page number following.

[15] The reference to "la hermosa Chile" in this line is clearly an anachronism since Chile was not discovered on the first voyage. Because the Indians were speaking, it is possible to assume that they knew of Chile, but clearly the Spaniards did not.

[16] Lemartinel and Minguet 68: "Le trésor de la cathédrale de Tolède possède une custodie qui, selon la tradition, est due à la générosité d'Isabelle." Neither Gómara nor Oviedo refers to such use of the gold.

[17] Gilman 112.

[18] Gilman 112–113.

[19] The Indies were conceived popularly as a land of great riches and a place to become wealthy. See Marcos A. Morínigo, *América en el teatro de Lope de Vega* (Buenos Aires: Instituto de Filología, 1946) 31–34.

[20] See the last sentence of Gómara's *Historia* in which he sides with Juan Ginés de Sepúlveda's theories concerning the conquest.

[21] Oviedo 30. The author states that the Indians had formerly been Christians but had lost or forgotten the Faith.

[22] Gómara 207–8. The author gives a full definition of the *areito*. Note the stage directions in Lope. One of the instruments used by the Indians was historically unknown to them—"panderos."

[23] The use of the words "sol" and "luna" are apt if not historically appropriate for the island natives. Lope wishes to indicate that the Indians worship the sun and the moon, which is borne out through references in the play. However, it was, of course, the Incas who worshiped the sun and the moon.

[24] The reference to Potosí in this passage is an anachronism since the mine was not discovered until the 1540s.

[25] See Lope's *Fuenteovejuna* and *Peribáñez* for similar rupture of social order by the nobility.

[26] Lemartinel and Minguet 59: "Lope a trouvé le nom de Dulcanquellín chez Alvar Núñez Cabeza de Vaca: *Naufragios* (1555). C'est ainsi que s'appelait un chef indien de Floride . . . " While the Indian chief is mentioned in chapter five of *Naufragios* (" . . . y aquellos indios de aquel señor, que se llamaba Dulchanchellin, hallaron el caballo, y nos dijeron donde hallaríamos a él por

el río abajo."—Ed. Justo García Morales [Madrid: Aguilar, 1945] 62.), it is extremely important to compare the depictions of the *cacique* by Cabeza de Vaca, Gómara and Lope. There is a similarity between Lope's and Gómara's representations, but not between Cabeza de Vaca's and Lope's. This indicates that Lope followed Gómara rather than Cabeza de Vaca in the development of his island monarch. Lemartinel and Minguet also believe that a host of other names of the Indian characters are taken from Cabeza de Vaca. Among them is Auté (Lemartinel and Minguet 61). In chapter six, Cabeza de Vaca says that Auté is a town in Florida, "Preguntámosles [i.e., the Spaniards to the Indians] luego por la tierra que estaba hacia el Sur, que pueblos y mantenimientos tenía. Dijeron que por aquella vía, yendo a la mar nueve jornadas, había un pueblo que llamaban Auté . . . " (García Morales 67). Gómara and Oviedo mention Auté, however. Gómara states that Auté is a town in Florida (Gómara 182), and this information is given in the same chapter, "Río de Palmas," with Dulcanchellín's name. Oviedo, likewise states that Auté is a town in Florida (Oviedo 290–92). Lope most probably took the name Auté from Gómara since both Dulcanchellín and Auté are mentioned in the same chapter. While I have not been able to locate in either Gómara or Oviedo the other Indian names that Lemartinel and Minguet believe are taken from Cabeza de Vaca (i.e. Tapirazú, Tacuana, and Mareama), a closer scrutiny of Oviedo and Gómara might reveal these names also. It is possible, however, that Lope has taken these three names from Cabeza de Vaca. As the explorer's name is mentioned in Gómara's chapter "Río de Palmas," it is possible that Lope was reminded of this explorer's work while reading Gómara and turned to his work for additional names.

[27] I have read the Madrid and Barcelona 1614 editions of *El nuevo mundo* at the British Library, London, England. Lemartinel and Minguet have inverted lines 2008–9 in their edition of the play: "y entre silvestres manjares/ los pon en la mesa asados." I have corrected the editors' mistake in the quote.

[28] Gómara writes that the royal couple was dismayed to learn of the cannibalistic tendencies of their new American subjects: "no pudieron sufrirse cuando oyeron que allá, en aquellas islas y tierras nuevas, se comían unos hombres a otros, y que todos eran idólatras." (167) See also Gómara, 183 and Oviedo, 35 for further details concerning the cannibalistic tendencies of the Indians.

[29] The date of composition of Lope's *Arauco domado* has been greatly debated. The subtle link between Lope's *El nuevo mundo* and Ercilla's *La Araucana* (Ongol-Ongolmo) further enhances my proposed 1607 date of composition of Lope's *Arauco domado* since the parallel shows the dramatist's interest in the Araucanian theme as *early* as the date of composition of *El nuevo mundo*. See Chapter 3. It is also possible that Lope saw in the name "Ongol" a similarity to the Spanish word, "ángel," i.e., the Fallen Angel, Lucifer. In act III Dulcanquellín says in a soliloquy, "pero si Ongol ángel fue . . . " (40)

[30] Dulcanquellín is not the only Indian who demonstrates a lack of understanding of the Christian sacrifice. In III, x, Tapirazú states to other Indians who anxiously await the celebration of mass: "Que nos dice [i.e., Buyl] que este Dios/ha de bajar a sus manos." (38) It is clear that Tapirazú understands the conversion of bread and wine into the body and blood of Christ as a miracle which will be physically seen by all the Indians. From this general confusion concerning the sacrifice of the mass, one is tempted to conclude that the dramatist perceived that the conversion effort in the New World was far from satisfactory.

[31] Oviedo reports the Spaniards' abuse of Indian women and their subsequent massacre by the Indian men in yet another passage: " . . . digo que después que pasó esta armada de la isla de Borinquén o Sanct Juan vino a esta de Haití, que llamamos Española, . . . E desde allí fue, por la costa abajo al Occidente, a la Isabela; e de allí pasó a Monte-Cristo, donde señoreaba el rey Goacanagarí . . . E allí habían quedado los treinta e ocho hombres que dejó el Almirante en el primero viaje, cuando descubrió esta tierra e isla; a los cuales todos habían muerto los indios, no pudiendo sufrir los excesos, porque les tomaban las mujeres e usaban dellas a su voluntad, e les hacían otras fuerzas y enojos, como gentes sin caudillo e desordenada. E habíanse apartado unos de otros, uno a uno, e dos a dos, e cuando más, tres o cuatro juntos, por diversas partes la tierra adentro, por donde querían, continuando su desorden: e como los indios los vieron así divisos e separados, acordaron de los matar, desconfiando de la vuelta del Almirante e creyendo que no habían de volver jamás otros cristianos; e así acabaron aquellos pocos que entre ellos estaban desaparecidos dándoles enojo." (35)

[32] The passage reveals again what I have termed "the call of the faith."

[33] A rather humorous anecdote is recounted by Oviedo and Gómara concerning the person who spotted land for the first time during the first voyage. Rodrigo de Triana was credited with the honor, but a sailor from Lepe was so outraged by his pronouncement since he claimed to have first spotted land that he left Spain, renounced Christianity and took up residence in Africa among the Moors. This account can be read in Oviedo on page 26 and in Gómara on pages 166 and 168. Lope makes no mention of this dispute in his *comedia*.

[34] Many linguistic confusions arose between the Indians and the Spaniards in their attempts to communicate with one another. See, for example, the humorous confusion which Gómara describes as a result of which the geographical area now known as Yucatán was named by the Spaniards—(185).

[35] Charles Gibson, *Spain In America* (Harper: New York, 1966) 12.

3

Visions of the New World in *Arauco domado*

Of all extant 16th and 17th century Spanish plays whose principal focus is the conquest of the New World, those which depict the ferocious and bloody wars between the Araucanians and the Spaniards are the most numerous.[1] The popularity of this particular theme of conflict among Golden Age dramatists is due, in part, to the publication of two epic poems which differed radically in their respective visions of the Spaniards and Indians who fought in Chile.

Alonso de Ercilla, a Spaniard who participated in the battles against the Araucanians, published his epic *La Araucana* in three parts (Part I, 1569; Part II, 1578; Part III, 1589) and revealed in his "Prólogo" to Part I a sympathetic attitude toward the Indians and an overt disdain for the brutality of his countrymen:

> Y si a alguno le pareciere que me muestro algo inclinado a la parte de los araucanos, tratando sus cosas y valentías más extendidamente de lo que para los bárbaros se requiere, si queremos mirar su crianza, costumbres, modos de guerra y ejercicio della, veremos que muchos no les han hecho ventaja, y que son pocos los que con tan gran constancia y firmeza han defendido su tierra contra tan fieros enemigos como son los españoles.[2]

The commanding general of the Spanish forces in Chile from 1557 until 1561 was don García Hurtado de Mendoza, and as some critics have shown, Ercilla greatly diminishes the role of this leader in the pacification of the Araucanians.[3] In Canto XIX, for example, during the assault on Fort Penco, the poet writes, "Don García de Mendoza entre su gente/su cuartel con esfuerzo defendía,/al gran furor y bárbara violencia/haciendo *suficiente* resistencia" (str. 47, 82—emphasis added). In the last Canto of the epic, Ercilla briefly refers to the incidents which unquestionably motivated him to leave don García in what Menéndez Pelayo terms "una celosa penumbra":[4]

> Ni digo al fin por acidente
> del mozo capitán acelerado
> fui sacado a la plaza injustamente
> a ser públicamente degollado;
> ni la larga prisión impertinente
> do estuve tan sin culpa molestado,
> ni mil otras miserias de otra suerte
> de comportar más graves que la muerte.
> (str. 70, 408–409)[5]

Ercilla's vituperation of many Spanish soldiers and his relative silence concerning the heroism of don García led the Chilean-born Pedro de Oña to write his epic poem *Arauco domado*, first published in Lima in 1596 and reprinted in Madrid in 1605.[6] Oña states in his "Prólogo" that he wishes to "traer a la memoria lo que él [i.e., Ercilla] dejó al olvido."[7] As Oña's work is dedicated to the son of the pacifier of Chile, don Juan Hurtado de Mendoza, it is clear that the poet's objective is to contest some of Ercilla's accusations against the Spanish conquerors of this region and to extol the heroic deeds of don García:

> Mas todas estas dificultades atropelló el solo deseo de hacer algún servicio a la tierra donde nací . . . celebrando en parte la parte de aquellos que, sirviendo en ella a su rey, dieron a costa de sus vidas plumas y lenguas a la fama, y el principal entre ellos, el marqués don García Hurtado de Mendoza . . . que es todo el sugeto deste libro. (352)

Lope de Vega was one of several peninsular playwrights whom don Juan Hurtado de Mendoza commissioned to write about his father's exploits during the Araucanian wars.[8] His "tragicomedia" *Arauco domado* was first published in Parte XX in 1625 and, like other plays and prose accounts, is there dedicated to don Juan Hurtado de Mendoza.[9] As would be expected, Lope praises in his "Dedicatoria" the valor of don García Hurtado de Mendoza, "freno español y yugo católico de la más indómita nación que ha producido la tierra . . . " (600)[10]

Students of Lope de Vega are by no means in agreement concerning the date of composition or the source(s) of Lope's *Arauco domado*. As it is my intention to show how Lope has used his sources in the creation of his play, and because there are many works which would have served as Lope's sources, it is important to have a clear understanding of its probable date of composition in order to ascertain which works were available to the dramatist at the time he wrote the play.

S. Griswold Morley and Courtney Bruerton date Lope's play between 1598 and 1603 in their study *Cronología de las comedias de Lope de Vega*, and they offer 1599 as the most probable year of composition.[11] The basis for their hypothesis rests principally upon the metric system of the play, and they believe Lope wrote his play shortly after the publication of Oña's epic in Lima (1596) since the dramatist mentions the Chilean poet in Canto III of his *La Dragontea*, published in 1598.[12] If Morley's and Bruerton's arguments are accepted, we would have to assume that Lope de Vega probably read one of the few copies of the Lima edition of *Arauco domado*.[13] But one difficulty remains with regard to dating the play.

Morley and Bruerton use Lope's own catalogue of plays published in the dramatist's 1604 and 1618 editions of his Byzantine novel *El peregrino en su patria* as a point of departure in determining the date of composition of Lope's plays.[14] Those plays which appear in the 1604 edition of *El peregrino* were obviously written prior to the publication of the novel; those plays which appear in the 1618 edition of the novel were, we assume, written between 1604 and 1618, i.e., between the first and second editions of *El peregrino*. While Morley and Bruerton have censured Menéndez Pelayo for his belief that Lope's play was composed ca. 1625 and have based their criticism on the fact that Menéndez Pelayo failed to notice that the title *Arauco domado* appears in the 1618 edition of *El peregrino*, they seem to have forgotten that *Arauco domado* does not appear in the 1604 list of plays. The fact that *Arauco domado* appears in the 1618 list of plays and not in the 1604 list seems to disqualify Morley's and Bruerton's conjectured 1599 as the date of composition of *Arauco domado*.

If one uses the *Peregrino* lists as a point of departure in determining the most probable date of composition of *Arauco domado*, it seems clear that Lope wrote his play sometime between 1604 and 1618. During this fourteen-year period, Cristóbal Suárez de Figueroa published a prose work entitled *Hechos de don García Hurtado de Mendoza, quarto Marqués de Cañete*. Published in 1613,[15] this work presents a highly favorable portrayal of Don García's tenure as governor of Chile. Suárez de Figueroa's work has led Menéndez Pelayo, José Toribio Medina and Juan M. Corominas to the conclusion that this 17th-century "preceptista" and avowed enemy of Lope de Vega was, to varying degrees according to the above-cited critics, a source of the dramatist's play.

Menéndez Pelayo believes that Lope's *Arauco domado* was composed ca. 1625, three years after the 1622 play *Algunas hazañas de las muchas de don García Hurtado de Mendoza*, composed by nine playwrights whom the critic dubbed "los nueve ingenios."[16] The critic states, "La comedia de los nueve autores merece particular atención por haber precedido en tres años a la de Lope, que seguramente fue escrita en victoriosa competencia con ella."[17] Although Menéndez Pelayo states that Pedro de Oña is the principal source of Lope's play, he seems to find some relationship between Lope's play and Suárez de Figueroa's book: "Aunque Lope de Vega tenía muy presente el libro del Dr. Suárez de Figueroa, y por de contado, *La Araucana*, lo que principalmente leyó en esta ocasión . . . fue el poema del joven chileno Pedro de Oña."[18]

As Morley and Bruerton have pointed out, Menéndez Pelayo fails to take into account the *Peregrino* lists in stating that the *comedia* was composed ca. 1625. Furthermore, Menéndez Pelayo is certainly vague when he states, "Lope . . . tenía muy presente el libro del Dr. Suárez de Figueroa . . . " Morley and

Bruerton assume that "muy presente" means that the dramatist read Suárez de Figueroa's account.

Medina states in the introduction to his edition of Oña's epic that the Chilean poet "fue la cantera de que todos ellos [i.e., Lope, Avila, Suárez de Figueroa, and the 'nueve ingenios'] se aprovecharon. . ."[19] Because Medina believes the date of Lope's play to be ca. 1620,[20] he states that Lope (and other writers) incorporated Suárez de Figueroa's account of the Mendozas' genealogy into his play:

> Lo que los sabios anotadores se olvidaron de apuntar, porque de seguro lo ignoraban, es que uno y otro genio la tomaron [i.e., the genealogy] del prólogo que a sus *Hechos de don García Hurtado* . . . puso el doctor Cristóbal Suárez de Figueroa.[21]

Many of Medina's theories are upheld in an article by Juan M. Corominas entitled "Las fuentes literarias del *Arauco domado* de Lope de Vega."[22] Corominas maintains Lope's play was composed ca. 1620 and that Suárez de Figueroa provided the historical basis for it. Although Corominas demonstrates the influence of Ercilla and Oña upon Lope, he declares:

> Dada la popularidad y prestigio literario de Suárez de Figueroa, dado que también estaba unido por la amistad a la familia de Hurtado de Mendoza, y dado que se había ocupado de Lope de Vega en sus escritos, lo más lógico es que se hubiese informado "históricamente" . . . en la obra de dicho autor. Y no hubiera sido nada extraño que el mismo hijo del marqués, a quien Lope dedicó su comedia, le hubiese regalado o prestado un ejemplar de la obra de Suárez.[23]

With regard to Medina's and Corominas' 1620 conjecture as to the date of composition of *Arauco domado*, I reiterate the importance of the 1618 *Peregrino* list in which the title of Lope's *comedia* appears. The appearance of the title in *El peregrino* clearly demonstrates that *Arauco domado* was written before the 1620 date offered by the above-cited investigators.

It is true that Suárez de Figueroa gives a long and detailed account of the Mendozas' illustrious lineage in the "Prólogo" to his *Hechos*. It is also true that in Act III, iv, the *gracioso*

Rebolledo informs two Indians, Tucapel and Gualeva, of the family's nobility. Since Menéndez Pelayo, Medina, and Corominas find a relationship between Suárez de Figueroa and Lope, I should like to compare the two passages:

Rebolledo: ....Toma
Veintitrés generaciones
La prosapia de Mendoza.
No hay linaje en toda España,
Tucapel, de quien conozca
Tan notable antigüedad:
De padres a hijos se nombran,
Sin interrumpir la línea,
Tan excelentes personas,
Y de tanta calidad,
Que fuera nombrarlas todas
Contar estrellas al cielo,
Y a la mar arenas y ondas:
Desde el señor de Vizcaya,
Llamado Zuria, consta
Que tiene origen su sangre . . . (627)

Suárez de Figueroa's passage is quite long; therefore, I shall quote here only the opening sentences because it is here alone that there is any perceptible similarity with Lope's verses cited above. The author writes:

Es mi intento escriuir la Christianidad, valentía, y prudencia de un Repúblico, Capitán y Gouernador, General y Virrey, del apellido de Mendoça; familia que ha sido y es secunda madre casi de los mayores y más antiguos Caualleros destos Reynos; grandes Christianos; defensores de la ley de Dios; restauradores de España; esforçados guerreros, que siempre en las batallas y conquistas assistieron al lado de sus Reyes. O quántos valerosos acuden para ser escritos solo con numbrar este linage. Pudiera començar de Lope Manso, que tras la pérdida de España, se retiró a las Asturias con algunos nobles. Hallóse en los principios de la restauración con Pelayo, y después con su yerno don Alonso. Ofrécese el infante don Zuria, primogénito del antecessor, y doña Memorana hija del Rey de Escocia. Este fue segundo de Altamira, y primero de Vizcaya, por elección de sus moradores que le hizieron cabeça contra los Leoneses en el Reynado del mismo don Alonso, casando con doña Munia, hija de don Bela, entonces Duque de Cantabria. (prelim. folio—6)

There are two important factors to be considered in comparing the above passages—common references and common meaning between the two references. Lope informs his audience that the family's origins begin with Zuria, lord of Vizcaya. Suárez de Figueroa informs his readers that Zuria was the first son of Lope Manso and doña Memorana. The dramatist, therefore, states that the family tree begins with Zuria, but Suárez de Figueroa states that one might begin the genealogy with Lope Manso. Therefore, while there is a common reference, Zuria, the meaning or interpretation of the common reference reveals a difference of opinion concerning the originator of the family. Suárez de Figueroa seems to imply that the family could be dated even further back when he states, "*Pudiera* començar de Lope Manso," but Lope, who is far less explicit, states that the family's noble blood originates with Zuria.

The variation between the two writers is noteworthy. Although Menéndez Pelayo, Medina and Corominas offer no concrete example to substantiate the assertion that Lope utilized Suárez de Figueroa, one would assume that their judgment is based upon the commonality of Zuria. However, while there is a common reference, the meaning or interpretation of the references is quite different.

It seems somewhat ingenuous to assume that Lope de Vega had to read Suárez de Figueroa's *Hechos* in order to learn about the Mendoza genealogy. In the first place, Pedro de Oña, whom the above writers all admit Lope read, and who never left the New World, certainly knew the social stature of don García. Although Oña does not offer a genealogical reference, he writes to don Juan, García's son, in the "Exordio,"

El vulgo fácil es el mar hinchado;
es la barquilla frágil mi talento;
yo soy el pobre Amiclas tremulento,
del recio temporal amedrentado;
mas sedme vos el César, don Hurtado,

> pues mucho más tenéis de nacimiento,
> y no me detendrá temor de Scila,
> ni fiera boca rábida y zoíla. (str. 11, 353)

Pedro de Oña was obviously aware of the nobility of the Mendoza family. Although Ercilla makes no mention of don García's nobility, one should not therefore conclude that he was unaware of the family's stature. Any of the writers about the Araucanian conflict would have to be aware of this fact with or without Suárez de Figueroa's account.

As all the critics discussed seem to err in their respective judgments concerning the date of composition of the play, and because some of them have mistakenly found an influence of Suárez de Figueroa upon Lope, I would like to offer my own conjecture concerning the date of composition of the play and show how Lope was connected to the Mendoza family and could have familiarized himself with their noble past.

Salvador Dinamarca's *Estudio del 'Arauco domado' de Pedro de Oña* states:

> Don García gobernó en Chile desde el 25 de abril de 1557 hasta el tres de febrero de 1561. En 1562, vuelto a España, se casó con doña Teresa de Castro y de la Cueva, hija del Conde de Lemos. Fue virrey del Perú desde el seis de enero de 1590 hasta abril de 1596. En 1591, por fallecimiento de su hermano Diego, heredó el título de Marqués de Cañete. Murió el 15 de octubre de 1609, a la edad de 74 años.[24]

In another chapter, Dinamarca writes as follows about the 1596 edition of *Arauco domado* published in Lima:

> Según el testimonio de Pedro de Oña y del impresor Antonio Ricardo, la tirada de la edición fue de 800 ejemplares. De estos se salvaron solo los 60 que don García llevó consigo para España. El resto . . . fue recogido por orden del doctor Pedro Muñiz, provisor del arzobispo de Lima, y depositado en el archivo de la Real Audiencia de Lima.[25]

Joaquín Entrambasaguas mentions in his *Vida de Lope de Vega* that the dramatist began service to the Marquis of Sarriá (the future Count of Lemos) in 1598 as his private secretary. Lope held the position until 1600.[26] As don Garciá was the Marquis of Sarriá's brother-in-law and since don García brought sixty copies of the 1596 Lima edition with him to Spain in that year, it is likely that one of these editions was given to his brother-in-law.

As stated, Lope published his *La Dragontea* in 1598, the year in which he began his service to the Marquis of Sarriá, and he praises Pedro de Oña in this poem. It seems reasonable to believe that Lope read one of the Lima editions of *Arauco domado* during his tenure as the Count's secretary.

Américo Castro and Hugo A. Rennert provide a further link between Lope de Vega and the Mendoza household in their study *Vida de Lope de Vega*. They report that the baptismal certificate of Lope's son, Lope Félix, reads:

> Madrid, 7 de febrero, 1607. En la iglesia parroquial de San Sebastián de la villa de Madrid, en siete de febrero de mil y seiscientos y siete años, yo, Alonso del Arco, bauticé un niño (nacido) en veinte y ocho de enero del mismo año, hijo de Lope de Vega Carpio y de Micaela de Luján, y le pusieron por nombre Lope; y fueron sus padrinos don Hurtado de Mendoza y Jerónima de Burgos. 'Alonso del Arco'.[27]

Rennert and Castro fortunately clarify the identity of the godfather:

> Don Hurtado de Mendoza, el otro padrino, es probablemente don Juan Andrés Hurtado de Mendoza, marqués de Cañete, al cual dedicó Lope después su comedia *Arauco domado*, inserta en la parte XX, Madrid, 1625.[28]

From the data the following salient points emerge:

1. Don García Hurtado de Mendoza married the Marquis of Sarriá's sister.
2. Don García brought 60 copies of the 1596 Lima edition of *Arauco domado* to Spain, and he may have given one of the copies to the Marquis. Lope may have read this copy soon afterward when he entered his service in 1598, since the

dramatist extols Oña's poetic abilities in *La Dragontea* in 1598.

3. The godfather of Lope's and Micaela's son in 1607 was don Juan Andrés Hurtado de Mendoza, whose mother was the Marquis de Sarriá's sister. Two years earlier, Oña's work had been published again in Madrid.

Lope's two *Peregrino* lists—1604 and 1618—seem to be the most reliable source for determining the date of composition of the dramatist's plays since he compiled them. Because of its inclusion in the second *Peregrino* list (1618), Lope's *Arauco domado* must have been written between 1604 and 1618, and I suggest that a likely time of composition was 1607–1609.

In the year 1607 Lope's child was born, and as Castro and Rennert state, don Juan Andrés Hurtado de Mendoza is most probably the Mendoza referred to as a godparent in the child's baptismal certificate. It seems reasonable that the dramatist would wish to celebrate the heroic deeds of don Juan Andrés' father at this time and demonstrate through his play his profound gratitude at having one of the country's most distinguished courtiers as his son's godfather.

When the old Marquis of Cañete, don García, died in 1609, passing his title on to his son Juan Andrés, Lope might also have thought the time propitious to compose a drama about the heroism of the new Marquis's father. One should recall Lope's "Dedicatoria" to don Juan Andrés in Parte XX (1625) in which he writes, "V. S. la reciba como prenda que restituyo a su dueño, y mi cuidado en estamparla, *por censo del tiempo que la he tenido*, si ya no se me tiene a grave culpa no haber comunicado al mundo cosas tan admirables." (600, emp. added) Lope indicates here that he has had the play for a considerable amount of time and begs don Juan's pardon for not having published the play earlier. Perhaps the play about don García published in 1622 by the team of nine writers jogged Lope's memory and spurred him to publish his own earlier and "better" treatment of the subject. Lope had composed the play no later than 1618, and the information I have presented seems to push the date of composition back to 1607–1609. There is no plausible reason to suppose that Suárez de Figueroa's 1613 *Hechos* exercised any influence upon Lope's *Arauco domado*. I must agree, therefore, with Menéndez Pelayo and others who state that Pedro de Oña was the principal source of Lope's play. There are, however, as has been pointed out elsewhere,[29] passages where Alonso de Ercilla's epic serves as a basis for Lope's drama. Referring to this epic, Menéndez Pelayo states that its "prestigio ha pesado y pesará eternamente sobre todo lo que se escriba de las cosas de Arauco."[30]

My purpose is to show how the "Monstruo de la Naturaleza" has utilized his primary sources, Ercilla and Oña, in the formation and recreation of his "tragicomedia." I will discuss the following aspects of the play in this chapter:

1. the character delineation of don García, commander of the Spanish expedition in Chile;
2. the character delineation of Caupolicán, commander of the Araucanian resistence;
3. the violence of the war and the objectives of the Spanish Empire in undertaking it;
4. the question of wealth and ambition;
5. the heroism of the Araucanian warriors;
6. the Araucanian religion vs. the Spanish religion;
7. Araucanian customs; and,
8. the mixture of the races.

Character Delineation of Don García

The stage directions to Act I, scene iii of Lope's play indicate, "Toquen chirimías, y córrase una cortina, detrás de la cual se vea un arco de hierbas y flores, y una gran alhoma debajo dél, tendido D. García en el suelo, y a los lados del arco los soldados que quepan, muy galanes, uno con el bastón, otro con la espada, y otro con el sombrero." (602) The scene is important because it develops the personality of the commander of the expedition. As the stage directions indicate, the first time the audience sees don García he is in a position of supplication, humility, prayer. Rebolledo, the "gracioso," explains to Tipalco and Pillarco, two Indian bondsmen who express their astonishment at the humility of don García, why the General prostrates himself:

> Al pasar el Rey del Cielo
> Le quiso servir de umbral;
> Que para daros ejemplo,
> Indios, por él ha pasado,
> En que su humildad contemplo,
> El sacerdote sagrado
> Con la Custodia a su templo. (602)

From the very first moments of the play, Lope links don García to the Christian faith; he is a humble and devout soldier who lies flat on the ground to allow the priest, carrying the monstrance containing the Body of Christ, to walk on him as he passes into the church. Other Spanish soldiers also underline the humility and exemplarity of don García. Don Alonso de Ercilla says, "Divino ejemplo tenemos;/yo no he visto humildad tanta." (602) Don Filipe de Mendoza adds:

> . . . Justo ha sido
> Que a todos ejemplo des:
> Al español, porque entienda
> Cómo se debe estimar
> Aquesta angélica prenda,
> Y al indio, porque al altar
> Llegar con respecto emprenda. (602)

Don García's salutation to his soldiers, which is his first utterance of the play, re-enforces the humility and religiosity of the commander:

> Caballeros, siendo yo
> Polvo y nada, él que del suelo
> Me levantó y me formó,
> Hoy me ha convertido en cielo,

Pues, como veis, me pisó.
Oficio de ángeles es
Este que agora he tenido,
Pues fui trono de los pies
Del mismo Dios . . . (602)

One needs only recall don Alonso de Ercilla's characterization of don García in the last Canto of his epic as a "mozo capitán acelerado" to surmise that the lavish praise of the General, quoted above, is unlikely to be found in this poet; indeed it is not.[31] The nucleus of Lope's scene is found in the third Canto of Oña's poem; of don García he writes:

El hecho fue que cuando el pan del cielo
En procesión al templo se traía,
Por dar ejemplo al indio que atendía,
Se derribó a medirse con el suelo,
Haciendo que el presbítero sin duelo
Por cima dél hiciese paso y vía,
Tratando con el pie su cuerpo humano,
Pues el de Dios trataba con la mano.

Fue el acto de humildad aventajada
Para dejar al bárbaro enseñado,
Que en las personas altas de su estado
Es la virtud que más a Dios agrada;
Pues cuanto bien parece la llanada
En la sublime cumbre del collado,
Parece la humildad allá en la cima
Del hombre que es tenido en más estima.

Con el manjar angélico divino
Quedó la gente llena de consuelo,
Y no se vido más barrer el suelo
El viento arrebatado en remolino;
Que como se deshace el torbellino
En asomando el délfico en el cielo,
Así tranquilidad el pueblo tuvo
Al punto que este sol en él estuvo.
(III, strs. 40–2, 364)

Both poet and playwright depict don García as a noble and humble Christian who teaches the multitude gathered in

Serena[32] by his saintly example. Lope has elaborated upon the scene through the Spanish soldiers' astonishment at don García's act of humility, and he even alludes here to don Alonso de Ercilla's admiration for the "mozo capitán acelerado."

One important difference between Oña's and Lope's accounts of this event revolves around the explicit details that the poet offers concerning the abuse by some Spaniards of the Indians and the power struggle between Aguirre and Villagrán. These details are barely perceptible in the passage from Lope above. I shall give a fuller account of these differences and their importance in another section of this chapter. Of importance here is the fact that the bulk of Lope's thought concerning don García is found in Pedro de Oña; in no line of Ercilla's *La Araucana* can one find a display of don García's humility or religiosity.

Character Delineation of Caupolicán

After the presentation of the historical problem (the arrival of don García in Chile to pacify the rebellious Araucanians) and the introduction of the exemplarity of don García in scenes 1 to 3, Lope inserts a dialogue between lovers into the fourth and fifth scenes in order to contrast the character of Caupolicán with don García's. While Lope unveils in the previous scenes the humility and devotion of don García, he characterizes the Araucanian leader as a man consumed with lust. Don García renders praise to God; Caupolicán renders praise to his wife, Fresia:

> Desnuda el cuerpo hermoso,
> Dando a la luna envidia
> Y quejaráse el agua por tenerte;
> Baña el pie caluroso,
> Si el tiempo te fastidia,
> Vendrán las flores a enjugarte y verte;
> Los árboles a hacerte
> Sombra con verdes hojas;

Las aves armonía
Y de la fuente fría
La agradecida arena, si el pie mojas,
A hacer con mil enredos
Sortijas de diamantes a tus dedos. (603)

Lope has taken this scene from Oña; Ercilla makes no mention at all of this event. Oña's love scene between Caupolicán and Fresia is found in Canto V, strophes 25 to 60:

Aquí Caupolicano caluroso
Con Fresia, como dije, sesteaba,
Y sus pasados lances le acordaba
Por tierno estilo y término amoroso:
No estaba de la guerra cuidadoso,
Ni cosa por su cargo se le daba,
Porque do está el amor apoderado,
Apenas puede entrar otro cuidado.

Por una parte el sitio le provoca;
La ociosidad por otra le convida
Para comunicar a su querida
Palabra, mano, pecho, rostro y boca,
Y al regalado son que amor le toca,
Le canta: "Dulce gloria, dulce vida,
¿Quién goza como yo de bien tan alto
Sin pena ni temor ni sobresalto?"

. . . .

"¡Dichosos los peligros desiguales
En que por ti me puse, amores míos!
Dichosos tus desdenes y desvíos,
Dichosos todos estos y otros males;
Pues ya se han reducido a bienes tales
Que entre estos altos álamos sombríos,
Tu libre cuello rindas a mis brazos
Y a tan estrechos vínculos y abrazos."

. . . .

Descienden al estanque juntamente,
Que los está llamando su frescura,
Y Apolo que también los apresura,
Por se mostrar entonces más ardiente;
El hijo de Leocán gallardamente

Descubre la corpórea compostura,
Espalda y pechos anchos, muslo grueso,
Proporcionada carne y fuerte hueso.

Desnudo al agua súbito se arroja,
La cual con alboroto encanecido,
Al recibirle forma aquel rüido
Que el árbol sacudiéndole la hoja;
El cuerpo en un instante se remoja,
Y esgrime el brazo y músculo fornido,
El peso que le dió naturaleza.

Su regalada Fresia, que lo atiende,
Y sola no se puede sufrir tanto
Con ademán airoso lanza el manto
Y la delgada túnica desprende;
Las mismas aguas frígidas enciende;
Al ofuscado bosque pone espanto,
Y Febo de propósito se para
Para gozar mejor su vista rara.
. . . .

Los pechos antes bellos que velludos,
Ya que se les prohibe el penetrarse,
Procuran lo que pueden estrecharse
Con reciprocación de ciegos ñudos;
No están allá los Géminis desnudos
Con tan fogosas ansias de juntarse,
Ni Sálmacis con Troco el zahareño,
A quien por verse dueña amó por dueño.
(V, strs. 25–6, 28, 33–5, 40, 374, 375)

Lope obviously wishes to contrast Caupolicán's behavior with don García's, as stated; furthermore, the playwright wishes to increase dramatic effect through the contrast. It is for the purpose of dramatic tension that Lope juxtaposes the scene of don García's humility with the scene of Caupolicán's lasciviousness. From the selections quoted from Oña, it is clear that the poet is quite explicit concerning the activity of Caupolicán and Fresia in the water. Oña was able to be so explicit because his epic poem was destined for private reading; Lope, of course, wrote for a diverse general public, and while he makes his public aware of the sensual preoccupations of Caupolicán and Fresia, he is understandably far less explicit.[33]

In Act I, scene vii, the public sees the results of Caupolicán's lust:

Caupolicán: ¡Fuego, fuego, que me abraso!
¡Déjame, Fresia!
Fresia: ¡Señor!
Orompello: ¿Qué es esto?
Talguén: ¡Extraño rumor!
Fresia: ¿Dónde vas? Detén el paso.
Caupolicán: ¡Ay, Fresia, no me detengas!
Tucapel: ¿Qué tienes, Caupolicán?
Caupolicán: ¡Hame abrasado Pillán!
Rengo: No es mucho que ardiendo vengas.
Caupolicán: Bañábame, Rengo amigo,
Con Fresia en aquesta fuente,
Cuando miro de repente
Todo el infierno conmigo.
Del agua brotaban llamas,
Y en medio dellas, Pillán,
Me dijo: "¡Oh, gran capitán,
Que tu heroico nombre infamas!"
(606)

Pillán, the Araucanian demon who, according to Oña and Lope, the Indians worship,[34] tells Caupolicán that don García has arrived at Concepción and has built a fort at Penco; it is due to Caupolicán's lust that infernal flames issue from the water to warn the *cacique* that don García has arrived. Lope's scene has its roots in Oña:

Estando en esto el uno y otro amante,
Linfáticos haciendo ya del agua,
A costa del amor chisposa fragua,
Que a tanto suele ser amor bastante;
Se les presenta súbito delante,
Con que el presente gusto se les agua,
La disfrazada furia de Megera,
Hablando al general desta manera:
"No es tiempo agora, príncipe araucano,

De darte a pasatiempos y placeres
Ni de rendirte al pie de las mujeres,
Pendiendo todo el reino de tu mano;
¿No ves el nuevo ejército cristiano,
Que, sin respeto alguno de quien eres,
Su huella imprime ya en la tierra tuya,
Con vana presunción de hacerla suya?"
(V, strs. 42–3, 375)

Lope has used his source wisely to present two important facts about Caupolicán: his time is idly spent in sensual distractions while his people are threatened by the mighty don García; and he has direct discourse with demonic spirits. The playwright presents in these scenes two images, fire and water, to symbolize the sin of Caupolicán (and, indeed, of all Araucanians) and his (their) future redemption through baptism.[35] The water motif reappears in the final act of the play with the purpose of creating structural unity and adumbrating the conversion and salvation of Caupolicán and his proud people. Nevertheless, Lope has unified Oña's third and fifth Cantos to starkly contrast the Spanish and Araucanian leaders. While don García states, "Caballeros, siendo yo/polvo y nada . . . ," Caupolicán boasts to Fresia, "No hay poder que me asombre;/yo soy el dios de Arauco, no soy hombre." (603)

The Violence of the War and the Empire's Objectives

Lope captures the violence of the war between the Indians and Spaniards with vividness, and he reiterates time after time the causes which stirred the Spaniards to undertake the bloody struggle. Here one sees how Lope suppresses events recounted in his sources and how he departs from their lead.

Two of the most violent (Senecan) acts which occur in the *comedia* are the amputation of the hands of the fearless Indian Galvarino and the crucifixion of Caupolicán and the amputation of his feet. Don García, who is depicted as a devout and religious "caballero" is, at the same time, a vehement warrior. *He* orders the severing of Galvarino's hands for having killed a Spanish soldier, Juan Guillén:

García: ¿Fue hazaña dalle la muerte
a *traición* a Juan Guillén?
Galvarino: Todo es guerra.
García: Pues advierte
Que haré yo que te la den,
Pues es guerra de otra suerte.
Cortalde luego las manos
Y envialde a Caupolicán,
Para que a sus araucanos
Diga que este premio dan
A un *rebelde* los cristianos.
Tomen ejemplo, y entiendan
De la suerte que castigo,
Para que otra vez no emprendan
Tomar las armas conmigo
Ni en su rincón se defiendan . . .
(625, emphasis added)

Lope's account of Galvarino's crime (the killing of Juan Guillén) and his sentence are derived from Oña, although there is a noteworthy difference. While Lope attributes Galvarino's sentence to don García, Oña attributes it to a group of Spanish soliders. Ercilla also records the sentence, but he does not state that it is retribution for Guillén's death, as do Lope and Oña. Furthermore, Ercilla is the vaguest concerning who ordered the sentence, although he was apparently there when it was pronounced.[36]

Oña writes that Juan Guillén was captured while searching for berries; the Indian Orompello wanted to spare Guillén's life, but Galvarino kills him. Orompello tells his prisoner:

"Pues vete luego en paz, y di a tu gente
En lo que reputo ardimiento,
Pues el poder y fuerzas le alimento,
Dejándole un soldado tan valiente";
Confuso y grato al hecho extrañamente

> Dejaba ya Guillén aquel asiento,
> Cuando tras él se lanza en el camino
> Con un bastón el impío Galbarino.
>
> Alcánzale ¡oh *traidor*! *a rostro vuelto*
> Y en medio la cabeza ¡oh dura suerte!
> Descarga el poderoso brazo fuerte,
> En furia desigual y en ira envuelto,
> Haciendo que, el alma el ñudo suelto
> Por la furiosa mano de la muerte,
> Déjase ya sin vida el cuerpo helado
> Entre su sangre y sesos revolcado.
> (X, strs, 68–9, 402, emphasis added)

Orompello is enraged by Galvarino's cruelty and asks him:

> ¿Qué te movió a querer quitar la vida
> al que de tantos la compró tan cara?
> ¿Por qué no le saliste cara a cara,
> y fuera tu braveza conocida,
> sino como *traidor* de aleve pecho?
> (X, str. 72, 402, emphasis added)

From the above passages one can understand why, in Lope, don García asks Galvarino, "¿Fue hazaña dalle muerte/a *traición* a Juan Guillén?" Oña is clear in informing his reader that Galvarino's crime is so heinous because it was committed while Juan Guillén's back was turned. Lope, on the other hand, omits Guillén as a character from his play; and it might, therefore, be difficult, if not impossible, to understand don García's pronouncement without the aid of Lope's direct source, Oña.

Ercilla does not give specific reasons for Galvarino's punishment; however, the poet records the following speech by don García to his troops concerning this form of treason:

> "Lo que yo os pido de mi parte y digo
> es que en estas batallas y revueltas,
> aunque os haya ofendido el enemigo,
> jamás vos le ofendáis a espaldas vueltas."
> (XXI, str. 55, 119–120)

Don García's advice is not at all related to Guillén's death, and Ercilla does not attribute Galvarino's sentence to this soldier's death. Ercilla's lines may have heightened Lope's understanding of Oña's account of Guillén's death; however, the lack of direct connection between don García's advice and the punishment of Galvarino makes it clear that Ercilla was not the principal source for Lope here.

In Oña's Canto XII, Galvarino is taken prisoner by a group of Indians allied with the Spanish soliders to be castigated for his crime:

No bien al trono claro del Oriente
A presidir el délfico subía,
Y de miralle el prado se reía
Limpiándose las rugas de su frente;
Cuando *un crecido número de gente*
Acompañando al bárbaro venía,
Así porque pudiesen con el preso
Como por ver el fin de tal suceso.
(XII, str. 15, 411, emphasis added)

. . . .

"¿Pensáis que por llevarme desta suerte
Ya me tenéis vencido, vil canalla,
O que forzado voy a la batalla
Y riguroso trance de la muerte?
Pues entended que el golpe menos fuerte
Y más a mi contento es el pasalla;
Por más pesado tengo y más esquivo
Quedarme de vosotros hombre vivo.

Mas aunque no lo puede hacer mi diestra,
No dejo de morir con alegría,
Muriendo por la dulce patria mía,
Que es una misma cosa con la vuestra;
Y no es mi voluntad llamarla nuestra,
Por no contarme en vuestra compañía,
Ni conceder, oh Chile, que te llames
Engendrador de hijos tan infames.

¿De qué nación tan bárbara se sabe
Que ofenda su linaje y propia tierra,
Por excusar el peso de la guerra,

Juzgando que el servir es menos grave?
Traidores, en vosotros solo cabe
Y en esos pechos pérfidos se encierra,
Según lo que tenemos hoy delante,
Atrocidad y crimen semejante.

Por no sufrir el peso de la lanza,
Un peso para el hombre tan pequeño,
Sufrís cargar la leña y aun el leño,
Que suele ser la parte que os alcanza;
Ponedme cada peso en su balanza,
Veréis, si ya no estáis en torpe sueño,
Que al cielo va de leve la primera,
Y al suelo de pesada la postrera.

¡Que déis la libertad, indignos della,
Por ser contra nosotros, en batalla!
¿Qué más pudiera hacerse por buscalla
De aquello que habéis hecho por perdella?
Así que así no veis que sin tenella
Andáis con el acero y con la malla,
Sin excusar trabajo de algún modo,
Sino que le tenéis doblado en todo.

Pues si pasáis la misma pesadumbre
Tan libres como siervos, gente dura,
¿No fuera más honor y más cordura
Pasalla en libertad que en servidumbre?
No veis que un libre tiene dulcedumbre
Para poder templar el amargura
Del áspero trabajo más acerbo,
Lo cual es imposible siendo siervo.

La natural premática ¿no manda
Que por la cara patria los mortales
Padezcan todo género de males
Aunque hayan de morir en la demanda?
Mirad que cometéis maldad nefanda,
Pues va contra las leyes naturales,
Y que es mostruosidad tan gran flaqueza,
Pues quita lo que da naturaleza."
(XII, strs. 19–25, 411)

Su justa increpación dejó con esto,
Y todos los amigos que escuchaban
Turbados y perplejos se miraban

Tan solamente hablando por el gesto;
Con que cesó el escarnio descompuesto,
Y la confusa grita que le daban,
Quendando a su decir enmudecidos,
Y del vencido bárbaro vencidos.

Mil cosas en el hondo de su pecho
Sus rostros en el suelo revolvían,
[i.e., the Indians who aid the Spaniards]
Que alzarlos al del Indio no podían,
Por ver lo bien que ha dicho y mal que han hecho;
Hasta que ya pasado poco trecho,
Llegaron al paraje do venían
Para que fuese el preso justiciado,
Según la gravedad de su pecado.

En cumplimiento pues de lo que digo,
Le sentenciaron luego los hispanos
En que se le cortasen ambas manos,
Para terror y ejemplo al enemigo;
Porque, temiendo el áspero castigo,
Dejasen de seguir intentos vanos,
Y a trueque de no vérselas cortados,
Las manos a la paz viniese atadas.
(XII, strs. 28–30, 412, emphasis added)

As stated before, Ercilla is extremely vague about Galvarino's executioners although the prisoner was brought to his barracks. Ercilla seems to attribute Galvarino's sentence to the mere fact that he was caught alone and defenseless—"se alargó del bando amigo."

Lope follows Oña's lead in attributing the severance of Galvarino's hands to his killing of Juan Guillén while his back was turned. However, the dramatist has disregarded both poets' accounts of the executioner. Both Ercilla and Oña attribute the deed to nameless Spaniards, the former being less explicit than the latter as to their identity. Lope attributes the order to don García himself.

Lope's departure from his sources adds to the dramatic tension of the play and broadens don García's character. Galvarino's castigation occurs at the beginning of the last act (scene ii), and it adumbrates Caupolicán's capture and execution. Act

III presents, then, the rapid disintegration of the Araucanian resistance beginning with Galvarino and culminating in Caupolicán. While Lope has depicted don García as a devout soldier in Act I, he has not detracted from the initial conceptualization at the end of the play by ordering Galvarino's castigation. Rather, he has added further depth to don García's character as commander of the imperial forces. Don García acts quickly and decisively concerning Galvarino; he does not hesitate to punish those Indians who have rebelled against the Monarchy. *He* is the pacifier of Arauco, and it is due to his decisions that Arauco is tamed.[37]

The killing of Caupolicán might seem even more cruel and illogical than the severance of Galvarino's hands since the Araucanian commander is baptized at the end of the play before his execution (don García is the godfather) and after repenting his past life of idolatry. However, from the vantage point of the Spaniards, one should not consider the crucifixion of Caupolicán or the amputation of Galvarino's hands as unjust or excessively cruel acts. Don García enumerates the offenses of Caupolicán which make him merit death:

> Mataste a Valdivia, echaste
> muchas ciudades por tierra;
> Tú diste fuerza a la guerra,
> Tú la gente *rebelaste*,
> Tú venciste a Villagrán
> y tú morirás por ello. (634, emphasis added)

In these lines, as in those between Galvarino and don García, the Araucanians are conceived as rebels against the Spanish Empire and its king, Philip II, and like all traitors, they deserve the penalty of death. There are many passages in the play which support and emphasize this posture. Before presenting supportive evidence within the play for this concept, let us first examine don García's pronouncement in relation to the play's sources. In the penultimate strophe of Oña's *Arauco domado* the poet decides to truncate his narration of the struggle, but he promises a sequel which, unfortunately, never came to fruition.

Oña leaves his readers with an incomplete narration of his central theme, the taming of Arauco. Caupolicán, therefore, is spared subjugation and death in Oña's unfinished poem.

For the conclusion of his play Lope turned to Ercilla, but he made evident modifications. The reasons Lope gives for Caupolicán's execution, spoken by don García in the above passage (the killing of Valdivia, the destruction of cities, etc.), are based, to a great extent, on words pronounced by Caupolicán in Ercilla's last Canto:

> Soy quien mató a Valdivia en Tucapelo,
> y quien dejó a Purén desmantelado;
> soy el que puso a Penco por el suelo
> y él que tantas batallas ha ganado;
> (XXXIV, str. 8, 350)

According to Canto III, it was not Caupolicán who actually killed Valdivia (Governor and Captain General of Chile from 1540 to 1552[38]) but one of the elders of the tribe named Leocato:

> Caupolicán, gozoso en verle vivo
> y en el estado término presente,
> con voz de vencedor y gesto altivo
> le amenaza y pregunta juntamente;
> Valdivia como mísero captivo
> responde, y pide humilde y obediente
> que no le dé la muerte, y que le jura
> dejar libre la tierra en paz segura.
>
> Cuentan que estuvo de tomar movido
> del contrito Valdivia aquel consejo;
> mas un pariente suyo empedernido,
> a quien él respetaba por ser viejo,
> le dice: "¿Por dar crédito a un rendido
> quieres perder tal tiempo y aparejo?"
> Y apuntando a Valdivia en el celebro,
> descarga un gran bastón de duro nebro.
> (III, strs. 64–5, 191)

In spite of the fact that Leocato actually killed Valdivia, Caupolicán takes full responsibility for the act since he is the leader of his people:

> Yo soy Caupolicán, que el hado mío
> por tierra derrocó mi fundamento,
> y quien del araucano señorío
> tiene el mando absoluto y regimiento,
> la paz está en mi mano y albedrío
> y el hacer y afirmar cualquier asiento,
> pues tengo por mi cargo y providencia
> toda la tierra en freno y obediencia.
> (XXXIV, str. 7, 349)

Therefore, according to Caupolicán's testimony, he is ultimately responsible for all the tumult that has occurred.

As indicated, Caupolicán repents his life of idolatry in the final act of Lope's play:

> Señor, si yo era bárbaro, no tengo
> Tanta culpa en no haberos conocido;
> Ya que me han dicho lo que os he debido,
> Sin pies a vuestros pies clavado vengo.
>
> Yo confieso que tarde me prevengo;
> Pero dicen que, estando arrepentido,
> Debo creer que en este día he nacido;
> Perdonadme, Señor, si me detengo.
>
> Pasé adorando al sol mis años tristes,
> Contento de mirar sus rayos de oro;
> Pero ya sé que vos al sol hicistes.
>
> Mi edad pasada arrepentido lloro:
> ¡Oh Sol, autor del sol, pues luz me distes,
> Con esa misma vuestro rayo adoro! (636)

In Ercilla's 34th Canto, Caupolicán begs for commutation of his death sentence in exchange for the conversion of his people to Christianity; his contrition hinges upon sparing his life; his death, states the *cacique*, would only prolong the hostilities:

> La paz común destruyes con mi muerte,

suspende ahora la espada rigurosa
debajo de la cual están a una
mi desnuda garganta y tu fortuna.
(XXXIV, str. 11, 350)

Y pues por la experiencia claro has visto
que libre y preso, en público y secreto,
de mis soldados soy temido y quisto,
y está mi voluntad todo sujeto,
haré yo establecer la ley de Cristo,
y que, sueltas las armas, te prometo
vendrá toda la tierra en mi presencia
a dar al Rey Felipe la obediencia.
(XXXIV, str. 14, 351)

While Lope has followed Ercilla in the presentation of Caupolicán's contrition, he has departed from the poet in that the *cacique* at no time attempts to bargain his life for his conversion or the conversion of his people. In the play, Caupolicán's conversion and surrender to death are unconditional. The dramatist seems determined to demonstrate to his audience that Arauco has been definitively subdued: Caupolicán: "Así baja y alza el vuelo/La fortuna de la guerra;/Pues hoy me derriba al suelo,/ Piérdase el cuerpo, que es tierra:/Gánese el alma, que es cielo." (635)[39] The proud and haughty spirit of Caupolicán exhibited throughout most of the play has succumbed to the will of the Christian state. By conversion he has gained the immeasurable benefit of possible eternal life in heaven.

There are other important distinctions to be made between Ercilla and Lope concerning the execution of Caupolicán. In Lope, it is don García who sentences Caupolicán to die, as has been noted. In Ercilla's Canto XXXIV, Caupolicán is brought before Reinoso who, after listening to the *cacique*, condemns him to death (strophe 4, 349). Furthermore, the Canto states that Caupolicán objected to being executed by a Negro:

Luego llegó el verdugo diligente,
que era un negro gelofo, mal vestido,
el cual viéndole el bárbaro presente
para darle la muerte prevenido,

> bien que con rostro y ánimo paciente
> las afrentas demás había sufrido,
> sufrir no pudo aquella, aunque postrera,
> diciendo en alta voz desta manera:
>
> "¿Cómo? ¿Qué en cristianidad y pecho honrado
> cabe cosa tan fuera de medida,
> que a un hombre como yo tan señalado
> le dé muerte una mano tan abatida?
> Basta, basta morir al más culpado,
> que al fin todo se paga con la vida
> y es usar deste término conmigo
> inhumana venganza y no castigo.
>
> ¿No hubiera alguna espada aquí de cuantas
> contra mí se arrancaron a porfía,
> que usada a nuestras miserias gargantas,
> cercenara de un golpe aquesta mía?
> Que aunque ensaye su fuerza en mí de tantas
> maneras la fortuna en este día
> acabar no podrá que bruta mano
> toque el gran General Caupolicano."
>
> Esto dicho, y alzando el pie derecho
> (aunque de las cadenas impedido)
> dió tal coz al verdugo, que gran trecho
> le echó rodando abajo mal herido;
> reprehendido el impaciente hecho,
> y él del súbito enojo reducido
> le sentaron después con poca ayuda
> sobre la punta de la estaca aguda.
> (XXXIV, strs. 24–7, 354–5)

Lope has completely suppressed the above-cited lines; there is not even the slightest reminiscence of them in the play, and one is left with the unavoidable question: Why? Is one to assume from the suppression that Lope had a favorable attitude toward Negroes?[40] This may or may not be the case; however, there is obvious humor in the way in which Ercilla has narrated the event. Although there are several moments in which Lope delights his audience with humorous anecdotes, the final solemn moments of the play in which the dramatist wished to show the utter subjugation of Arauco to the newly-crowned King Philip were not appropriate for a scene which might lend itself to laughter. It seems that Lope exercises good dramatic sense in not rupturing the solemnity of the moment of the subjugation of "la más indómita nación que ha producido la tierra" ("Dedicatoria," 601) with a scene which might reduce the audience to laughter.

In addition to these differences between Lope and Ercilla, there is yet another. As stated, Ercilla's sympathy lies frequently with the Indians and not the Spaniards. After Caupolicán's execution, the poet records his personal feelings regarding the act:

> Paréceme que siento enternecido
> al más crüel y endurecido oyente
> deste bárbaro caso referido
> al cual, Señor, no estuve yo presente,
> que a la nueva conquista había partido
> de la remota y nunca vista gente;
> que si yo a la sazón allí estuviera
> la cruda ejecución se suspendiera.
> (XXXIV, str. 31, 355–6)

There is no Spanish character in the play whose sentiments remotely approximate Ercilla's. In fact, there is great jubilation at the end of the play for the Spaniards who have achieved their purpose in Chile—the taming of the Araucanians:

> (Salga toda la compañía, muy galana,
> de soldados, con música, con nueve
> banderas, y detrás Don García;
> vuélvase a descubrir aquel arco, y
> sobre una basa se vea, armado con un
> bastón, el rey Filipe II, muy mozo,
> como que fuese estatua.)
>
> García: Invictísimo Filipe,
> Nuevamente coronado
> Por rey de España y del mundo
> Que a vuestros abuelos santos

Halló Colón, y después,
Tantos españoles brazos,
A costa de sangre suya
Os dieron y conquistaron:
Ves aquí nueve banderas,
Nueve battallas de Arauco
Que en vuestro nombre he vencido,
Pacificando su Estado.

. . . .

Filipe: Señor, mirad que os servimos,
Tiñendo estos verdes campos
De sangre de cien mil indios
Por daros un reino extraño:
Quien calla, señor, otorga.
(636–637)

Don García's brother, don Filipe, rejoices with all the actors who played the role of Spanish conquerors in the defeat of the Indians and the ascent of Philip to the throne. The Indian blood which has been shed on verdant fields is the cause for celebration and not for lamentation.

That Caupolicán is a rebel against the religious and secular establishments of Spain is a concept reiterated throughout this play. Don García makes this charge against Caupolicán as justification for his execution; these charges against Caupolicán are derived most probably from Ercilla. In the fifth scene of Act II Caupolicán admits rebellion against the Spanish Monarchy:

Ya veis, valientes chilenos,
Y gallardos araucanos,
Como al español Filipe
Nos habemos rebelado
Porque muchos de nosotros
Éramos ya sus vasallos. (616)

Caupolicán and his followers are rebels against Spain because they have risen up against their lawful lord to whom they had previously sworn allegiance. The mission of don García is, therefore, to reduce the rebellion of the king's vassals. In Act I, scene iii, don García states his purpose in Chile:

Dos cosas en Chile espero
Que su gran piedad me dé,
Porque con menos no quiero
Que el alma contenta esté:
La primera es ensanchar
La fe de Dios; la segunda
Reducir y sujetar
De Carlos a la coyunda
Esta tierra y este mar. (602–603)

Ercilla records the dual mission of the Spaniards in Chile which don García expresses in the play, and he considers the Araucanians as rebellious vassals because they have forsaken Christianity and Crown:

(Y causa principal de la jornada
era la religión y salvamento
de la rebelde gente bautizada,
que en desprecio del Santo Sacramento
la recibida ley y fe jurada
habían pérfidamente quebrantado
y las armas ilícitas tomado;

Pero si quisiesen convertirse
a la cristiana ley que antes tenían,
y a la fe quebrantada reducirse
que al grande Carlos Quinto dado habían,
en todas las más cosas convenirse
a su provecho y cómodo podrían,
haciéndoles con prendas, firme y cierto
cualquier partido lícito y concierto).
(XVI, strs. 29–30, 18–19)

It should be noticed that in Ercilla the mission of the Spaniards is not pronounced by a specific individual. Oña, however, attributes the statement of purpose to don García:

La cifra dellas [i.e., of don García's *obras*
and razones] fue certificarlos [i.e., the Indians]
Que solo era su blanco y su motivo
Hacer que conociesen un Dios vivo
Que quiso con su sangre rescatallos,

Y que se confesasen por vasallos,
Con someter al yugo el cuello altivo,
Del sacro don Felipe sin segundo,
Monarca universal de todo el mundo.

Mostróles por el título y derecho
Que los cristianos esto pretendían;
En especial de aquellos que se habían
Apóstatas, después de fieles, hecho;
Propúsoles el público provecho
Que dando al Rey la paz, recibirían,
Con los terribles daños que en su tierra
Causaba el uso fierro de la guerra.

Añade al fin que en nombre y en persona
Del solo invicto rey de los hispanos
Si más no toman armas en las manos,
Por las tomadas antes les perdona;
Mas que si, despreciando su corona,
Hicieran cruda guerra a los cristianos,
Se les habrá de hacer a sangre y fuego,
Sin dárseles minuto de sosiego.
(IV, strs. 32–4, 369)

Although Ercilla and Oña offer the same reasons for the presence of the Spanish soldiers in Chile, Lope seems to follow Oña because it is don García who specifically states the purpose of the mission. Oña and Lope raise the stature of the commander by demonstrating his allegiance to his faith and his monarchs; all his actions point toward the conversion of the Indians and the pacification of one of the king's rebellious realms. Ercilla, by contrast, never attributes these goals to don García; for this poet pacification and conversion are the goals of all soldiers who travel from Peru to Chile—"la causa principal de la *jornada . . .* "

While Ercilla, Oña, and Lope all claim that the Indians are rebels against the Spanish monarchy, it is only Lope who actually has the natives admit this. Thus, Caupolicán's statement in which he rejoices in the rebellion against Philip II—"Eramos ya sus vasallos . . . " —is wholly Lope's invention. Lope would not have his Indians ignorant of their crimes; they are aware of the allegiance which they have broken. Although Lope departs from Ercilla and Oña in attributing to the Indians total awareness of their rebellion, he exhibits some ambiguity in his attitude. In Act III, scene xii, Caupolicán is captured, and don García asks him, "¿No eras vasallo del Rey/De España?" Caupolicán responds, "Libre nací,/La libertad defendí/De mi patria y de mi ley;/La vuestra no la he tomado." (633) Again one is confronted with statements which have no parallel in either Ercilla or Oña. On the one hand, Lope assures his public that Caupolicán is fully aware of the fact that he is a rebellious vassal; on the other, he seems to contradict himself by Caupolicán's statement that he has never accepted Spanish domination or faith. Caupolicán's struggle seems to have been in legitimate defense of his natural liberty. The apparent contradiction in Lope's thought reveals, perhaps, the dramatist's own intellectual struggle with a difficult issue. If Caupolicán is cognizant of the fact that he is a rebel, his punishment might be totally justifiable from the point of view of international law; however, if Caupolicán has never sworn allegiance to the Crown or its religion, he is not legally bound to its jurisdiction.

It is here that Lope de Vega's *ingenio* struggles with some of the controversial issues raised by Francisco de Vitoria concerning just war. In the second half of the second *Relección* Vitoria informs his students that differences in religion do not justify the right to wage war; such a war waged on these grounds is unjust; furthermore, war cannot be waged for the glory of the prince or for his personal advantage.

As shown, Lope follows Ercilla and Oña (principally the later) in stating the purposes of the Spanish mission: evangelization of the Indians and the reduction of the natives to the Spanish crown. To this extent Ercilla, Oña, and Lope are not in accord with Vitoria's assessment of just war.

In the first part of the second *Relección* Vitoria states that if the Indians freely accept the prince of Spain as their ruler, they, as vassals, must accept Spanish laws. As stated, Lope stands alone in actually having Caupolicán say that he is a rebellious vassal—"Eramos ya sus vasallos." Likewise, it is Lope alone who has Caupolicán deny vassaldom: "Libre nací,/La libertad defendí/De mi patria y de mi ley;/La vuestra no la he tomado." The apparent contradiction reflects, perhaps, Lope's personal ambiguity with respect to whether the Araucanians had ever *freely* chosen to be governed by the Spanish Monarchy, its laws and its religion.

The Question of Wealth and Personal Ambition

El nuevo mundo descubierto por Cristóbal Colón and *Arauco domado* coincide in their presentation of the Spaniards quest for gold. However, while one clearly sees the greed of Terrazas, Arana, and other Spaniards in the former play, in the latter it is the Indians who make this charge against the Spaniards, but at no time in the play does one see the Spaniards in quest of monetary gain in Chile. Lope radically departs from Ercilla and Oña, who clearly report the abuses of some Spaniards in search of wealth; the dramatist suppresses much of the information his sources offer concerning this matter and only vaguely alludes to those Spaniards who sought wealth and thereby provoked the rebellion of the Araucanians.

One can find numerous examples in Ercilla's poem to substantiate the Spaniards' thirst for wealth in Chile.[41] In words that could have been written by Friar Bartolomé de las Casas, Ercilla states:

> La sincera bondad y la caricia
> de la sencilla gente de estas tierras
> daban bien a entender que la cudicia
> aun no había penetrado aquellas sierras;
> ni la maldad, el robo, y la injusticia
> (alimento ordinario de las guerras)
> entrada en esta parta habían hallado
> ni la ley natural inficionado.
>
> Pero luego nosotros, destruyendo
> todo lo que tocamos de pasada,
> con la usada insolencia el paso abriendo
> les dimos lugar ancho y ancha entrada;

y la antigua costumbre corrompiendo,
de los nuevos insultos estragada,
plantó aquí la cudicia su estandarte
con más seguridad que en otra parte.
(XXXVI, strs. 13–14, 381–2)

Ercilla informs his readers of the causes which led to the death of Pedro de Valdivia, governor of Chile before don García's arrival in 1557. Valdivia was, according to the poet, en route to fight the Araucanos:

Pero dejó el camino provechoso,
y, descuidado dél, torció la vía
metiéndose por otro, codicioso,
que era donde una mina de oro había,
y de ver el tributo y don hermoso
que de sus ricas venas ofrecía,
paró de la codicia embarazado,
cortando el hilo próspero del hado.

A partir, como dije, antes, llegaba
al concierto en el tiempo prometido,
mas el metal goloso que sacaba
le tuvo a tal sazón embebecido;
después salió de allí, y se apresuraba
cuando fuera mejor no haber salido.
Quiero dar fin al canto, porque pueda
decir de la codicia lo que queda.
(II, strs. 92–3, 173)

Valdivia's excursion in search of gold leads him into the hands of his enemies, who execute him. As shown, Lope accuses Caupolicán (through don García) of killing Valdivia; however, at no time does any character state or imply that Valdivia's greed was the ultimate cause of his death. Ercilla implies that had Valdivia kept his course, he would not have fallen prey to the enemy. According to Ercilla, don García offers his soldiers the riches of Chile:

"Y pues es la sazón tan oportuna
y poco necesarias las razones,

> no quiero detener vuestra fortuna
> ni gastar más el tiempo en oraciones.
> Sús, tomad posesión todos a una
> destas nuevas provincias y regiones
> donde os tienen los hados a la entrada
> tanta gloria y riquezas aparejada."
> (XXXV, str. 8, 367)

Although Lope has probably followed Ercilla's concept of booty at the end of the play when don García orders the "repartimiento" of the Araucanians ("Vosotros, soldados míos/Llegad a besar su mano [i.e., the hand of the picture of Philip II]/Porque los repartimientos/Que de los indios os hago,/Confirme en ausencia suya/Este famoso retrato." 637), there is no incident in the play where the General is depicted as a soldier desirous of, or in quest of, gold.

Pedro de Oña does not deny the Spaniards' thirst for gold either. According to the Chilean poet, don García, upon arrival in Chile, wished to investigate some of the charges about Spanish abuse of the Indians:

> Queriendo pues saber qué modo había
> Sobre pagar el indio sus tributos
> Y si conforme a sacros estatutos
> El amo acerca desto procedía;
> Echó de ver su mucha demasía,
> Y como andaban todos absolutos
> Sin regla, sin medida, ley ni fuero,
> Con el ansioso hipo del dinero.
>
> No solamente echaban a las minas
> Los diputados ya para este oficio,
> Sino también el personal servicio,
> Hambrientos por las vetas de oro·finas;
> Y contra humanas leyes y divinas,
> Que todo estaba entonces por el vicio,
> Aun no eran reservados desta cuenta
> Los viejos tremultosos de noventa.
>
> ....
>
> ¡Oh qué desaforado desafuero
> Usado con los pobres naturales!

¡Oh qué de imposiciones desiguales
En gente que era al fin de carne y cuero!
¡Oh siempre viva hambre del dinero,
Dismulada muerte de mortales,
Polilla de las almas gastadora,
Hinchada sanguijuela chupadora!
(III, strs. 15–16 and 21, 363)

Lope's primary source, the poet Oña, who wished to recall to memory what Ercilla had forgotten, still admits Spanish abuse of Indians in mines and their insatiable desire for gold. In his fourth Canto, Megera, an infernal spirit, speaks to Caupolicán concerning don García:

Ya veis como este próspero mancebo
En su gobierno va por tal camino,
Que, o yo seré malísimo adevino,
O él será el estrago de Erebo;
Pues ultra de que al fin es renuevo
De aquel fecundo tronco Mendocino,
Le presta Dios auxilios eficaces,
Y mueve sus ejercicios y haces.

No sé por dónde pueda ser entrado,
Pues no hay en él resquicio ni repelo,
Ni agalla en que se trabe aquel anzuelo,
Que a sus antecesores han trabado;
Porque del cebo en que ellos han picado,
Que es el metal del fértil indo suelo,
Tiene tan apartado el apetito,
Que no hay por él cogelle en el garlito.
(IV, strs. 81–2, 372)

These lines from Oña probably inspired Lope to write lines which seem quite similar. The "gracioso" Rebolledo makes a distinction between the intentions of the first conquerors of America and the intentions of don García in a soliloquy in I, xxii:

Los que las Indias hallaron,
Vinieron por oro y plata;
Halláronla tan barata,

Que por vidros la compraron.
No viene así don García,
Ni plata intenta buscar;
Que viene a pacificar
Su bárbara rebeldía. (612)

Perhaps Lope has utilized Oña's depiction of don García as a point of departure for the treatment of gold and ambition in the play. In spite of the testimonies of Ercilla and Oña concerning the Spaniards' quest for gold, Lope seems to lead his audience to believe that wealth has no bearing upon the wars in Chile. Indeed, the Indian Tucapel informs Rebolledo, "Yo no tengo ricas joyas/Que darte, que como sabes,/Arauco produce pocas." (627) The Indian's statement certainly contradicts Ercilla's and Oña's pronouncements; for them gold not only exists in Chile but has been a prime mover of Spanish greed. Furthermore, Oña shows how the thirst for gold led to the exploitation of the Indians in mines. Lope's obvious departure from his sources is, perhaps, due to his admiration for the Mendoza family and his optimistic belief that the evils perpetrated by some Spanish soldiers no longer occurred under the direction of don García.

Lope does not ignore the past disturbances in Chile before don García's arrival. In the opening scene of the play Lope refers briefly to the state of affairs in Chile as don García arrives from Peru. Rebolledo, the "gracioso," informs the Indian bondsman:

Si Aguirre y Villagrán tan excelente
Nombre de capitanes merecieron,
Muerto Valdivia, General valiente,
Las discordias de entrambos, pues quisieron
Ser cada cual gobierno desta tierra,
De aquesta rebelión la causa fueron. (601)

The play begins in a moment of political and social crisis in Chile. Governor Valdivia has been killed, and Francisco de Villagrán and Francisco de Aguirre vie for control of the government. However, Rebolledo's brief historical background concerning the power struggle between these two Spanish soldiers soon gives way to jubilation; don García has arrived. Lope indicates, however, that Villagrán and Aguirre are responsible for the rebellion which has occurred in Chile. The exploitation of the Indians in the gold mines (referred to by Oña) occurred during Valdivia's tenure as governor and after his death when Aguirre and Villagrán struggled to gain power. Lope does not mention this fact; the dramatist limits his discourse to the political disturbances precipitated by these two Spanish soldiers. Ercilla does not report the dispute between Villagrán and Aguirre; however, Oña gives a detailed account of the event. Lope follows Oña, who states that the disturbances between Villagrán and Aguirre have left the entire realm in disorder:

> Mas viendo que otros soplos más violentos,
> y tempestad mayor furiosa y brava
> a todo el reino alborotaba
> queriéndole volar por los cimientos,
> y la furia sola de dos vientos
> revueltos y encontrados lo causaba,
> da traza el verdadero dios Eolo
> como encontrallos por su mano él solo.
> (IV, strs. 43–50, 364)

One might possibly explain Lope's departure from his sources concerning the quest for gold and the exploitation of the Indians to obtain it by the fact that these events occurred before don García's arrival. Lope's play leaves the impression that the new commander corrected the abuses which had taken place in Chile under Valdivia, Villagrán and Aguirre. The rebellion of the Araucanians is due, according to Oña and Lope, to the greed and abuses of previous administrations. For Lope gold was no longer a factor in the rebellion; according to Tucapel, there is none to be found on Araucanian soil.

The passages in the play in which the Indians accuse the Spaniards of greed have a basis in the sources; however, no Indian in Ercilla or Oña ever makes the accusation. In Lope's play several Indians do charge the Spaniards with greed. These

Indians, it would seem, refer to their past experiences under the yoke of former Spanish leaders in Chile and not to present leadership which, according to Rebolledo, has no interest in the precious metals that other conquerors of the past sought.

The Heroism of the Araucanian Warriors

Lope demonstrated feminine valor in many of his plays, and *Arauco domado* offers many examples of it.[42] In the sixth scene of the final act the controversy over peace with the Spaniards or continued resistance arises again. Fresia offers her opinion to the Araucanian warriors who dispute the question:

> Que si ya por pareceres
> Queréis rendir vuestros nombres
> Dejad las armas los hombres
> Y daldas a las mujeres;
> Que yo seré capitán
> De muchas a quien faltaron
> Sus maridos, que emplearon
> Mejor que los que aquí están,
> Que irán contra don García
> Y contra el mundo. (628)

There is no line in either Ercilla or Oña in which Fresia decides to take up arms against the adversary; however, Lope's verses are an elaboration of Ercilla's statement about Araucanian women in the "Prólogo del Autor" to Part I of *La Araucana*. He writes, "Vienen también las mujeres a la guerra y peleando algunas veces como varones, se entregan con grande ánimo a la muerte." (122)

In III, xiv, after the final defeat of the Araucanians and the captivity of Caupolicán, Fresia appears "con un niño en los brazos, en lo alto" to vilify the cowardice of her husband:

> ¡Cobarde marido mío,
> Que el valor de Chile afrentas!
> Tú que prenderte dejaste,

Pudiendo morir sin ella,
¿Cómo perdiste el sentido
Al salir de aquella puerta?
Qué, ¿te han atado las manos
Esos que temblaron dellas?
. . . .
Que tan afrentada estoy
De que mi marido seas,
Que este hijo que de ti
Entre los brazos me queda,
Por no tener de un cobarde
A mis ojos tan vil prenda,
Le estrello en estos peñascos.
. . . .
¡Españoles, si no hubiere
Alguno allá que se atreva
A ser de Caupolicán
Verdugo, llamad a Fresia;
Que yo misma iré a quitarle
La vida, porque con ella
Vengue Chile sus agravios
Pues él sin patria no venga! (634)

As Caupolicán is not taken prisoner in Oña's unfinished poem, he is spared Fresia's vituperations in *Arauco domado.* Lope has taken the narration of this event from Ercilla:

"¡Ay de mí! ¡Cómo andaba yo engañada
con mi altiveza y pensamiento ufano
viendo que en todo el mundo era llamada
Fresia, mujer del gran Caupolicano!
Y agora miserable y desdichada,
todo en un punto me ha salido en vano,
viéndote prisionero en un desierto,
pudiendo haber honradamente muerto.

¿Qué son aquellas pruebas peligrosas
que así costaron tanta sangre y vidas,
las empresas difíciles dudosas
por ti con tanto esfuerzo acometidas?
¿Qué es de aquellas vitorias gloriosas
de esos atados brazos adqueridas?

> ¿Todo al fin ha parado y se ha resuelto
> en ir con esa gente infame envuelto?
>
> Dime: ¿faltóte esfuerzo, faltó espada
> para triunfar de una mudable diosa?
> ¿No sabes que una breve muerte honrada
> hace inmortal la vida y gloriosa?
> Miraras a esta prenda desdichada
> pues que de ti no queda ya otra cosa,
> que yo, apenas la nueva me viniera,
> cuando muriendo alegre te siguiera.
>
> Toma, toma tu hijo, que era el ñudo
> con que el lícito amor me había ligado;
> que el sensible dolor y golpe agudo
> estos fértiles pechos han secado.
> Cría, críale tú que ese membrudo
> cuerpo en sexo de hembra se ha trocado;
> que yo quiero no título de madre
> del hijo infame del infame padre."
>
> Diciendo esto, colérica y rabiosa,
> el tierno niño le arrojó delante
> y con ira frenética y furiosa
> se fue por otra parte en el instante.
> (XXXIII, strs. 78–82, 345–6)

Lope follows Ercilla's lead in that Fresia kills her child. However, the major difference between Ercilla's and Lope's versions is that in the play Fresia offers to take up arms to resist Spanish subjugation; Lope has again recalled Ercilla's pronouncement in his "Prólogo" concerning the valorous Araucanian women who go to war.[43]

Araucanian Religious Practices

The religiosity of don García stands in stark contrast to the paganism, cannibalism, and demonic worship of the Araucanians in Lope's play. From the beginning of the play the dramatist unites the Indians with satanic forces during the conjuration of the demon Pillán. Although Ercilla shows many examples of the pagan rituals of the Indians, Lope clearly used Pedro de Oña in the formulation of the demonic scene.

In I, v, some of the Araucanian warriors have learned of don García's arrival in Chile and decide to invoke the spirit of Pillán to determine the intentions of the new governor. Pillalonco, a tribal elder, is the Indian who will summon Pillán and speak with him:

Robolledo: Haz tu oficio, Pillalonco,
Consulta a nuestro Pillán.
Pillalonco: *¿Traéis la lana?*
Talguén: Aquí están,
Sacerdote, *lana y tronco.*
Pillalonco: Retiraos todos allí,
Mientras comienzo el conjuro.
Orompello: Pues presto, porque te juro
Que el furor revienta en mí.
Pillalonco: Yo daré prisa, Orompello,
No te fatigues, que ya
Pillán la verdad dirá.
Orompello: Pues aquí aguardo a sabello.

(Retírense, y el viejo ponga un ramito en el suelo
y una vedija de lana encima.) [Scene VI]

Pillalonco: Ya pongo el ramo *y la vedija encima*
De la lana más cándida apartada:
¿Qué aguardas, pues, que tu tiniebla oprima?
Ponte en ella, [i.e., the wool] Pillán, y la dorada
Faz descubierta, dime lo que sabes
Deste español y su vecina armada.
¿Para qué quieres que con voces graves
Te importune, si amigo y dueño eres,
Pudiendo responder a las suaves?

(Salga por el escotillón Pillán, demonio, con un
medio rostro dorado y un cerco de rayos, como sol,
en la cabeza, y en medio cuerpo con un justillo
de guadalmecí de oro.)

Demonio: ¿Qué me oprimes, amigo, qué me quieres?
Pillalonco: Cuéntame, Pillán divino,
Quién es aqueste famoso
Capitán, que del Pirú

Viene a Chile, y sobre el hombro
Del mar Antártico, dando
Tanto miedo a nuestro polo
Que los fieros araucanos,
De Valdivia victoriosos,
Los nunca vencidos pechos
Bañan en cobarde asombro.

Demonio: Noble sacerdote mío,
Generoso Pillalonco,
Este capitán que viene,
Puesto que le ves tan mozo,
En vuestros rebeldes cuellos
Pondrá el yugo poderoso
De Carlos quinto y Felipe,
No más de en dos años solos.
Es el Virrey del Pirú
Su padre, aquel generoso
Marqués de Cañete, que él
Le envía contra vosotros.
Muy bien sabe a quien envía;
Que su brazo poderoso
Vencerá nueve batallas.
Al fin, rindiéndoos a todos,
En vuestro desierto suelo
(Ved si es hombre prodigioso)
Fundará siete ciudades.

Pillalonco: ¿Qué me dices? ¿Cuándo? ¿Cómo?

Demonio: El cuándo, agora será;
El cómo, del presuroso
Tiempo lo sabréis; mas creo
Que después de estos enojos
Le habéis de querer de suerte,
Por tantos hechos heroicos,
Que le llaméis San García
Y le hagáis, estatuas de oro.
Yo solo seré el que pierda,
Y no pienso perder poco,
Pues si entra la cruz de Cristo,
Luego mis banderas rompo.
(604–605)

One of the details which leads to the conclusion that Pedro de Oña was Lope's principal source for the play is the dramatist's reference to wool as an aid in conjuring Pillán. This minute detail is only found in Oña and would seem to indicate that the dramatist is following the Chilean poet rather closely. Certainly, Lope's audience must have been perplexed when Pillalonco asks Talguén if he has brought wool; for those who saw the performance of the play and for those who read it today, the reference to wool would have, perhaps, little significance without Oña's explanation. In his Canto II Oña explains the use of wool:

> En medio de la rueda compasada,
> Después que el suelo a soplos alisaron,
> Aquellas manos pérfidas hincaron
> Una ramilla luenga deshojada
> De cuya extrema punta doblegada,
> Por un sútil estambre le colocaron
> Un burujón de lana de la tierra,
> Que es donde su Pillán se les encierra.
>
> De tal superstición y extraño rito
> Usa la miserable gente vana,
> Y a la vedija va de buena gana
> El regidor perpetuo del Cocito;
> De suerte que cual pece en el garlito,
> Le tienen con el átomo de lana,
> Porque le llevaron donde es llamado
> Con solo un hilo della maniatado.
>
> Otro mayor abuso temerario
> Y un género infernal de idolatría
> Es fama haber entre ellos hoy en día,
> Más especial y menos ordinario;
> Que ya que no es al cuento necesario,
> Pues del tan poco o nada se desvía,
> Y todo lo que es nuevo aplace oíllo,
> Me pareció de paso referillo.
> (II, strs. 50–2, 360)

The Araucanians gather to hear Pillalonco conjure the infernal spirits to foretell their destiny under the leadership of don García. Oña's incantation is quite long; therefore, I shall underline those passages from the poem which have their parallel in Lope's play.

Colgado pues *el copo de la vara,*
Con un zuzurro bajo y escarbroso,
Como de negro tábano enfadoso
Cuando revuela en torno de la cara,
Apresta la infelice gente avara
Su pérfido conjuro tenebroso,
Haciendo que tomase en él la mano
Quien de la facultad era decano.

Tomóla de derecho *Pillalonco,*
Un viejo descarnado formidable
De cuerpo retorcido como un cable,
Ramificado más que el pie de un tronco;
Y del sumido y magro pecho ronco
Sacó esta voz horrenda y execrable:
"A vos invoco, barato profondo,
Escuro centro y concavo del mundo."
(II, strs. 62–3, 361)

. . . .

Pendiente del *oráculo de lana,*
Y alerta por si el ídolo venía,
Ni párpado ni ceja se movía
De la congregación perdida y vana;
Mas viendo ya propincua la mañana
Y que el *Eponamón* se detenía,
Así de nuevo el Mágico le invoca
Echando espumarajos por la boca:

"*¿Qué es esto, cómo agora te detienes?*
Espíritu infernal, ¿por qué te tardas?
¿No acabas de venir? ¿A cuándo aguardas?
Sabiendo que te llamo yo, ¿no vienes?
Hola, que se me quiebran ya las sienes,
Y el término debido no me guardas;
No quieras que de hoy más a tu estalaje
Ninguna destas ánimas abaje."
(Strs. 70–1, 361)

. . . .

Un proceloso y negro torbellino
Distinto de la noche, en su espesura,

Y envuelto más que en agua en piedra dura,
Dejó turbado el cielo cristalino;
Con esta majestad y pompa vino
El Rey que siempre está en región escura,
Tomando la vedija por su tronco,
De donde así les habla en bajo tono:

"Más presto vengo yo do soy llamado,
Si mi venida causa algún consuelo,
Y si detuve agora el sordo vuelo,
Ha sido por no dar un mal recado;
Pues ya que está dispuesto por el hado
Que os venga tanto mal y desconsuelo,
Quisiera por lo mucho que me toca,
Que nunca se supiera de mi boca.

Sabed que ya las vítreas ondas abre
Con espolón herrado y raudo remo
Uno, de quien con justa causa temo
Que mi cabeza dura descalabre;
Este será el que a fuego puro os labre,
Y quien os mudará de extremo a extremo,
En vuestra rendición haciendo tanto,
Que espante al mismo reino del espanto.

Sabed que el hijo y nieto de virreyes,
Uno de Lima, y otro de Navarra,
Renuevo de la vid y fértil parra
Que tiene su majuelo en altos reyes,
Sobre poneros vínculos y leyes,
Que no sé, amigos, yo según lo miro,
Que brazo le podrá llegar al tiro.

Mas ¡ay! que ya pacífico el Estado
Ha de trataros de manera,
Que los que fuere entonces y lo que era
Serán como lo vivo y lo pintado;
Lo que por fuerza fue será de grado
Lo que de pedernal, de blanda cera,
Y al que os hubiere dado mil enojos
Le lloraréis después con ambos ojos.

Yo soy ¡ay duro mal! ¡ay grande afrenta!
En quien está la pérdida notoria,
Porque a la fin vosotros, su victoria
Por propia la pondréis a vuestra cuenta;

> *Mas yo, que su virtud se me presenta,*
> *Y siento aparejársele la gloria,*
> *De sus intensos méritos el pago*
> *Con entrañable rabia me deshago."*
> (II, strs. 75–80, 361–362)

Salvador Dinamarca notes similarities and differences between Ercilla's and Oña's treatment of the conjuration:

> Los elementos básicos del conjuro de Pillalonco, con la excepción de la vedija que es original de Oña, se hallan en diversos pasajes de *La Araucana*. La contribución de Oña consiste, pues, en haber elaborado el material que halló disperso en *La Araucana*, tomando como punto céntrico del episodio un elemento nuevo, el de la vedija, y en haberlo escrito con verdadero arte dramático.[44]

Dinamarca is correct in stating that the basic difference between the two poets' presentation of the Araucanian incantation is Oña's introduction of the tuft of wool upon which the demon Pillán appears. Although there is no reference in Oña's incantation to don García as a saint, which one finds in Lope's incantation scene, the dramatist has taken the concept from the poet's "Exordio de esta Primera Parte:"

> Mas ¡oh sublime garza Sant García!
> Que es nombre con que el bárbaro os honra,
> Y bien os cuadra y viene desde ahora,
> Si en la virtud está la nombradilla.
> (str. 14, 353)

Lope's incantation scene works effectively to foretell the Indians' fate at a point early in the *tragicomedia*. The audience witnesses the unraveling of the foretold destiny of the Indians, which they vainly attempt to avert. Furthermore, the dramatist reveals to his public the benign nature of the new general whom the Indians will one day consider a saint. In addition, Lope underscores the need to convert the Indians to Christianity, to wrest the natives from diabolic worship.

Araucanian Customs

As stated in the previous chapter, an "areito" is a celebrative song and dance ceremony performed by Caribbean and Central American Indians. The "areito" was not a custom of the Araucanians;[45] it is a pure invention of Lope's *ingenio* which serves a structural and thematic purpose in the play, as a similar *areito* in *El nuevo mundo* had also done. The "areito" appears in the final act, scene x:

> (Todos asentados, Quidora y Leocotón bailen,
> cantando los músicos.)
>
> Músicos: Pir*agua*monte, pir*agua,*
> Pir*agua,* jevizariz*agua*
> En una pir*agua* bella,
> Toda la popa dorada,
> Los remos de rojo y negro,
> La proa de azul y plata,
> *Iba la madre de Amor,*
> *Y el dulce niño a sus plantas;*
> El arco en las manos lleva,
> *Flechas* al aire dispara;
> *El río se vuelve fuego,*
> *De las ondas salen llamas.*
>
> A la tierra, hermosas indias,
> *Que anda el amor en el agua.*
>
> Pir*agua*monte, pir*agua,*
> Pir*agua,* jevizariz*agua;*
>
> *Bío, Bío,*
> *Que mi tambo le tengo en el río.*
>
> Yo me era niña pequeña
> Y enviáronme un *domingo*
> A mariscar por la playa
> Del *río de Bío-Bío;*
> Cestillo al brazo llevaba,
> De *plata* y *oro* tejido;
> Hallárame yo una *concha,*
> *Abríla con mi cuchillo;*
> *Dentro estaba el niño Amor,*

Entre unas perlas metido;
Asióme el dedo y mordióme;
Como era niña, di gritos.

Bío, Bío
Que mi tambo le tengo en el río.

Pir*agua*monte, pir*agua,*
Pir*agua,* jevizariz*agua.*

Entra, niña, en mi canoa
Y daréte una *guirnalda,*
Que lleve el sol qué decir
Cuando amanezca en España.
Iremos al tambo mío,
Cuyas paredes de *plata*
Cubrirán paños de plumas
De pavos y guacamayas.
No tengas miedo al Amor,
Porque ya dicen las damas
Que le quiebra el interés
Todos los rayos que fragua.

Pir*agua*monte, pir*agua,*
pir*agua,* jevizariz*agua;*

Bío, Bío,
Que mi tambo le tengo en el río.

La blanca niña, en cabello
Salió una mañana al río,
Descalzó sus pies pequeños,
Comenzó a quebrar sus *vidros.*
Andaba nadando Amor,
Y acercándose quedito
Asióle del uno dellos
A quien llorando le dijo:
"Deja el pie, toma el cabello,
Pues que la ocasión he sido
Y porque mejor la goces,
Vente a mi tambo conmigo."

Bío, Bío,
Que mi tambo le tengo en el río.

Pir*agua*monte, pir*agua,*

> Pir*agua*, jevizariz*agua*.
> (631–632, emphasis added)

It is highly improbable that Lope's audience understood what a "piragua" was, as it is a word used by the Caribbean Indians which means "canoe." Lope certainly knew the meaning of "piragua" from his reading of Ercilla.[46] Lope must have understood that "piragua" would have no meaning for his public; however, Lope's purpose in the "areito" was not to confuse his audience but to suggest through "piragua" the Spanish word for water, "agua." The repetition of the refrain "piraguamonte, piragua . . . " creates a hypnotic effect upon the audience and hurls the public into a strange and unknown level of consciousness. The constant repetition of "piragua" recalls the image of water and leads the careful listener back to Act I, scenes iii and v in which Caupolicán and Fresia enjoy sensual pleasures in the river from which fire erupts as chastisement for their lust. The "areito," therefore, is a structural device which aids in the unity of the play.

The thematic unity between I, iii and v and the "areito" in act III is evident: love. Many of the poetic images in the scene between Caupolicán and Fresia are also present in the "areito": "arco," "flechas," "vidrio," "agua," "conchas," "oro," "plata," etc. Although these images are quite common in Golden Age poetry, it is not a mere coincidence that both theme and images are parallel in the love scene and the "areito." Lope demonstrates his dramatic skills by recalling to memory the theme and images presented in Act I.

The hypnotic effect which the "areito" produces heightens the sensual images presented. When Lope writes, for example, "hallárame yo una concha,/abríla con mi cuchillo . . . ," he is highly suggestive. The "concha" is symbolic of the vagina and the "cuchillo" symbolizes the penis. The two images aid in recalling the sensual nature of Caupolicán's and Fresia's activites in the river. When Lope writes, "El río vuelve fuego,/De las ondas salen llamas," he again recalls the lust of the two lovers as well as their punishment. The reiteration of "que mi tambo le tengo en el río" (i.e., My inn is in the river) recalls the place, the river, in which Caupolicán and Fresia made love.

Water is an ancient symbol used frequently in the Bible and in secular literature to represent the forces of destruction and redemption (Noah's Ark—water = destruction; the parting of the Red Sea and the Jews' flight across—water = redemption; the baptism of Jesus—water = redemption). The water motif presented in the first act of the play reappears at the end in the "areito." Water is symbolic of both Caupolicán's destructive passion and his future redemption through baptism. Lope has masterfully utilized his "areito" to unify his play through theme and images and adumbrate the salvation of Caupolicán and, by extension, the Araucanian people. One perceives in the "areito," which, with little authenticity, purports to depict an Araucanian custom, the dramatist's belief in the need to convert the natives to Christianity.[47]

A clear example of Lope's use of Oña occurs in the fifteenth scene of Act I. Quidora, Gualeva, and Millaura (Indian women) appear on stage "con unas cestillas de fruta y unas botillas o barros de agua" (609) to carry to their husbands. Lope seizes the moment to introduce his public to some of the exotic and unknown foods of the Araucanians:

Gualeva: *Madí* traigo en mi cestillo;
Pérper traigo que beber;
Mas no veo a mi querido
Tucapel.
Millaura: Yo traigo aquí
El *ulpo* mejor que vi,
Por si cansado o herido
De aquesta batalla sale,
Fresia, mi adorado Rengo.
Quidora: Por aquí un *cocavi* tengo
Que no hay cosa que le iguale,
Y también truje *muday*
Porque beba mi Talgueno,
Aunque es de mi amor ajeno,
Si sangre en mis venas hay. (610 emphasis added)

At the end of Oña's epic poem is a "Tabla" which he wrote

so that his readers might understand "algunos términos propios de los indios . . . " (456) Of the five foods which Lope mentions, all appear in Oña's "Tabla." Oña offers the following definitions for the comestibles mentioned by Lope:

> "Ulpo" que los indios llaman, si se puede escribir, *ulldpu*, es el principal y más ordinario mantenimiento dellos, el cual solamente es harina de maíz o cebada tostada, desleída en agua fría; sírveles de comida y bebida juntamente.
>
> "cocoví" y desto hacen su *cocaiv* y matalotaje cuando caminan, llevando una talega de esta harina y en cestillo para hacer el ulldpu, tan tejido, que nunca el agua echada en él se vierte ni rezuma. Es alimento muy fresco y más sustancial y regalado cuando la harina lleva de aquel madí que arriba se declara.
>
> "muday" es la misma chicha de maíz, más suave.
>
> "chicha" es vino hecho las más veces de cebada y maíz tostado y molido, y algunas de frutilla o murta.
>
> "madí" es una semilla negra, que seca y molida se hacen della unas bolas envueltas en harina; son de gran regalo y sustento para los indios.
>
> "pérper" es también la de maíz, más gruesa y menos fuerte que todas (i.e., "pérper" = a type of "chicha").

Lope has used Oña's "Tabla" to create a scene which illustrates the Araucanian women's love for their husbands and their concern for their welfare.

If Lope was able to intrigue his audience with an exotic list of comestibles, it is certain that he horrified it with the exposition of the cannibalistic nature of the Araucanians. The *gra-*

cioso, Rebolledo, is taken prisoner while looking for a banana to eat. Upon seeing the prisoner Tucapel orders: "Asale entero, que quiero/Comérmelo todo entero/De rabia de don Filipe." (615). There are several instances in both epic poems which refer to the Araucanian practice of cannibalism; however, the comical scene in which Rebolledo is taken prisoner and later, through his "ingenio," released, is not found in Ercilla or Oña. Oña does state that Juan Guillén was taken prisoner while searching for berries and was killed, but he does not say that Guillén was eaten by his captors; nevertheless, the rather weak parallel between Rebolledo's captivity while in search of a banana and Guillén's captivity while in search for berries might possibly suggest that Lope has developed the scene from Oña. Lope changes the fruit from berries to bananas and heightens dramatic effect by Tucapel's desire to eat Rebolledo. Although Lope follows both Ercilla and Oña in reporting the cannibalistic tendencies of the natives, his purpose was certainly to horrify his public and emphasize the need to eradicate such practices through pacification, Hispanization, and Christianization.

In the final act of the play the Araucanian warriors gather together to encourage one another before battle. One of the means by which they encourage one another is to drink the blood of Valdivia's corpse. While Oña and Ercilla address the Araucanian fondness for wine,[48] neither poet claimed that the Araucanians drank Valdivia's blood or anyone else's. This vampire-like detail, of Senecan tradition, is wholly Lope's invention, and its purpose is to re-enforce the impression of the "barbaric" customs and rituals of the natives. Caupolicán proclaims to his warriors:

> Yo tengo engastado en oro
> De Valdivia el mismo casco,
> Donde con alegre fiesta
> Quiero que todos bebamos
> Sangre de algún español,
> Y con música y aplauso,
> Juremos morir o echar
> Los españoles de Arauco. (630)

Lope has certainly departed from sources in the above depiction of the Araucanians. The notion of drinking human blood is repulsive; however, one should not conclude from Caupolicán's statement that Lope felt disdain for native Americans and their culture.

Lope was a dramatist. Sometimes exaggerated effects such as this one are used to captivate the audience, to maintain its attention. Furthermore, the presentation of bloody and gory details on stage stems from a classical source: Lope, like many of his predecessors in the 16th-century theater, follows the Senecan tradition in many plays for the purpose of compelling his audience's attention through the appeal of horror.[49] Lope may have found many Indian customs worthy of contempt, but, given the Senecan tradition of the Spanish theater, it cannot be asserted that Lope's depiction of the Indians' drinking blood bears any explicit or implicit relation to the dramatist's views about the Araucanians, whose bravery and simplicity he has in no wise disparaged.

The Mixture of Races

In various scenes of *Arauco domado* Lope speaks of amorous intrigues between Spanish soldiers and Indian women. However, what seems both interesting and astute is Galvarino's rejection of the mixture of races. The warrior proclaims to his tribesmen as they view his severed hands:

> ¿Será mejor que estos hijos
> Vayan de leña cargados,
> Y que sus madres les den,
> Con vuestra afrenta y agravio,
> Siendo amigas de españoles
> Otros mestizos hermanos,
> Que los maten y sujeten
> Con afrentas y con palos? (629)

There is no exact parallel to Galvarino's statement in Oña or

Ercilla; the latter poet reports that Galvarino tells the Araucanian warriors who view his castigation that the Spaniards are adulterers:

> Su pretensión de la codicia mana,
> que todo lo demás es fingimiento,
> pues los vemos que son más que otras gentes
> adúlteros, ladrones, insolentes.
> (XXIII, str. 13, 138)

In Ercilla's passage the word "adúlteros" may indicate that Spanish men and Indian women shared intimacy without marriage; and in Ercilla's Canto XII one learns with amusement that the Indian Lautaro wants Marco Váez to import Spanish women to Chile for the pleasure of Araucanian men. Express mention of *mestizaje* occurs nowhere, however, in Ercilla or Oña. Galvarino's bitter reference to it in Lope's play reflects the dramatist's reading of Oviedo and Gómara and others rather than the two famous poets of the Chilean conquest. The theme of amorous contact between Spaniards and Indians is pursued in still other episodes.

After don García has passed sentence on Galvarino, the Commander addresses another concern with his brother, don Filipe:

> García: Filipe, hablaros quisiera.
> Filipe: ¿Qué me mandas?
> García: ¿Qué se ha hecho
> La india de Tucapel?
> Filipe: Lo que presumes sospecho.
> García: No porque el indio es cruel,
> No es por temor de su pecho;
> Pero porque los soldados,
> De vuestro ejemplo movidos,
> No intenten . . .
> Filipe: Justos cuidados,
> Y justamente advertidos;
> Pero ya están remediados,
> Porque luego que la hablaste,
> La honraste, la regalaste,

Con mayor honestidad
Que el Romano, cuya edad
Con esta hazaña igualaste,
La envié con Rebolledo
A Tucapel, y allá está.
García: Encareceros no puedo
Lo que, de tenerla acá,
Tuve a vuestros años miedo.
Filipe, si Cipïón,
Si Alejandro, aunque gentiles,
Dignos de alabanza son,
No se manche en hechos viles
La cristiana estimación.
Su ejemplo merece un templo.
Filipe: La fama le dé a tu ejemplo. (626)

Don García's concern for the private and intimate affairs between Indian women and Spanish soldiers is not found in either Ercilla or Oña. The love intrigue between don Filipe de Mendoza and Gualeva, wholly Lope's invention, begins in II, vi, when Rebolledo, serving as intermediary, introduces them to one another. While Filipe, earlier characterized as a donjuanesque figure, anxiously pursues his amorous inclinations, Gualeva, although admitting her attraction to the Spanish soldiers, never succumbs to his advances.

Don Filipe's frustrated love and don García's warning to his brother are highly illustrative of Lope's views concerning the intimacy between Spaniards and Indians. The dramatist most probably recalled his earlier reading of Gómara and Oviedo, who record the disastrous results of such entanglements, to which Lope vaguely referred in *El nuevo mundo* . . . Furthermore, Ercilla's accusation, through Galvarino, of the adulterous Spaniards, would have been yet another reminder of the persistence of amorous adventures between Indians and Spaniards.

Lope de Vega has built upon his readings concerning sexual intrigues in America in order to demonstrate again the exemplary nature of the pacifier of Chile, don García. The juxtaposition of the scene in which don García reprimands his brother for his dishonorable conduct with the previous scene in which don García orders the severance of Galvarino's hands, is significant. Lope demonstrates that don García has come to Chile to redress *all* abuses—those committed by the Indians (Galvarino's assassination of Juan Guillén) as well as those committed by the Spaniards (the coupling of Spaniards and Indians). Lope admits to his audience, through don García's speech, that abuses of this nature continue; however, such behavior by Spanish soldiers (especially one of noble birth such as Filipe de Mendoza) is not only intolerable but also unbecoming a Christian. Through the good example of don García, Lope stresses the fact that there are Christian soldiers who work honorably and nobly in the Americas for the benefit of all mankind.

Conclusions

I have attempted to show that *Arauco domado* was composed ca. 1607, basing my hypothesis on the 1604 and 1618 *Peregrino* lists; in the earlier list *Arauco domado* does not appear, which indicates that the play was composed after the 1604 publication of *El peregrino en su patria*. The title of the play does appear in the 1618 edition of *El peregrino*, which leads to the conclusion that *Arauco domado* was composed between the first and second editions of *El peregrino*, i.e., 1604 and 1618. My theory as to the 1607 date of composition is based on the fact that in that year, Juan Hurtado de Mendoza, to whom Lope dedicated his play, was the godfather of the dramatist's son.

I categorically dismiss the notion that Suárez de Figueroa exercised any influence upon Lope de Vega. It is clear that Lope de Vega has generally followed Pedro de Oña's epic poem minutely and used Alonso de Ercilla's epic occasionally.

There are, indeed, several moments in Lope's *Arauco domado* where the dramatist has departed from the lead provided by Ercilla and Oña and has offered the public his personal visions of the New World. When Caupolicán is crucified, Lope spurns

Ercilla's reference to the Negro who was to serve as the executioner. The dramatist has rejected Ercilla's "negro gelofo mal vestido" because he realized that the final solemn moment of the play in which the proud Araucanians resubmit themselves to Spanish dominion was inappropriate for the introduction of a character who traditionally symbolized frivolity, humor, dishonor, etc. Lope's omission of the Negro does not necessarily indicate that the dramatist had a favorable attitude towards Negroes, rather that his sense of dramatic fitness perceived the inappropriateness of this executioner when Arauco is subdued.

Lope has also departed from Ercilla concerning the person who orders Caupolicán's execution. Ercilla states that Reinoso condemns Caupolicán to death, whereas Lope attributes the execution order to don García in order to demonstrate that he is the pacifier of the rebellious realm.

The dramatist has also departed from Ercilla in terms of the reaction to the *cacique's* death. Ercilla states that he felt pity for Caupolicán—" . . . Siento enternecido." Lope's reaction is quite the opposite. All Spaniards rejoice at the end of the play because don García's mission in Chile has been accomplished. Arauco is tamed. Furthermore, Ercilla says that Caupolicán attempted to strike a bargain with the Spaniards in exchange for his life; Caupolicán says that he or his people will convert to Christianity if his life is spared. There is no such deal in Lope. Caupolicán, states Lope, must die for his crimes against the State.

The dramatist differs from his two sources concerning the charge of sedition. Lope follows both Oña and Ercilla in stating that the Indians are rebels against the Monarchy; however, it is only in the *comedia* that the Indians admit to the charge leveled against them. The dramatist, nevertheless, seems to have had serious reservations about the status of the Araucanian Indians within the Empire. When Caupolicán proudly proclaims that he has never foresworn allegiance to Spanish law, the dramatist's personal ambiguity is evident. On the one hand Lope says that the Indians are Spanish vassals, but on the other he states, through the *cacique,* that the natives are not. Lope clearly seems to have struggled with a thorny problem posed by Francisco de Vitoria in the classrooms at the University of Salamanca. Vitoria believed that the monarch could only claim that the Indians were vassals if they had freely accepted Spanish laws. Lope de Vega reveals in this play, through the apparent contradiction in his thought, that he was not wholly convinced that the American Indians had ever willingly accepted Spanish law.

The accusation of Spanish greed—the indefatigable search for gold—appears in *El nuevo mundo* and *Arauco domado*. In neither play does Lope deny his countrymen's passion for the precious metal; however, this theme has been severely muted in the second play. Unlike Ercilla and Oña, who report that there is gold in Chile for the gathering, Lope insists that the hills of Arauco are devoid of it. The dramatist contradicts the testimony of his sources because this mundane compulsion is diametric to his main concern in the drama: the portrayal of the Christian principles upon which don García establishes his new government. While Ercilla and Oña have clearly indicated don García's interest in the wealth of America, no such reference is found in the *comedia*. Indeed, no Spanish character in the play seems minimally interested in seeking gold. Although Ercilla implies that Pedro de Valdivia's demise was the result of his quest for gold, there is no such indication in the play.

The intimate affairs between Indian women and Spanish soldiers is another point touched on in both *El nuevo mundo* and *Arauco domado* but with differing emphases. In the latter play, Lope clearly states through don García that Spanish soldiers might be better advised to tend to the tasks of exploration and conquest. Lope had learned from Gómara and Oviedo that the intermingling between Spaniards and Indian women could lead to the massacre of soldiers by the Indian men. Furthermore, Lope declares that such pursuits are not in keeping with the Christian mission in America.

Lope was neither historian nor philosopher. His personal vision of the Araucanian wars and the participants in them is difficult to discern because he was a dramatist principally concerned with conveying events in a manner that would instruct and delight. As his prestige ultimately rested upon the acceptance or rejection of his work by the public, and because Lope's public was so diverse (noblemen, intellectuals, peasants, etc.), Lope tended to avoid controversy which might offend his heterogeneous audience. Although Lope wrote few plays about the New World, it is clear that he did seriously question the events which occurred across the Atlantic but seemed confused or perturbed by the many conflicting reports which he read and heard. Lope was unquestionably proud that his nation had discovered the Indies and was attempting to implant Christianity there, but he was equally perplexed by the philosophical, historical, and poetic accounts, so often conflicting and confusing, which either condemned the Spanish presence for its cruel treatment of the Indians or exalted his nation and its soldiers for their bravery, courage, and evangelic mission. It is to his credit, in the long run, that recognizing the epoch-making character of the discovery and conquest of the New World, he struggled with the task of dramatizing significant moments of this Spanish enterprise, however painful, conflictive and troubled the enterprise had been.

Notes

[1] Other playwrights and plays on the Araucanian wars are:

a. Pedro de Rejaule y Toledo, *La bellígera española*. The play was first published in 1616.
b. Gaspar de Avila, *El gobernador prudente*. The play was first published in 1663.
c. Guillén de Castro, et al., *Algunas hazañas de las muchas de don García Hurtado de Mendoza, Marqués de Cañete*. The play was first published in 1622.
d. Francisco González de Bustos, *Los españoles en Chile*. The play was first published in 1665.

[2] Alonso de Ercilla, *La Araucana*, Eds. Marcos A. Morínigo and Isaías Lerner (Madrid: Clásicos Castalia, 1979) 121–2. All further quotes are from this edition. I will indicate the Canto, strophe, and page after further quotes.

[3] For the dates of García's tenure as Governor of Chile see Salvador Dinamarca, *Estudio de "Arauco domado" de Pedro de Oña* (New York: Hispanic Institute in the United States, 1952) 84. Among the critics who note the diminished role of García in Ercilla's poem are Marcelino Menéndez Pelayo, *Obras completas: Estudios sobre el teatro de Lope de Vega*, 65 Vols. (Santander: Aldus, 1949) 34: 193; J.P. Wickersham Crawford, *Vida y obras de Cristóbal Suárez de Figueroa*, Trans. Narciso Alonso Cortés (Valladolid: Colegio de Santiago, 1911) 49.

[4] Menéndez Pelayo 193.

[5] Wickersham Crawford 49: " . . . Sabido es que Ercilla y Juan de Pinela altercaron en una justa en 1566, y que el joven y energético gobernador los amenazó con ahorcarlos." For further discussion see Marcelino Menéndez Pelayo, *Antología de poetas hispano-amricanos* 4 Vols. (Madrid: Sucesores de Rivadeneyra, 1895) 4: 16 and following.

[6] Dinamarca 50 and 63.

[7] Pedro de Oña, *Arauco domado*, Ed. Cayetano Rosell, *BAE* 29 (Madrid: M. Rivadeneyra, 1854) 352. All further quotes are from this edition with the Canto, strophe, and page following. I have also consulted the edition by José Toribio Medina (Santiago de Chile: Imprenta Universitaria, 1917) and the translation of the epic, *Arauco Tamed*, Charles Maxwell Lancaster and Paul T. Mancester (Albuquerque: U of New Mexico P, 1948).

[8] Menéndez Pelayo 193.

[9] Lope de Vega, *Arauco domado*, Ed. Marcelino Menéndez Pelayo, RAE 12 (Madrid: Sucesores de Rivadeneyra, 1913). All quotes are from this edition with the page number following. I have added scene divisions. See Wickersham Crawford 47 and 51. He points out that Suárez de Figueroa first dedicated his *Hechos de don García Hurtado de Mendoza, quarto marqués de Cañete* to the Duke of Lerma but subsequently changed the dedication to Juan Hurtado de Mendoza.

[10] Lope's "Dedicatoria" has been problematic for some critics who have attempted to ascertain the date of composition of the play (e.g. Medina, Corominas, Menéndez Pelayo). I will discuss these critics' theories in this chapter and offer my probable date of composition. It is my belief that the "dedicatoria" was written long after the composition of the play, probably at the time of publication of *Parte XX*, 1625.

[11] S. Griswold Morley and Courtney Bruerton, *Cronología de las comedias de Lope de Vega*, (Madrid: Gredos, 1968) 285. I have also consulted their earlier English edition of the study (New York: MLA, 1940). There is no difference in opinion concerning the play from one edition to the other.

[12] Lope de Vega, *La Dragontea*, Ed. Gregorio Marañón (Burgos: Aldecoa, 1935) 79. Referring to Oña, Lope writes, "La cual como pasó nadie se atreva/Contar mejor en verso castellano,/Aunque parezca en Chile cosa nueva,/Que Pedro de Oña, aquel famoso indiano:/Este día mejor de vuestra cueva/Que es monte

de Helicona soberano,/Gran don Beltrán, que no mi vega humilde,/Que apenas soy de aquellas letras tilde." Lope also remembered Oña in his 1630 *Laurel de Apolo,* silva II. See Lope de Vega, *Laurel de Apolo,* Ed. Federico Carlos Sainz de Robles 2 Vols. *Lope de Vega*: Obras escogidas: *Poesía y Prosa* (Madrid: Aguilar, 1964) 2: 1556.

[13] Lancaster and Mancester, give the reasons for the suppression of the Lima edition: "De Oña was a student at the College of San Felipe and San Marcos in 1590, and afterwards participated in an expedition sent to quell a rebellion in Quito, Equador. Cantos XIV, XV, and XVI of *Arauco domado* tell of this insurrection; and, indeed, the intemperate language used by the poet against the insurgent leaders of Quito who had refused to pay taxes imposed by García in all the regions under his jurisdiction provoked complaints from the capitular members of the 'audiencia' of Quito, who succeeded in suppressing the first edition of *Arauco domado,* after only 120 of the 800 copies published had been sold . . . At the time of the suppression of the poem, it was charged that *Arauco domado* had appeared without the usual ecclesiastical sanction. Suit was brought against the author, before he could sail from Callao, and the printer, who in order to escape imprisonment, had to seek refuge in the cloisters of a monastery." (18)

[14] Morley's and Bruerton's bibliography in their *Cronología* indicates that they have used the 1604 and 1618 editions of *El peregrino en su patria.* I have used the edition prepared by Myron A. Peyton (Chapel Hill: U of North Carolina P, 1971). Peyton states that his edition of Lope's novel is based upon the 1604 text. Peyton reproduces the 1604 and 1618 lists of Lope's plays. *Arauco domado* appears in the 1618 list but not in the 1604 list.

[15] Cristóbal Suárez de Figueroa, *Hechos de don García Hurtado de Mendoza, quarto Marqués de Cañete,* (Madrid: Imprenta Real, 1613). I have used this edition at the rare book room, Bryn Mawr College. All further quotes are from this edition with the folio number following. For a discussion of Suárez de Figueroa's literary theories and his relationship to Torres Rámila and Lope see, Joaquín Entrambasaguas, *Estudios sobre Lope de Vega,* 3 Vols (Madrid: CSIC, 1946).

[16] Menéndez Pelayo, *Estudios* 194.

[17] Menéndez Pelayo, *Estudios* 194.

[18] Menéndez Pelayo, *Estudios* 195.

[19] Medina, *Arauco domado* x.

[20] José Toribio Medina, Ed. *Dos comedias famosas y un auto sacramental* (Santiago de Chile: Litografía Barcelona, 1915) 7.

[21] Medina, *Dos comedias* . . . 51.

[22] Juan M. Corominas, "Las fuentes literarias del *Arauco domado,*" *Lope de Vega y los orígenes del teatro español: Actas del I Congreso Internacional sobre Lope de Vega* (1981): 161–70.

[23] Corominas 162.

[24] Dinamarca 85.

[25] Dinamarca 58.

[26] Joaquín Entrambasaguas, *Vida de Lope de Vega* (Barcelona: Labor, 1936) 131–132.

[27] Américo Castro and Hugo A. Rennert, *Vida de Lope de Vega* (Salamanca: Anaya, 1968) 102.

[28] Castro and Rennert 103.

[29] In addition to the cited studies by Menéndez Pelayo and Corominas see: C.M. Fernández Shaw, "América en Lope de Vega," *Cuadernos hispano-americanos* 54 (1963): 675–697. See also: Aurelio Miró Quesada S., *América en el teatro de Lope de Vega* (Lima: n.p., 1935).

[30] Menéndez Pelayo, *Estudios* 195.

[31] In fact, when Lope puts praise of García into Ercilla's mouth in this scene, he appears knowingly to be playing a rather mean trick on his great dead predecessor.

[32] Canto III, strophe 13 of Oña's poem indicates that the place of action is Serena. Lope makes no reference to the place of action.

[33] A similar suppression of sensual elements present in Lope's sources occurs in *Adonis y Venus*, which Morley and Bruerton date between 1597–1603. The source of this play is Ovid's *Metamorphoses*, Book X, lines 289–739. In Ovid the metamorphosis of the lovers, Hipómenes and Atlanta, is due to the ingratitude which Hipómenes shows Venus, who had promised to win the hand of Atlanta for him. To take revenge Venus awakens lust in Hipómenes, who takes Atlanta to a sacred place in the temple of Cibeles where their passions are consumed. Ovid is quite clear in the revelation of the offense of Hipómenes and Atlanta. Lope, however, is far less explicit about the sexual offense. See Lope de Vega, *Adonis y Venus*, Ed. Marcelino Menéndez Pelayo, RAE 2 (Madrid: Sucesores de Rivadeneyra, 1913). One of the impulses of the Counter Reformation in Spain was the attempt to eliminate erotic episodes which had developed in Renaissance theater and prose. See Américo Castro, *Pensamiento de Cervantes* (Madrid: Hernando, 1925) 26–8.

[34] Ercilla and Oña also inform their readers that Eponamón is another demon worshiped by the Araucanians; Lope does not refer to this deity in his play. For other names of Araucanian demons see Dinamarca 106. See chapter 7 of his study also.

[35] See Gustavo Umpierre, *Songs in the Plays of Lope de Vega* (London: Tamesis, 1975) 100. The writer notes the symbolism of "agua" in the "areito."

[36] Ercilla XXII, str. 45, 132: "Nuestro campo por orden recogido,/retirado del todo el enemigo,/fue entre algunos un bárbaro recogido [i.e., Galvarino],/ que mucho se alargó del bando amigo; el cual acaso a mi cuartel traído/hubo de ser, para ejemplar castigo/de los rebeldes pueblos comarcanos,/mandándole cortar ambas manos."

[37] In Lope's play it is don Alonso de Ercilla who exhibits regret over the castigation of Galvarino.

[38] Dinamarca 84.

[39] Caupolicán's character development is certainly remarkable. In the initial scenes of the play in which he and his wife bathe in the river, the *cacique* is depicted in sensual terms. Later, of course, the spectator/reader learns about Caupolicán's valor as a warrior. Finally, the lover/warrior succumbs to the Church. Caupolicán's words here, " . . . Pues hoy me derriba al *suelo* [i.e., Fortune],/Piérdase el *cuerpo*, que es *tierra*: Gánese el alma, que es *cielo*," are reminiscent of don García's initial pronouncements, "Caballeros, siendo yo/ *Polvo* y nada, el que del *suelo*/Me levantó y me formó/Hoy me ha convertido en *cielo*." At the end of the play Caupolicán expresses the same theological concept that don García expressed at the beginning. I shall show in my discussion of the "areito" that Lope has made a masterful attempt to unify his play structurally. Caupolicán's reiteration of don García's theological precept serves as a means of thematic unity: pacification through Christianization.

[40] The portrayal of the Negro in Golden Age literature is seldom favorable; he is usually a source of comic relief or an example of dishonor (e.g., *Lazarillo de Tormes*, *Don Quijote*). C.M. Fernández Shaw points out in his article "América en Lope de Vega," "En uno de los cantos del poema *La Dragoneta* se refiere a los mulatos, y en él, de paso, nos expresa su opinión sobre el problema de las diferencias raciales: 'Un mulato, perdónenme, si quieren,/algunos que hay de su color honrados,/que en fin los que lo son, como lo adquieren,/por su virtud merecen ser loados./Que los que salen tales no difieren/de hidalgos bien nacidos y enseñados,/más que en haberles dado el sol más fuerte/en el común camino de la muerte.'" (683) Lope indicates that the "mulato" differs from other men only in the color of his skin and seems to reveal a favorable attitude toward the Negro.

[41] See Canto I, str. 68, 146; II, strs. 88 and following, 172; III, strs. 1–3, 174; XXXVI, str. 14, 381–2.

[42] The third act of *Fuenteovejuna* (Morley and Bruerton: 1612–14), for example, has many examples of feminine valor. Laurencia says at the beginning of the third scene, "Dejadme entrar, que bien puedo,/en consejo de los hombres;/que bien puede una mujer,/si no a dar voto a dar voces." (120) Later in the scene she proclaims, "Vive, Dios, que he de trazar/que solas mujeres cobren/la honra destos tiranos,/la sangre destos traidores/y que os han de tirar piedras, hilanderas, maricones,/amujerados, cobardes,/y que mañana os adoren/nuestras tocas y basquinas,/solimanes y colores!" (122) See also scenes viii and ix of the same act. See: *Diez comedias del Siglo de Oro*, Eds. J. Martel and H. Alpern, 2nd ed. (New York: Harper and Row, 1968).

[43] Fresia's valor is not an isolated case in the play. Gualeva is an equally ferocious warrior. In I, xix, she denounced Rengo for having abandoned Tucapel in battle, saying, "¡Ay, cobarde, pues yo vivo/Y si Tucapel murió/Por él saldré al campo yo! . . ./(Quítele la macana). Hacer, infame que sientas/ Que este femenil cabello/cubre un alma varonil." (611) This scene is taken from Oña, Canto VII.

[44] Dinamarca 181–2.

[45] See Gustavo Umpierre, *Songs in the Plays of Lope de Vega* (London: Thamesis, 1975) 99–100. He offers an interesting interpretation of certain words in the "areito." He says, "'Jevizarizagua' (sic) or 'Genicaris agua' (from Turkish 'yeni' (new) and 'cheri' (troops)); 'jenizaro' in Spanish colonial times means 'mixed breed' or, more specifically, a person of Chinese and American Indian ancestry. Is the termination of 'agua' ruled by the rhyme? Is 'Bío Bío' in the next line simply reference to the river which marked the boundry between the Spaniards and the Araucan Indians or, is 'bio,' the Greek word for 'life,' meant here as an illusion to Baptism, one of the motives of the conquest of America?"

[46] Ercilla canto XXXVI.

[47] Umpierre, 99 has posed the question concerning the possible symbolic use of water in the "areito." What he has not seen is the unifying effect between the "areito" and Act I, iii and v.

[48] Oña, Canto II, strs. 11, 13–16, 358. Ercilla, Canto III, str. 73, 80. According to both poets, wine was drunk to celebrate victory in battle.

[49] Juan de la Cueva clearly follows the Senecan tradition in his play *El infamador*, Ed. Francisco A. de Icaza (Madrid: Castellanos, 1941). Two examples of Lopean plays in which Senecan scenes of horror appear are *El mayordomo de la Duquesa de Amalfi* and *El castigo sin venganza.*

4

Visions of the New World in *El Brasil restituido*

El Brasil restituido is one of Lope de Vega's many historical dramas. The manuscript, presently located at the New York Public Library, bears the dramatist's signature as well as the date of composition of the play, October 23, 1625. The *comedia* celebrates the victory of the combined Imperial forces of Spain and Portugal over the Dutch invaders of the Bay of All Saints and its port city, Salvador, on April 30, 1625.

The identification of Lope's source or sources for this play has been a difficult and frustrating task for the few critics who have made the attempt. In his *Estudios sobre el teatro de Lope de Vega* Marcelino Menéndez Pelayo lists several possible sources of Lope's information.[1] They are: Bartolomeu Guerreiro's *Jornada dos vassalos da coroa de Portugal* . . . ,[2] João de Madeiros Correia's "Relaçam verdadeira . . .",[3] Francisco de Avendaño y Vilela's "Relación del viaje y sucesso . . .",[4] and Fadrique de Toledo's "Relación de la carta . . .",[5] "Verdadera relación . . .",[6] and "Relación del sucesso . . ."[7] In the end, Menéndez Pelayo finds the accounts so similar that he refuses to designate any one as Lope's source: "Siendo tan semejantes entre sí, no puedo determinar a punto fijo la que prefirió Lope . . ."[8]

Gino de Solenni was the next critic to address the question of the source of *El Brasil restituido*. In his article entitled "On the Sources of *El Brasil restituido*" he affirmed that the direct source of the play was the "Relación que envió Diego de Ruiz . . ."; however, at a later date Solenni published a critical edition of the play in which he retracted his former assertion concerning the source.[9]

In an article Diego Martínez Torrón states that the source of the play is Fadrique de Toledo's "Relación de la carta."[10] He says Fadrique de Toledo's "Relación" is to be preferred to Diego de Ruiz's because the former "Relación" served as a model for the latter. Although Martínez Torrón discovered the almost word-for-word similarity between these two letters, he is not correct in stating that Ruiz's letter is modeled after Toledo's "Relación de la carta." Diego de Ruiz's "Relación" is an exact duplicate of another letter written by Toledo entitled "Relación del sucesso . . . " Examination of the two letters by Toledo reveals that the "Relación de la carta" and the "Relación del sucesso" are almost identical, the latter having some small omissions found in the former. A comparison between Toledo's "Relación del sucesso" and Ruiz's "Relación," however, reveals not one difference between them. One can conclude, therefore, that Diego de Ruiz's letter is no more than a reprint of Toledo's "Relación del sucesso."

As Solenni has indirectly dismissed Toledo's "Relación del sucesso" as the source of *El Brasil restituido,* Martínez Torrón undertakes the task of showing how the "Relación de la carta" is, indeed, the source. Martínez Torrón uses, as did Menéndez Pelayo and Solenni before him, the letter of approval written by the censor, Pedro de Vargas Machuca, six days after Lope completed the drama, in order to show that the censor's statements about the source refer to Fadrique de Toledo's "Relación de la carta." Vargas Machuca states:

> Esta gloria de las armas dEspaña en la restitución del Brasil . . . la ha escrito Lope de Vega Carpio, muy ajustada y conforme a la mejor relación que deste suceso tenemos, calificada de un textigo jnstrumental que se halló en esta guerra y trajo de ella honroșas señales en sus heridas. En la comedia se habla dél y de otros muchos caballeros con la honrra y alabança que se les deue . . .[11]

Therefore, according to the censor of the play, Lope's source comes from a witness who fought in the Brazilian campaign, was wounded, wrote about the war, and is cited in the play. Martínez Torrón concludes from Vargas Machuca's letter: "Don

Fadrique de Toledo bien pudo ser el testigo de excepción que menciona Vargas Machuca, y qué duda cabe que su relación sería la más ajustada a los hechos."[12]

Fadrique de Toledo, unlike the other possible sources mentioned by Menéndez Pelayo, fits three of the four qualifications mentioned above. As the Commanding General of land and sea forces, he was the most important officer and, presumably, the most qualified witness. It was he who drafted the terms of surrender found in both his letters cited as well as in Lope's play. He did indeed write about the war, and he is one of the central characters in Lope's drama. There is, however, no mention either in Lope's drama or in Toledo's letters, or in any of the other possible sources, of the general's having been wounded.

Martínez Torrón states that Lope de Vega's use of Fadrique de Toledo's "Relación de la carta" begins in Act II and that the events narrated in Act I " . . . están muy literaturizados, y no parecen basarse en ninguna relación concreta, sino quizá en los hechos conocidos de oídas."[13] Act I, however, intertwines the historical event, the Dutch invasion of the Bay of All Saints with a love theme, don Diego's rejection of doña Guiomar because of her Jewish birth (vv. 41–50). It is this rejection which causes her father, don Bernardo, to announce an occasion for revenge against don Diego (and by extension, against the Spanish and Portuguese): the arrival of the Dutch to Brazil to free the Judaizers residing there from the rigors of the Inquisition:

Don Bernardo: Teniendo que el Santo Officio
enuía un visitador,
de cuyo graue rigor
tenemos bastante indicio,
los que de nuestra nación
viuimos en el Brasil,
que tiene por gente vil
la Cristiana Religión,
por escusar las prisiones,
los gastos, pleitos y afrentas,
y ver deste yugo essentas
de tantas obligaciones

nuestras familias, que ya
a tal miseria han llegado,
porque dizen que enojado
Dios con nosotros está,
hauemos escrito a Olanda,
que con armada se apresta,
de que tenemos respuesta,
que sobre sus aguas anda,
juzgando será mexor
entregarnos a olandeses
que sufrir que portugueses
nos traten con tal rigor. (147–170)

While Martínez Torrón is correct in stating that there are more historical details in Acts II and III than in Act I, the accusation of Jewish complicity in the fall of the Bay of All Saints may be Lope's borrowing from João de Madeiros Correia's "Relaçam verdadeira," as he is the only pamphleteer who makes this allegation:

> Tomaraõ [i.e., the Hispanic soldiers] hũ Olandes, que disse estauaõ muy fortes, & que tinhaõ dentro muitos judeus, & judias, que de Olanda vieraõ com elles, & que estes excitaũaõ os Olandeses, a que se defendessem, & ihes dauaõ muito dineiro, & que hauiaõ mandado noue navios a costa de Guinè a roubar, & oito ao Rio de Ianeiro, & que esperauaõ de Olanda setenta nauios, segundo ihe hauiaõ ausiado . . .

Contrary to Martínez Torrón's assertion that Act I is not based upon any specific pamphlet, it seems that there is at least one reference in this act which has a parallel in one of the sources cited by Menéndez Pelayo. Following Madeiros Correia's lead, Lope has capitalized upon the fact that the security of an American colony has been undermined by two of Spain's historical enemies—Protestants and Jews.

It is important to note that Martínez Torrón never offers his readers the results of his investigation concerning the source of the play. He satisfies himself with the following statement: "Aunque por la brevedad exigida en esta ponencia no detallaré la estrecha afinidad entre la relación de Fadrique de Toledo y el texto de Lope, debe destacarse que la analogía entre ambos textos es impresionante."[14] My investigation of the source of the play reveals no detectable relation between Toledo and Lope.

In view of the confusion concerning Lope's sources for this play, I propose to examine each source mentioned by Menéndez Pelayo—Guerreiro's *Jornada,* Madeiros Correia's "Relaçam," Avendaño y Vilela's "Relación del viaje y sucesso," and Toledo's "Relación de la carta"—in order to determine which of the narratives Lope might have used in writing *El Brasil restituido.* I have chosen three principal areas for examination. They are: the departure for and arrival of the Spanish fleet at the Bay of All Saints, the dead and wounded, and the incident of the soldier who captures the flag from the enemy camp.[15] Furthermore, it will be shown that the *relaciones* which Lope used were provided to him by the Count Duke of Olivares (or perhaps an intermediary) with his specific instructions concerning details of the play, which was first performed at court on November 5, just two weeks after its completion.

The narration in Act II by the personified "Brasil" of the departure and arrival of the Imperial armada is very long; I have, therefore, summarized Lope's historical facts and indicated their line numbers in the play. Lope writes that Philip IV, upon learning of the Dutch invasion, named Fadrique de Toledo y Osorio as the Commanding General of the armada (883–889 and 893–894). The Spanish fleet departed from Cadiz on a Tuesday with thirty-one ships (901–904 and 920–922). The Spanish fleet went to Tenerife and then to the Cape Verde Islands where the Portuguese fleet had been awaiting its arrival (935–938). After being detained at the Cape Verde Islands a few days due to a lack of water, the combined Spanish and Portuguese armadas sailed toward the Bay of All Saints rather than Pernambuco (977–982). The arrival at Brazil was delayed further by the calmness of the winds (991–992). The arrival occurred during Holy Week, and on Good Friday Fadrique de Toledo ordered the scouting of the Bay (999–1014). A captain reported to Toledo that the city was fortified and that the enemy awaited reenforcements from Holland (1015–1019). Disembarkation of the

Imperial soldiers occurred on the southern bank on Good Friday without resistance from the enemy (1020–1040).

A comparison between Lope's lines and the four possible sources reveals an extraordinary similarity between Avendaño y Vilela and Lope de Vega. Both the soldier and the dramatist state that thirty-one ships left Cadiz for the Bay of All Saints on a Thursday, that the Spanish fleet went first to Tenerife and then to the Cape Verde Islands where it was met by the Portuguese fleet, that the calmness of the winds prevented an earlier arrival at Brazil, that the Imperial armies arrived at their destination on Holy Thursday, and that the city, Salvador, was fortified.

Fadrique de Toledo's "Relación" offers far too little information for one to assert that the dramatist has taken his information from the Commanding General.[16] As many of the details offered by Guerreiro and Madeiros Correia do not coincide with the information Lope presents,[17] it seems that the dramatist has followed Avendaño y Vilela's narration here.

One should notice, however, an important difference between Avendaño y Vilela and Lope. The dramatist declares that the disembarkation occurred on Good Friday at the southern coast of the Bay. The soldier states that the disembarkation happened on Monday, March 31, on the eastern coast of the city. It is probable that Lope altered Avendaño y Vilela's Monday disembarkation for poetic reasons. As Good Friday is, according to the New Testament, the day on which Jesus was crucified, Lope apparently made the change from Monday to Friday in order to suggest the supreme sacrifice that the Imperial soldiers made for their country.

In Act III of *El Brasil restituido* the mythological figure of Apollo narrates to the personified "Brasil" a battle between the Imperial forces and the Dutch. It is here that the dramatist lists the casualties of war. Lope informs his audience that don Pedro de Porras was wounded in the hand: "pero casi al mismo tiempo/vna bala narangera/le ha roto el muslo siniestro,/con que le van retirando,/y queda en el canpo muerto" (1465–1469). Captain Pedro de Santisteban also dies: "Don Pedro de Santisteuan/cayó de vn balazo muerto" (1514–1515). Francisco Manuel also meets his end in the battle: "Y al capitán don Francisco/Manuel que gallardo y diestro/la cruz de San Juan onraua,/ y murió con ella al pecho" (1524–1527). Juan de Torreblanca is another victim: "Al alférez del Maestre/de Canpo tanbién han muerto,/y don Juan de Torre Blanca/fue blanco del plomo negro,/con algunos portuguesses/que hasta la muralla fueron . . . " (1528–1533).

The dramatist states that Enrique de Alagón was wounded: "A don Enrrique tanbién/lleba de la mano vn dedo . . . " (1470–1471). Diego de Guzmán was also injured "¡Qué valeroso le sigue/el animoso don Diego/de Guzmán!: Pero tanbién/ le retiran porque al suelo/le ha derribado vna bala/pasándole el muslo diestro" (1486–1491). Diego Ramírez survives a wound in the chest: "¡O duro y sangriento Marte,/ay, Musas, entristezeos,/porque a don Diego Ramírez/le passa vna bala al pecho!/ Notable ha sido la herida; pero no querrán los cielos/que muera, aunque su balor/viuiera en la fama eterno" (1506–1513). Diego de Espinosa narrowly escapes death: "Sale cantidad de picas,/ pero yeren a don Diego/de Espinosa, a quien la muerte/ preuiene lloroso entierro" (1520–1523).

At the close of the play don Manuel de Meneses, Commander of the Portuguese fleet, praises two of his countrymen who gave their lives: "Que me cuestan mucha sangre/de portuguesses que han muerto./Don Alfonso de Alencastro/y Martín Alfonso fueron/gran pérdida a Portugal" (2321–2325).

Guerreiro's list of soldiers who were wounded or killed coincides not at all with that of Lope de Vega.[18] Indeed, as the title of the work suggests, Guerreiro offers minimal information concerning the wounded or killed Spanish soldiers. Of the five wounded soldiers mentioned by Madeiros Correia, three are mentioned by Lope: Enrique de Alago, Diogo Ramirez, and Diogo de Guzmão; only two of the soldiers he reports as having died appear in Lope's play: Pedro de Santiesteban and Francisco Manoel.[19]

Examination of Toledo, Avendaño y Vilela, and Lope reveals that all the dead and wounded soldiers mentioned by the dramatist are found in these two possible sources with the exception of Alfonso de Alencastro and Martín Alonso.[20] It is possible that these two names indicate that there are other sources unknown to us which Lope followed. I am inclined, however, to believe that Lope drew his information concerning the dead and wounded from Avendaño y Vilela because it seems clear that Lope has taken the departure and arrival data from this writer.

The most heroic feat of Lope's play occurs when the *gracioso,* Machado, captures one of the enemy flags and offers it to don Fadrique as a symbol of the *gracioso's* valor. The scene in Act III is as follows:

> Fadrique: ¿Qué es esto?
> Enrique: Vn soldado es
> que por el muro trepó,
> que lo desigual le dió
> en que pusiese los pies. (1896–1899)
> ....
> [Machado con la vandera.]
> Machado: Da los pies, balor de España,
> Toledo por justa herencia,
> a quien ofreze a tu gloria
> esta vandera enemiga,
> la primera que te obliga
> a pensar en la vitoria. (1902–1907)
> ....
> Fadrique: Esta cadena te doy,
> y ocho escudos de ventaja.
> (1932–1933)

The event in which an enemy flag was taken was so impressive that it was narrated by all four writers. Fadrique de Toledo and Avendaño y Vilela, however, make no mention of the monetary reward which the Portuguese writers say Toledo gave to this nameless soldier. This fact leads to the conclusion that Lope de Vega read one of the Portuguese pamphlets. Because Madeiros Correia's narration seems to be the source of the accusation of Jewish complicity in the fall of the Bay of All Saints, I am inclined to believe that Lope has followed this writer here.

There are two significant instances where Lope departs from all known sources. These departures may be due to the fact that *El Brasil restituido* was first performed before the royal family and the Count Duke of Olivares on November 6, 1625,[21] and therefore, I suspect, Lope conformed his play to certain requirements perhaps specified by the Count Duke himself.

Machado's nationality is one clear instance of such a departure. In several scenes[22] the *gracioso* indicates that he is of Castilian and Portuguese lineage:

> Guiomar: ¿Y cómo os llamáis?
> Machado: Machado;
> y si es que lleba la silla
> todo cauallo en Castilla,
> de portugués tengo vn lado,
> los tres castellanos son. (2230–34)

It is interesting to note that while Toledo does not indicate the nationality of the valiant soldier who stole an enemy flag, Madeiros Correia and Guerreiro state that the soldier was Aragonese, and Avendaño y Vilela declares that he was Basque. None of the writers states that the nameless soldier was Portuguese or Castilian. This alteration is Lope's addition. Because the expedition to Brazil was a joint undertaking by Spain and Portugal, it is likely that Lope, departing from the historical sources, which in any event were in disagreement, created a heroic Spanish-Portuguese soldier in order to celebrate the victory achieved by the nations under the united crown of Philip IV.

The dramatist's insistence upon Machado's dual nationality may very well point to the Count Duke of Olivares' direct intervention into the composing of the play, his desire to extol the Spanish military victories achieved during the 1620s and 30s in Europe and America and, to defend his foreign-policy decisions before a court growingly skeptical of his actions. The new royal residence, the Buen Retiro, begun in 1629 and completed in October, 1632, was the idea of the Count Duke.[23] Furthermore, one of the rooms of the new palace, the Hall of Realms, a great center for court festivities and reunions, and also conceived by Olivares, displayed twelve paintings[24] depicting Spanish armed victories in Europe and America, "each carefully chosen to advance the claims of the Hapsburg kings of Spain as the universal defenders of the faith and the promoters of peace and justice . . . and to show friends and enemies of the regime alike that the affairs of the Monarchy were"[25] in the capable hands of the Count Duke. Among the twelve paintings hung in the Hall between ten windows was the *Recapture of Bahia* by the Dominican Juan Bautista Maino,[26] and as J. H. Elliott and J. Brown write, Lope's play "gave Maino the inspiration for the treatment of his theme."[27] Elliott and Brown state that Maino's indebtedness to Lope de Vega is perceived in the foreground of the painting where a wounded Castilian soldier is tended by a Portuguese woman:

> In Lope's play, an escaped soldier says how he saw in "these deserted fields old men, children and women, a pitiful sight." It would have been logical for Maino to include these returning refugees as a counterpoint to the defeated and departing Dutch who had deprived them of their homes. It would also have been appropriate to show a Portuguese woman tending a Castilian who had shed his blood on her behalf, as a further symbol of that union of hearts which Olivares was striving to encourage through the Union of Arms.[28]

It is no mere accident that the dramatist and the artist stress the union of the reigns of Castile and Portugal, Lope through his insistence upon Machado's Spanish-Portuguese blood and Maino through the portrayal of a Portuguese woman's care of a wounded Castilian soldier. That Lope de Vega reiterates time and again the Spanish-Portuguese heritage of his valiant *gracioso* seems to point to the Count Duke's desire to celebrate the union of the Spanish and Portuguese crowns under Philip IV.

Lope's other clear departure from his sources concerns the

king's pardon of the Dutch soldiers. In the play the victorious don Fadrique addresses a portrait of King Philip and says:

> Magno Filipe, esta gente
> pide perdón de sus yerros
> ¿Quiere Vuestra Magestad
> que esta vez les perdonemos?
> Pareze que dixo sí. (2289–2293)

Such a rapid communication between Toledo and the king is certainly not found in any of these historical pamphlets. Rather, the depiction of a clement and magnanimous king seems to be another example of the Count Duke's connection to the *comedia*. Again Elliott and Brown link Lope and Maino. Referring to the background of Maino's painting, they write:

> At the king's feet lie in defeat the personifications of his enemies—Heresy . . . Discord . . . and Treachery or Fraud . . . better known in those days as the Dutch, the English, and the French . . . If God was on Philip's side, so too was the count-duke. In a motif of considerable audacity, Olivares had himself depicted with Minerva as the joint author of Philip's victories. With one hand he lays the laurel wreath on the king's brow, and with the other he hands a sword and the olive branch, a symbol both of the olive groves of his title and of reconciliation. Olivares offered victory to his sovereign and clemency to his defeated enemies. The scene thus becomes an emblematic synopsis of the leading idea of the Hall of Realms. A powerful and victorious king defeats his enemies: a merciful king offers them peace and reconciliation. And behind it all, in this perfect representation of the concept of rule by favorite or "valimiento," is the figure of the minister. The sword and the olive branch, victory and clemency—these are the themes that unite the plays by Calderón [i.e., *El sitio de Bredá*] and Lope and the paintings of Velázquez [i.e., *La rendición de Bredá*] and Maino, and link them to Olivares. In all four works, the victorious generals offer their enemies the forgiveness of the wise, just king. The concept of magnanimity in victory represented in the plays and battle pieces may be traced back to Olivares, who explicitly interpreted the two victories in that light.[29]

The proximity between the date of composition of *El Brasil restituido*, (October 23, 1625), its date of approval by Vargas Machuca, (October 29, 1625), and its first performance at court, (November 6, 1625), suggest that the *comedia* was written with some haste, specifically for representation before the royal family. It seems altogether possible that Olivares provided Lope with several pamphlets of the Brazilian campaign along with specific instructions concerning details of composition: the depiction of the union of crowns of Spain and Portugal and the victorious and clement Philip IV. These two details do not appear to be fortuitous similarities between Lope's play and Maino's painting. Indeed, Lope had sought to gain the Count Duke's favor since 1621.[30] The censor's declarations about Lope's source, which confused Menéndez Pelayo, Solenni, and Martínez Torrón, need not be taken literally. Rather, Vargas Machuca's statement should be interpreted as the censor's assurance to the Count Duke and the royal family that the historical facts were the best available. Vargas Machuca may have been totally unaware of Lope's precise sources. After all, *none* of the pamphleteers fits all four qualifications which the censor outlines as the source, and although the censor states that the play is based upon "*la* mejor relación," it appears that Lope has followed at least *two* writers—Avendaño y Vilela and Madeiros Correia.

In his book entitled *América en el teatro de Lope de Vega,* Aurelio Miró Quesada correctly states that the role of America in *El Brasil restituido* is secondary to the principal concern of the depiction of the war between the Portuguese and the Spaniards against the Dutch:

> La referencia a América es en todo momento incidental y ocasional. A diferencia de las obras de Lope ya estudiadas, como *El nuevo mundo descubierto por Cristóbal Colón* y el *Arauco domado* en que se presenta, aunque solo sea con caracteres fragmentarios y en su mayor parte convencionales, el contacto de las dos civilizaciones y las luchas que sostienen los españoles para lograr dominar a los indios; en *El Brasil restituido* el argumento es diferente. Lo que importa en este caso es sólo la disputa—verdad que en tierra americana—de dos elementos no americanos: de un lado los holandeses, y de otro los portugueses y españoles unidos, que combaten por el dominio del Brasil y confrontan

> sus limitados y particulares intereses. El único elemento que no se consulta es precisamente el que debía ser el decisivo: el propio país americano.[31]

Miró Quesada is, of course, arguing from a quantitative point of view—i.e., the number of lines dedicated to the portrayal of America and its inhabitants is minimal. However, because Lope's brief references to America are not found in any source—a noteworthy distinction between this play and the two American plays which precede it—one may assume that the dramatist's comments about the New World are his own or a reflection of the popular beliefs of his countrymen or the product of earlier readings on the subject. One might argue, therefore, that from a qualitative viewpoint, Lope informs his audience/reader much more than previously about his own impressions of the New World, because his words are not here the reflection of another writer.

The personified figure of "Brasil" is illustrative of Lope's basic impressions of America and Americans. The stage directions which precede "Brasil's" first appearance on stage read: "Salen algunos yndios, con arcos y flechas, y el Brasil en figura de dama yndia, con vna rueda de plumas y vna flecha dorada como dardo." (26) The costume worn by this personified figure represents a standard image of American Indians—feathers and a bow and arrows. However, because personifications are symbolic generalizations, one might argue that "Brasil" is, in a generalized way, a reflection of the dramatist's thought concerning American dress. Furthermore, the image of a woman, rather than a man, dressed as "Brasil" evokes, perhaps, sensuality; Lope's generalized portrait of American women reveals his belief in their sensuous nature. Indeed, in *El nuevo mundo descubierto por Cristóbal Colón* the dramatist does reveal his belief that Indian women were more inclined to the display of their sensuous nature than Spanish women. The bow and arrows are symbolic of the bellicose nature of the natives. The fact that the arrow is golden recalls, perhaps, gold as well as the erroneous assumption that all Americans worshiped the sun. Therefore, it appears that among the dramatist's most basic concepts concerning the American Indians are the sensuality of the women, their war-like nature, their adoration of the sun as a god, and their use of feathers as part of their attire.[32]

In her initial speech to the Indians surrounding her, "Brasil" contrasts her pagan past with her new Christian nature. Of her religious practices, she states:

> En tienpo que gentil estaua ociosa,
> y el mar etiópico reynaua,
> que de perlas mis plantas adornaua,
> injusto dueño y sin razón tirano
> de mi balor la posesión tenía
> desde que fue del çielo soberano,
> donde cándida aurora amanecía,
> desterrado a viuir opuesto en vano
> en noche eterna al senpiterno día,
> nunca desta verdad desengañada,
> entre las olas de la mar sentada. (490–500)

The "injusto dueño" and the "sin razón tirano" of whom "Brasil" speaks is Lucifer, who was expelled from heaven due to his rebellion against God's supremacy. The allegorical figure informs the audience that she and her people were deceived by the powers of darkness; their religious practices were inspired by Satan and not by God. The arrival of the Portuguese signified a new and illuminated direction in the lives of "Brasil's" people:

> Sus portugueses conquistaron fuertes
> mi tierra y mar, con otras la ganaron
> después que con Castilla echaron suertes
> y mis famosos yndios sujetaron;
> porque xamás el hijo de Laertes
> y los que su balor aconpañaron
> quando de Troya mísera boluieron,
> tantos peligros y naufragios vieron,
> Entonces reçiuí la fee de Christo
> y supe que era Dios único y sólo;
> con el tirano antiguo me malquisto

> y niego adoración al claro Apolo;
> y los fieros ydólatras resisto,
> que ocupan la más parte deste polo,
> y linpia del antiguo barbarismo
> me baño en las corrientes de bautismo. (509–524)

"Brasil" continues her review of past and present religious practices of her inhabitants by demonstrating her understanding of basic Catholic thought: the transubstantiation of bread and wine into the body and blood of Christ, the immaculate conception of Jesus, the unblemished virginity of Mary throughout her life, the death of Jesus on a cross, and his redemption of mankind.

Lope de Vega had insisted from his earliest American play, *El nuevo mundo*, on the necessity of converting the Indians to Christianity. In this play the same central thought re-emerges. The Iberians had brought salvation and enlightenment to a people who had hitherto been deceived by polytheistic beliefs. Furthermore, "Brasil's" impressive demonstration of knowledge about and understanding and acceptance of Christianity might reveal the dramatist's conviction (certainly not universally accepted by all Europeans) that native Americans were indeed capable of reason.[33]

"Brasil" continues her speech by linking her past religious deception to her present political situation. The arrival of the Dutch, abetted by the Jews living in Brazil, is a pernicious attempt to destroy the salvation attained through Catholicism.

> Pues viendo que no puede persuadirme, [i.e., Lucifer]
> vltimamente soliçita a Olanda
> por medio de vnos bárbaros hebreos
> que le han comunicado sus desseos;
> que por este camino yntenta en vano
> yntroduçir su herror y apostasía,
> y que le nieguen a Filipo Hispano
> estas riberas la obedenzia mía.
> Y sin temer su poderosa mano,
> que rayos como Júpiter enbía,
> ronpen el mar, y aunque las olas gimen,

las fuertes proas en su espalda ynprimen.
Presso el gouernador, que sin deffensa
estaua, desta offensa diuertido,
triunfan a costa de mi injusta offensa
los que han llegado, y los que me han vendido. (545–560)

While it appears that Madeiros Correia was Lope's source for this information, it is, nevertheless, significant that the dramatist has linked the invasion of the city to two enemies of the Faith: the Dutch Protestants and the Jews. It is the threat of the introduction of heterodoxy which concerns "Brasil." Her inhabitants were once idolators, separated from God's grace. Salvation was achieved through the evangelic teaching of the Portuguese and Spanish colonizers. At present the salvation of her people is jeopardized by unbelievers who, as agents of the "injusto dueño," attempt to dislodge those who have successfully implanted the true word of God in the country.

Jews, Protestants and Indians possess at least one common defect for the dramatist—all are removed from God's salvation because they are not members of His Catholic communion. The American Indians, however, have never had the opportunity to hear and receive the Good News and, therefore, need the Spaniards and the Portuguese to save their souls from eternal damnation. Lope returns again to the central theme of all three American plays: the necessity of evangelization and conversion.

One of the most curious aspects of *El Brasil restituido* is the dramatist's repeated insistence that Brazil is an island found in the Ethiopian Sea:

Ongol: ¿Posible puede ser que en tu belleża
puede caber, Brasil, ysla famosa,
contra nuestro valor tanta tristeza?
Brasil: Fortuna, en mis desdichas rigurosa,
corona con laureles mi cabeza.
En tienpo que gentil estaua ociosa,
y en mar etiópico reynaua,
que de perlas mis plantas adornaua . . . (485–492)

Lope's apparent confusion about American geography is certainly not derived from any of the possible sources of the play. It is, perhaps, the result of his own consultation of medieval maps, some of which refer to the southern portion of the Atlantic Ocean between Africa and South America as the "Oceanus AEthiopicus." Furthermore, the *Enciclopedia Universal Ilustrada* states the following concerning early conceptions of the location of Brazil:

> Los cartógrafos de aquella época [13th and 14th century] lo tenían por una isla, que pintaban en medio del Atlántico y en la misma latitud del cabo Finisterre de Inglaterra o Land's End de los ingleses. Todavía llaman los ingleses Peña de Brasil a un islote situado a poca distancia del extremo Sur de Irlanda.

Indeed, many early maps of the world do show a small island called Brazil in the "Mare Atlanticum" near Ireland.[34]

Lope's allusions to the natives of Brazil as cannibals is derived from his readings of Gómara, Oviedo, Ercilla, and Oña. In Act I the "gracioso" Machado informs the Indian Ongol (the name is reminiscent of Ercilla) that Bernardo and his daughter Guiomar have effectuated their plan of revenge by having don Diego de Meneses killed by the Indians.

Behind the comic tone of the dialogue between Machado and Ongol concerning the disposal of the corpse is a far more serious comment about the natives:

> Machado: Pues qué, ¿bays a sepultarlo?
> Ongol: Sí, pero en nuestros pechos
> después que está asado a quartos.
> Machado: ¿Honbres coméys?
> Ongol: ¿Qué te admiras?
> ¿Ay manjar más delicado? (776–780)

The immediate reaction to the dialogue most certainly should be laughter, but the notion of cannibalism was obviously repugnant to the European. That Lope would include this detail in *El Brasil restituido* seems to indicate the profound impression left upon him after his earlier readings concerning this custom in some parts of America. The supposed practice of cannibalism by the natives of Brazil re-enforces the dramatist's conviction that instruction in Catholicism was ultimately the most effective means of eradicating the custom.

Conclusions

An attempt to discover the sources of *El Brasil restituido* is a difficult task. In the first place the pamphlets which were available were, as Menéndez Pelayo has pointed out, quite similar in many respects. Furthermore, the process of determining the source is hampered by the censor's comments concerning Lope's source since none of the possible writers about the Brazilian campaign fulfills all the requirements stated by Vargas Machuca: a soldier who fought in the war, was wounded in it, subsequently wrote about it and is mentioned in the *comedia*.

My investigation points to Lope's use of more than the *single* source which Vargas Machuca vaguely claims to be the historical basis for the play ("la mejor relación"). It is, indeed, not surprising that Lope has pulled his historical information from more than one writer since the dramatist's two earlier American plays demonstrate the use of more than one source.

I have identified Francisco de Avendaño y Vilela as one of the sources of *El Brasil restituido*. The similarities between the soldier's and the dramatist's references to the departure and arrival of the Imperial forces are the principal bases for this contention. Avendaño y Vilela is the only writer who states that the fleet departed Spain on a Thursday with thirty-one ships. While Mareiros Correia refers to the reunion of the Spanish and Portuguese fleets, and although Guerreiro mentions the arrival at Bahía during Holy Week, and while Toledo mentions the fact that Salvador was well-fortified, it is *only* Avendaño y Vilela who states *all* these facts. It is, therefore, reasonable to conclude that Lope drew this information from Avendaño y Vilela.

Lope's references to the soldiers who died or who were

wounded during this campaign reveal similarities with both Toledo and Avendaño y Vilela. Each soldier to whom Lope refers is found in the pamphlets of these two writers. Since Avendaño y Vilela is clearly the source of the departure/arrival information in the play, I suspect that this writer served as Lope's model in this case.

João de Madeiros Correia, a Portuguese pamphleteer, seems to be Lope's other source. Because this writer stands alone in attributing the fall of the city of Salvador to the Jews, it seems that Lope has followed the pamphleteer's lead on this issue. Furthermore, Lope's reference to the chain given to Machado by don Fadrique seems to have its origins in one of the Portuguese narratives. Since Madeiros Correia was probably used in reference to the role of the Jews in the fall of the city, I have speculated that the reference to the monetary reward has also come from this writer.

Although Fadrique de Toledo, the Commanding General of land and sea forces of the Imperial fleet, might appear, by virtue of his rank, to be the writer upon whom Lope relied for the creation of his play, I find no evidence for this assumption. Indeed, Toledo offers almost no information concerning the departure from Spain, the difficulties on the high seas, or the union of the two fleets in the Cape Verde Islands. Guerreiro's long work emphasizes the role of the Portuguese in recapturing Bahia, as the title suggests, and therefore, was not complete enough in scope for a dramatist who wished to celebrate the combined victory of Spain and Portugal.

Lope's two significant departures from all possible sources emphasize the combined triumph of two great nations under a magnanimous and clement monarch, Philip IV. The *gracioso* Machado's repeated boasting of his Castilian-Portuguese lineage and Philip IV's pardoning of his enemies at the close of the play, through Fadrique's rather mystifying consultation with his monarch via a portrait, link the *comedia* to the Count Duke of Olivares' desire to represent the monarchy as triumphant and victorious over its enemies yet magnanimous and clement toward them and, at the same time, to remind his own detractors at court that the affairs of State were guided by his capable hands.

The new royal palace of the Buen Retiro, completed in 1632, was the idea of the Count Duke. One of its rooms, the Hall of Realms, decorated by the Count Duke, Diego de Velázquez and Juan Bautista Maino, displayed twelve paintings all depicting Spanish armed victories. One of the paintings, the *Recapture of Bahia* by Maino, owes its depiction of a Portuguese woman's aid to a fallen Castilian soldier to the ruling idea of Olivares' Hall of Realms. This same bond between the Iberian people is reflected in Lope's play through the proud, heroic *gracioso* whose heritage combines the greatness of Spain and Portugal.

Lope's other significant departure from his sources concerns the depiction of the king. Philip IV's clemency and magnanimity in victory, expressed through Fadrique at the close of the play as the enemies are pardoned, is seen in the background of the painting as Minerva and Olivares jointly crown the victorious Philip IV, who crushes under foot his enemies yet forgives their transgressions.

These strong ideological connections between Lope's play and Maino's painting (which, like the other eleven paintings in the Hall of Realms, was intended to fulfill the Count Duke's specifications of victory, magnanimity, and clemency) seem to also point toward the Count Duke's intervention, directly or through an intermediary, in the play. That the play was performed first at court before King Philip and the Count Duke (November 6, 1625) just two weeks after Lope had completed it (October 23, 1625) provides further evidence which strongly suggests the Count Duke's involvement in the composition of the play. It is possible that the Count Duke, whose favor Lope had sought during this time, gave Madeiros Correia's and Avendaño y Vilela's pamphlets to Lope and offered specific instructions concerning the depiction of the union of crowns and the victorious and clement king.

Because the focus of each writer of the Brazilian campaign is upon the war itself, there is very little information about America or the Americans. As this is the case, one might assume that the information Lope provides concerning the natives reflects some of his most basic concepts about the New World.

The attire worn by the allegorical figure, "El Brasil," demonstrates, in a primitive way, the dramatist's conceptualization of the Indians: their use of feathers as a decorative part of their attire, their worship of the sun (suggested by the gold arrows), their bellicose nature (inferred from the arrows), their sensuality (suggested by the feminine personification of the country). This is not to say that Lope believed all Indians dressed and worshiped as the images suggest they do; rather, such a depiction forms a generalized notion of the natives.

Lope may have felt certain sympathies for the plight of the new Spanish vassals, but he certainly does not romanticize them here or elsewhere. As in earlier plays, Lope seems to suggest that cannibalism is a practice of all American Indians. That Lope really believed what he portrayed on the stage concerning this matter is most improbable since earlier readings had clearly demonstrated otherwise. Lope's insistence upon this trait is intended to inform his countrymen of the utter necessity to acculturate the Indians in Spanish ways of life and in its religion.

Lope's belief in the benefits of the Christianization of America cannot be denied. As in earlier plays, Lope reiterates here the need to incorporate the Indians into the Church of Rome. His vision of the role of the Spaniards in America as crusaders for Catholicism gains a new dimension in *El Brasil restituido*. Spain, as depicted in this play, becomes a universal champion of Christianity. Its world mission is to eradicate all forms of heterodoxy. The idolatrous Indians are only one example of Spain's struggle for religious uniformity. The Dutch and the Jews also form part of the equation. Protestants, Jews, and Indians all seem to fall short of divine grace because they do not form part of the Universal Communion.

The constant references to Brazil as an island in the Ethiopian Sea is possibly more revealing than scandalous. The apparent ignorance of Lope reveals, perhaps, the artist's poetization of the American continents. As in *Persiles y Sigismunda,* in which

Cervantes stretches the truth concerning the location of Northern European islands and towns, Lope likewise knew that he could state in a public forum that Brazil was an island in the Mare AEtiopicum without shattering verisimilitude because he understood that the vast majority of his audience would not know otherwise.

Notes

[1] Marcelino Menéndez Pelayo, *Obras Completas*: *Estudios sobre el teatro de Lope de Vega*, 65 vols. (Santander: Aldus, 1949) 34: 237–238.

[2] Bartolomeu Guerreiro, *Jornada dos vassalos da coroa de Portugal*, Ed. Wilson Lousada. (Rio de Janeiro: Divisão de Publicaçoes e Divulgação, 1966). I have used this modern edition.

[3] João de Madeiros Correia, "Relaçam verdadeira de todo o succedido na restauação de Bahia de todos os Sanctos . . . " (Oporto: João Rodriguez, 1625). I have used the Oporto edition of this rare pamphlet in the University of Minnesota.

[4] Francisco de Avendaño y Vilela, "Relación del viaje y sucesso de la Armada que por mandato de su Magestad partió al Brasil a echar de allí a los enemigos que lo ocupaban." (Seville: n.p., 1625). I have used a photostat copy of this rare pamphlet at the New York Public Library.

[5] Fadrique de Toledo, "Relación de la carta que enbió don Fadrique de Toledo, general de las Armadas y poderoso exército que fué al Brasil . . . " (Seville: Simón Faxardo, 1625). I have used the copy of this rare pamphlet in the John Carter Brown Library, Brown University.

[6] —. "Verdadera relación de la grandiosa vitoria que las Armadas de España han tenido en la entrada del Brasil . . . " (Cadiz, 1625). I have not been able to locate this pamphlet. There is no reference to it in the *National Union Catalogue, Pre-1956 Imprints*, the British Museum's *General Catalogue of Printed Books*, the Bibliothèque National's *Catalogue Général des Livres Imprimés*, the *Catálogo de incunables de la Biblioteca Nacional*, the *Catálogo de la biblioteca de Menéndez Pelayo*. One may presume that this pamphlet varies little from Toledo's other two pamphlets, "Relación de la carta" and "Relación del sucesso," which are almost identical, as explained above.

[7] —. "Relación del sucesso del Armada y exército que fué al socorro del Brasil . . . " (Cadiz: n.p., 1625). I have used this pamphlet at the John Carter Brown Library, Brown University.

[8] Menéndez Pelayo 238.

[9] Gino de Solenni, "On the Sources of *El Brasil restituido*," *Revista de estudios*

hispánicos 1 (1928): 168–169. Also *El Brasil restituido,* Ed. Gino de Solenni (New York: Instituto de las Españas en los Estados Unidos, 1929) ix-x.

[10] Diego Martínez Torrón, "Valores informativos en el teatro de Lope de Vega: La fuente de *El Brasil restituido,*" *Lope de Vega y los orígenes del teatro español: Actas del I Congreso Internacional sobre Lope de Vega* (Madrid: Edi-6, 1981) 155.

[11] I have used the edition prepared by Gino de Solenni (New York: Instituto de las Españas en los Estados Unidos, 1929) 114. All further quotes are taken from this edition with the line number following. I have compared Solenni's edition to one by Marcelino Menéndez Pelayo, RAE 13 (Madrid: Sucesores de Rivadeneyra, 1902) 76–106, with Lope's autograph manuscript in the New York Public Library and the copy by Agustín Durán, found in the Biblioteca Nacional de Madrid, a microfilm copy of which I possess. Because Solenni's edition is based upon Lope's manuscript and not upon the Durán copy, used by Menéndez Pelayo, Solenni's edition is preferable. Solenni notes the variations between his edition and Menéndez Pelayo's.

[12] Martínez Torrón 155.

[13] Martínez Torrón 157.

[14] Martínez Torrón 157.

[15] These are the same principal areas which Solenni examined when he discovered the error with regard to his earlier belief that Ruiz was the source.

[16] Fadrique de Toledo's "Relación de la carta" is addressed to King Philip IV. He states that (1) he arrived at the Canary Islands on January 28, 1625, at the Cape Verde Islands on February 10, and at the Bay of All Saints on March 29, Holy Saturday; (2) he ordered scouting of the city and San Benito and Carmen; (3) he ordered Pedro Osorio, the Marquis of Torrecuso, and Francisco de Almeyda to make headquarters at San Benito; (4) he went to Carmen Fort with Juan de Orellana and Antonio Muñiz Barreto.

[17] Guerreiro's *Jornada dos vassalos da coroa de Portugal* is the longest of the four possible sources. He states (1) the Imperial forces arrived at the Bay of All Saints on March 29, 1625; (2) the initial scouting of the area was undertaken by Joseph Furtado and Sebastião Loureiro; (3) the city was not fortified; (4) Toledo and other generals gathered for consultation on Easter, March 30; (5) the decision was made to send the troops ashore to Forts Carmen and San Bento. Madeiros Correia offers the following information concerning the departure and arrival (1) the arrival at the Bay of All Saints occurred on March 29, 1625; (2) Spanish and Portuguese fleets had met at Cape Verde; (3) the enemy was fortified within the city of Salvador, having abandoned San Bento on the northern coast and San Carmo on the southern; (4) Governor Francisco de Moura informed the Imperial forces that there were more than 2,800 enemy soldiers—Dutch, French, and English; (5) On April 1, Toledo went ashore.

[18] Guerreiro offers little information concerning the names of those soldiers wounded or killed. Referring to the battle near San Bento, he gives the fol-

lowing names: *DEAD*—Pedro Osorio, Francisco de Almeida; *WOUNDED*—Pedro Cesar de Meneses, Henrique Henriques de Miranda.

[19] Madeiros Correia offers the following list of casualties during the same battle near San Bento: *DEAD*—Pedro Osorio, Pedro de S. Estauam, Alonso de Gama, Francisco Manoel; *WOUNDED*—Enrique de Alago, Diogo Ramirez, Pedro Mallea, Diogo Guzmão, Pero Manso.

[20] Fadrique de Toledo gives the following casualties: *DEAD*—Pedro Osorio, Pedro de Santiesteuan, Francisco de Aguilar, Alonso de Gama, Francisco Manuel, Juan de Oviedo, Juan de Torreblanca, Josefe Manrique, Lucas de Figueroa, Diego de Espinosa, Simón de Vidácar; *WOUNDED*—Enrique de Alagón, Diego Ramírez, Diego Espinosa, Diego de Guzmán, Pedro Medrano, Diego de Mallea. Avendaño y Vilela reports the following: *DEAD*—Pedro Osorio, Francisco Manuel de Aguilar, Alonso de Gama, Pedro de Santiesteuan, Juan de Torreblanca, Pedro Barba, Simón de Bidácar, Juan de Lima (an *indiano*); *WOUNDED*—Enrique de Alagón, Diego Ramírez, Diego de Guzmán, Diego de Espinosa.

[21] The date of the first performance is given by N.D. Shergold, *A History of the Spanish Stage From Medieval Times Until the End of the Seventeenth Century* (Oxford: Clarendon, 1967) 224. See also N.D. Shergold and J.E. Varey, "Some Palace Performances of Seventeenth-Century Plays," *Bulletin of Hispanic Studies* 40 (1963): 218. The cast of actors in Andrés de la Vega's company who performed before the royal family is found in the autograph manuscript and copied by H.A. Rennert, "Notes on Some 'Comedias' of Lope de Vega," *MLN* 1 (1905–6): 109.

[22] "¿No sabe que soy Machado,/castellano y portugués? (479–80); "No soy de linaje escuro;/que, Machado y portugués,/soy hidalgo, como lo es/melón bueno y no maduro." (1128–31); "Conmigo hablaua, que soy/castellano y portugués." (1862–3). It is Machado's repeated references to himself as Castilian and Portuguese which lead me to believe that Lope was fulfilling Olivares' request that the drama celebrate the combined victory of Castile and Portugal.

[23] Shergold *A History of the Spanish Stage . . .* 276. See also H.A. Rennert, *The Spanish Stage in the Time of Lope de Vega* (New York: The Hispanic Society of America, 1909) 238–239.

[24] For a list of the paintings hung in the Hall of Realms see Luis Diez del Corral y Pedruzo, *Velázquez, la monarquía e Italia* (Madrid: Espasa-Calpe, 1979) 48. Among the twelve paintings was Diego de Velázquez's *La rendición de Bredá* which celebrates Ambrosio de Spínola's victory over the Dutch in the Netherlands on June 5, 1625. Pedro Calderón de la Barca commemorates this victory in his play *El sitio de Bredá* which, according to Shirley B. Whitaker, "The First Performance of Calderón's *El sitio de Bredá*," *Renaissance Quarterly* 31 (1978): 515–531, was first performed for the court in 1625 and served as Velázquez's source for the painting. *El sitio de Bredá* is similar to *El Brasil*

restituido in that Olivares hoped that both plays would strengthen his own position at court and justify his military adventures in Europe and America. Whitaker states that Olivares furnished a map of Bredá which was used at the palace performance of Calderón's play, and it would, therefore, not be surprising that the Count Duke would ask Lope to conform his play to certain specifications. Karl Justi, *Velázaquez y su siglo*, Trans. Pedro Marrades (Madrid: Espasa-Calpe, 1953) 338, indicates that Olivares, Maino, and Velázquez planned the decoration of the Hall of Realms.

[25] John Huxtable Elliott and Jonathan Brown, *A Palace for a King: The Buen Retiro and the Court of Philip IV* (New Haven: Yale, 1980) 192.

[26] Diego Angulo Iñíguez and Alfonso E. Pérez Sánchez, *Historia de la pintura española* (Madrid: CSIC, 1969) 319, offer 1635 as the date of completion of Maino's painting.

[27] Elliott and Brown 187.

[28] Elliott and Brown 188.

[29] Elliott and Brown 188 and 190.

[30] Lope's attempt to win the Count Duke's favor is discussed by H.A. Rennert, *The Life of Lope de Vega* (Glasgow: Gowans and Gray, 1904) 314–315. Lope dedicated *El premio de la hermosura* (1621) and *Circe* (1624) to Olivares. In September, 1625, one month before completing *El Brasil restituido*, Lope dedicated his *Triunfos divinos con otras rimas* to the Countess of Olivares.

[31] Aurelio Miró Quesada S., *América en el teatro de Lope de Vega* (Lima: n.c., 1935) 78.

[32] The reference to the bellicosity of the Brazilian Indians may be the dramatist's recollection of the Araucanians.

Lope erroneously insisted in *El nuevo mundo* and in *Arauco domado* that the Caribbean Indians and the Araucanians worshiped the sun. It was, of course, a practice of the Incas.

See *Américas*, Vol. 28, n. 4 (1976) for photos of depictions of America in sculpture and painting, e.g., Meissen's "America," a porcelain figure on a gilded bronze base, ca. 1745; Lorenzo Vaccario's "America," a figure in silver with incrustations of precious metals, 1692; Joseph Wright's "The Indian Widow," an oil painting, 1785. All the above works of art depict America as an Indian woman. Meissen's porcelain figure emphasizes the exotic and sensuous aspects of America; Vaccarrio's and Wright's depictions suggest the bellicose aspects of America.

[33] See Chapter One. Vitoria stated that if one could prove that the Indians were "amentes," it would be advisable for the Spaniards, who are mentally superior, to protect the Indians (i.e., enslave them) as one would protect a child who had not come to the age of reason.

[34] *Enciclopedia Universal Ilustrada*, Vol. 9, 619. See also Emerson David Fite and A. Freeman, Eds., *A Book of Old Maps* (Cambridge: Harvard UP, 1926) 71 and 96.

Conclusion

The purpose of this study has been to reveal the thought of Lope de Vega concerning the discovery, conquest, and colonization of America. To this end I have compared the dramatist's three extant American plays—*El nuevo mundo, Arauco domado,* and *El Brasil restituido*—to their sources to ascertain the degree to which Lope adheres to these historical and poetic accounts or departs from them to offer his public his own personal views, observations, and preoccupations. Two facts are patently clear concerning the dramatist's use of source material in the creation of these American plays:

1. Lope tended to adhere closely to his sources;
2. He never relied upon one writer alone in gathering information about the affairs of America.

Francisco López de Gómara's *Historia de las Indias* (1552) and Gonzalo Fernández de Oviedo's *Historia general* (Pt. I—1535) are Lope's sources for *El nuevo mundo* although certain of the Indian names may, as Lemartinel and Minguet suggest, derive from Alvar Núñez Cabeza de Vaca's *Naufragios* (1555) and *Comentarios* (1555). While Lope relies more heavily upon Oviedo's account (e.g., the messianic intentions of the enterprise, the erection of and devotion to the cross at Concepción de la Vega), Gómara is most tellingly used in the depiction of the lustfulness of Indian women, the Indian names Dulcanquellín and Auté, and the reference to the intercourse between the Indians and the devil.

Alonso de Ercilla's epic poem *La Araucana* (Pt. I—1569; Pt. II—1578; Pt. III—1589) and Pedro de Oña's *Arauco domado* are the sources of Lope's *Arauco domado*. Lope turned to Ercilla to dramatize the crucifixion of Caupolicán and the subjugation of the Araucanians as Oña's unfinished epic ends before narrating these events. Oña was, however, the poet upon whom Lope relied most, due in part, to Ercilla's unfavorable portrayal of don García Hurtado de Mendoza. In addition to the detail of the tuft of wool, the list of Araucanian food (pérper, madí, etc.) and the reference to don García as "San García," are further indications of how closely and minutely Lope has followed the Chilean poet.

Francisco de Avendaño y Vilela and João de Madeiros Correia seem to be two detectable sources of *El Brasil restituido*. The information concerning the departure and arrival of the fleet as well as the list of casualties seem to come from Avendaño y Vilela. The accusation of Jewish complicity in the fall of Bahia and the monetary reward given to Machado by Fadrique seem to originate in Madeiros Correia's "Relaçam."

Lope's two significant departures from all writers of the Brazilian campaign, Machado's Spanish-Portuguese heritage and Philip IV's clemency and magnanimity in dealing with the defeated enemy, emphasize the combined triumph of two great nations united under one monarch. Lope's departures from all historical accounts seem to point toward the Count Duke of Olivares' connection with the *comedia*, which was performed before the royal family and the Count Duke on November 6, 1625, just two weeks after Lope had completed composition of the play.

El Brasil restituido inspired Juan Bautista Maino's painting, *The Recapture of Bahia* (1635), in the depiction of the close bond between the two nations (the Portuguese woman tending the fallen Spanish soldier), and the clement and magnanimous king (crowned by Olivares and Minerva with his enemies under foot). The painting was one of twelve which hung in the Hall of Realms in the palace of the Buen Retiro, which was completed in 1632. Because each painting in the Hall of Realms fulfilled the Count Duke's wish to celebrate the Spanish military victories, a triumphant nation's forgiveness of its enemies, and the union of the crowns of Spain and Portugal, it seems very probable that the Count Duke is responsible for Lope's two above-mentioned departures from his sources.

While Lope generally follows his source materials closely, his adherence to them is not absolute. His departure from their lead can often be attributed to the ideological purpose of the play. With no regard to chronology, Lope freely combined in *El nuevo mundo* events from Columbus' first and second voyages. Although no clerics accompanied Columbus on his first voyage, as Gómara and Oviedo state, Lope included Friar Buyl in the play to indicate the messianic intentions of the Spanish nation in America. While La Deseada was not discovered until Columbus' second crossing of the Atlantic in 1493, Lope stated otherwise in order to re-enforce the idea of joy, safety, and refuge after a perilous trip across the ocean. The veiled references to the halting of communion by Friar Buyl and the massacre of Spanish soldiers for molesting native women are severely muted in order to avoid distractions from the messianic nature of the Spanish enterprise.

Lope de Vega's vision of America, its natives, and the Spaniards who went there is intimately united to his belief in the redemptive benefits of his Catholic religion. If there is one single unifying thought among *El nuevo mundo, Arauco domado,* and *El Brasil restituido,* it is that the teachings of the Roman Catholic Church must be sown and nurtured in America.

The depictions of Christopher Columbus and don García demonstrate the importance Lope placed upon the role of his Church in America. While Columbus initially lures European monarchs with the promise of wealth, he reiterates time and time again that the salvation of the natives is his principal concern. The dramatist goes as far as to suppress reports found in his sources concerning the Commander's attempt to conceal the wealth he had acquired in America in order to present this explorer as an example of the Christian zeal of the Spanish mission.

Don García is also portrayed as a Christian knight-warrior whose only concerns in America are the defense of nation and king, and the pacification of the rebellious Araucanians. Lope glosses over the reports from his sources which tell of the abuses of the Indians under Valdivia, Villagrán, and Aguirre and suggests that the former disturbances caused by unscrupulous leaders bear little relation to the Christian administration of don García. Furthermore, Lope suggests that don García succeeded where others had failed because he is devoutly religious and not swayed by a desire for material gain.

It is, perhaps, in *El Brasil restituido* where Lope demonstrates most clearly his conviction about the spiritual role his country must play in America. The natives of Brazil, after receiving the gift of salvation through the early Spanish and Portuguese missionaries, have been led astray by two of Spain's greatest spiritual rivals: Protestants and Jews. As the title of the play indicates, the role of the Imperial armies in this play is, in part, to restore spiritual health to inhabitants of this American colony. God, for Lope de Vega, was clearly behind the efforts of his nation to bring the American Indians into a new age of salvation.

Despite Lope's unalterable belief in the need to evangelize the Indians, he reveals in *El nuevo mundo* and *Arauco domado* his sensitivity to the emotional and intellectual upheaval which accompanies conversion to a new faith. Both Indian *caciques*, Dulcanquellín and Caupolicán, in their struggle to understand Christian precepts, reveal their skepticism about their new faith due to the discrepancy between its teachings and the contradictory actions of some of its adherents; however, in the end, both chieftains profess their acceptance of Christianity and their belief in its redemptive powers.

The appearance of the devil in each of the American plays is illustrative of the Indians' spiritual blindness. In each play the devil's message is unchanged: the Spaniards have come to America to destroy Satan's rule, to rob and plunder, abuse and exploit. Lope wanted to remind his public that the overwhelming problem for the Spanish nation was to eradicate the pagan practices of the natives. Satan stands in each play as the ultimate enemy of the aims of the Spanish nation in America.

Still, while Lope de Vega exalts the noble missionary effort of his nation, he does not ignore his countrymen's quest for material gain. That the greed of the Spaniards was a perturbing reality for Lope is evidenced by the gradual diminution of its importance in each play. The lust for gold is most clearly seen in the first American play, is severely muted in the second, and has little importance in the last.

Lope, much to his credit, chose not to mask this compulsion of his countrymen; rather, he gave this monetary interest a diminished role in relation to the missionary effort of his country. The conquistadores of *El nuevo mundo*, Terrazas and Arana, finally conclude that the inordinate quest for wealth distracts man from life's central and spiritual purpose. Contrary to the sources of *Arauco domado*, Lope insists that there is no gold in Chile to be exploited. This belief seems to reflect the dramatist's wish that the precious metal disappear, vanish from the Americas so that Spain might go on with its evangelic mission. The desire to diminish the role money plays in the disturbances between Americans and Spaniards is patent when Lope declares, in *Arauco domado*, the optimistic belief that the past exploitative practices of former conquistadores have no bearing upon the present administration of don García. Lope seemed to have been so disturbed by the reports of Spanish abuse of gold that he cleverly tried to link the extraction of precious metals from American mines to its use for religious purposes. He would have his audience believe that the first gold that Columbus brought to Spain was given to the Catholic Monarchs to make a monstrance for the Cathedral of Toledo.

Lope does not view the American Indians with the same benevolent eyes as did Bartolomé de las Casas. In all three plays, the dramatist charges the natives with idolatry and cannibalism, despite the fact that such customs were not, in many cases, part of the practices of the tribe he describes. Furthermore, if Dulcanquellín and Caupolicán are to stand as generalized conceptions of the Americans, one can only conclude that there is little favorable about the dramatist's impressions of the Indians. Dulcanquellín is depicted as a subverter of private and public order. He disregards the sanctity of true love by removing Tacuana from her home and her fiancé; he ruptures peace with the surrounding islands through incessant war. Caupolicán is no more favorably portrayed. He is consumed by earthly lusts and considers himself to be divine. Like Dulcanquellín, Caupolicán is also a subverter of societal order since he has led his indomitable people to rebel against their sworn allegiance to the Spanish nation.

On the other hand, I do not mean to suggest that Lope's vision of the Indian approximates that of Juan Ginés de Sepúlveda. The dramatist reveals his ambiguity as to whether the Indians had ever willingly sworn allegiance to the Spanish monarchy in *Arauco domado*.

While Lope clearly viewed the Indians as a bellicose people—witness Caupolicán, Dulcanquellín, or the martial representation of "Brasil"—he seemed to have admired their heroism in defending their homelands. Fresia is, in the final analysis, a freedom fighter. Her denunciation of her husband and her defiance of Spanish domination are intended to impress upon the audience her uncompromising love for her nation and people. It is here that Lope's admiration for Araucanian heroism is perceived. Lope believed his nation fulfilled a messianic purpose in America which was essential to the Indians' well-being; however, he seems to lament the fact that the evangelization effort was accompanied by excessive violence and the loss of the natives' sense of identity.

The mixture of Spanish and Indian blood is an issue Lope pondered considerably. Lope seemed to have been disturbed by the reports of soldiers' abuse of native women, if one is to judge from his relative silence in *El nuevo mundo* about the massacre of Spanish soldiers because of their sexual abuse of Indian women or don García's lesson to his brother Filipe in *Arauco domado*. Lope suggested to his audience that amorous entanglements between Spanish soldiers and Indian women generally brought disastrous results, should be avoided, and undermined the evangelic nature of the mission.

For all Lope's misgivings about some of the occurrences overseas, he, like many of his contemporaries, maintained a poeticized vision of America and the Americans. That he would maintain the untruth that La Deseada was discovered on Columbus' first voyage, or insist that Brazil was an island in the "Mar Etiópico," indicates a curious distance from the reality of the New World—especially curious in view of the fact that he closely followed historical accounts in his American plays.

Lope's three American plays reveal no firm ideological connection between them and the writings of Francisco de Vitoria or Bartolomé de las Casas. The dramatist has not used his plays as a vehicle to publicly denounce ruthless conquistadores or to question the legal rights of his country to conquer the American Indians.

Lope seems to respond to Las Casas' allegations about Spanish cupidity by suggesting that the spiritual role of Spain is ultimately of far greater importance for the natives as well as the peninsulars. He also seemed to struggle intellectually with a question posed by Vitoria—i.e., whether the Indians had ever knowingly pledged allegiance to the Spanish Crown—but Lope offers his public no firm decision or commitment on this question.

There were justifiable reasons for the dramatist's relative silence concerning these thorny matters. As I have stressed throughout this study, Lope's audience was too heterogeneous for him to expound such controversial ideas without offending someone. Furthermore, it seems that Lope wisely chose to stay on the margins of this fray because some of his own opinions were conflictive and unresolved. That Golden Age theater was relatively silent concerning the conquest of America is a fact. Lope de Vega dealt with the enterprise in his theater more than other dramatists of his generation, thus revealing once again his exceptional awareness of the scope and meaning of Spain's role in world history.

Works Cited

I. *Principal Works by Lope de Vega*

Vega Carpio, Lope de. *Arauco domado.* RAE 12. *Obras de Lope de Vega Carpio.* Ed. Marcelino Menéndez Pelayo. 15 vols. Madrid: Sucesores de Rivadeneyra, 1913.

—. *El Brasil restituido.* RAE 13. *Obras de Lope de Vega Carpio.* Ed. Marcelino Menéndez Pelayo. 15 vols. Madrid: Sucesores de Rivadeneyra, 1902.

—. *El Brasil restituido.* Ed. Gino de Solenni. New York: Instituto de las Españas en los Estados Unidos, 1929.

—. *El nuevo mundo descubierto por Cristóbal Colón.* Ed. J. Lemartinel and C. Minguet. Paris: Presses Universitaires de Lille, 1980.

—. *El nuevo mundo descubierto por Cristóbal Colón.* RAE 11. *Obras de Lope de Vega Carpio.* Ed. Marcelino Menéndez Pelayo. 15 vols. Madrid: Sucesores de Rivadeneyra, 1913.

—. *El peregrino en su patria.* Ed. Myron A. Peyton, Chapel Hill: University of North Carolina P, 1971.

II. *Plays and Epic Poems by Other Writers*

Avila, Gaspar de. *El gobernador prudente. Dos comedias famosas y un auto sacramental.* Ed. José Toribio Medina. Santiago de Chile: Litografía Barcelona, 1915.

Calderón de la Barca, Pedro. *La aurora en Copacabana.* Vol. 1. *Obras completas.* Ed. A. Valbuena Briones. 3 Vols. Madrid: Aguilar, 1966.

Castro y Bellvis, Guillén de, et al. *Algunas hazañas de las muchas de don García Hurtado de Mendoza, Marqués de Cañete.* Vol. 3. RAE *Biblioteca selecta de clásicos españoles: Obras de don Guillén de Castro y Bellvis.* 3 Vols. Madrid: Tipografía de la "Revista Archivos," 1925.

Carvajal, Micael de and Luis Hurtado de Toledo. *Las cortes de la muerte. . . . BAE* 35. Ed. Justo de Sancha. 271 Vols. Madrid: Atlas, 1950. 1–41.

Ercilla, Alonso de. *La Araucana.* Ed. Marcos A. Morínigo and Isaías Lerner. Madrid: Clásicos Castalia, 1979.

González de Bustos, Francisco. *Los españoles en Chile. Parte Veinte y dos de Comedias Nuevas, Escogidas de los mejores ingenios de España.* Madrid: Andrés García de la Iglesia, 1665.

Oña, Pedro de. *Arauco domado. BAE* 29. Ed. Cayetano Rosell. 271 Vols. Madrid: M. Rivadeneyra, 1854.

—. *Arauco domado.* Ed. José Toribio Medina. Santiago de Chile: Imprenta Universitaria, 1917.

—. *Arauco Tamed.* Trans. Charles Maxwell Lancaster and Paul T. Manchester. Albuquerque: U of New Mexico P, 1948.

Rejaule y Toledo, Pedro de. *La bellígera española. Dos comedias famosas y un auto sacramental.* Ed. José Toribio Medina. Santiago de Chile: Litografía Barcelona, 1915.

Télez, Gabriel. *Todo es dar en una cosa, Amazonas en las Indias, La lealtad contra la envidia.* Vol. 2. *Obras dramáticas completas.* Ed. Blanca de los Ríos. 3 Vols. Madrid: Aguilar, 1969.

III. *Historical Accounts of the Conquest*

Avendaño y Vilela, Francisco de. "Relación del viaje y sucesso de la Armada que por mandato de su Magestad partió al Brasil . . . " Seville: Francisco de Lyra, 1625.

Colón, Cristóbal. *El primer viaje de Cristóbal Colón*. Madrid: Instituto Histórico de Marina, 1943.

Fernández de Oviedo, Gonzalo. *Historia general y natural de las Indias*. *BAE* 117. Ed. Juan Pérez de Tudela Bueso. 271 Vols. Madrid: Atlas, 1959.

Guerreiro, Bartolomeu. *Jornada dos vassalos da coroa de Portugal*. Ed. Wilson Lousada. Rio de Janeiro: Divisão de Publicaçoes e Divulgação, 1966.

Las Casas, Bartolomé de. *Tratados*. Prol. L. Hanke. Mexico: Fondo de Cultura y Económica, 1965.

López de Gómara, Francisco. *Historia de las Indias*. *BAE* 22. *Historiadores primitivos de Indias*. Ed. Enrique de Vedia. 271 Vols. Madrid: M. Rivadeneyra, 1852.

Madeiros Correia, João de. "Relaçam verdadeira de todo o succedido na restauração de Bahia de Todos os Sanctos . . . " Oporto: João Rodriguez, 1625.

Núñez Cabeza de Vaca, Alvar. *Naufragios*. Ed. Justo García Morales. Madrid: Aguilar, 1945.

Ruiz, Diego. "Relación que enbió Diego Ruiz . . . " *El Brasil restituido*. Ed. Gino de Solenni. New York: Instituto de las Españas en los Estados Unidos, 1929.

Suárez de Figueroa, Cristóbal. *Hechos de don García Hurtado de Mendoza, Quarto Marqués de Cañete*. Madrid: Imprenta Real, 1613.

Toledo y Osorio, Fadrique de. "Relación de la carta . . . " Seville: Simón Faxardo, 1625.

—. *Relación del sucesso . . . " Cádiz: n.p., 1625.*

Vitoria, Francisco de. Relecciones sobre los indios y el derecho de guerra. Trans. Armando D. Pirotto. Buenos Aires: Espasa-Calpe, S.A., 1946.

IV. *Secondary Sources*

Angulo Iñiguez, Diego and Alfonso Pérez Sánchez. *Historia de la pintura española*. Madrid: CSIC, 1969.

Bleiberg, Germán, ed. *Diccionario de historia de España*. 2 Vols. Chapel Hill: U of North Carolina P, 1967.

Castro, Américo. *El pensamiento de Cervantes*. Madrid: Hernando, 1925.

—. *The Spaniards*. Trans. Willard F. King and Selma Margaretten. Berkeley: University of California P, 1971.

Castro, Américo and Hugo A. Rennert. *Vida de Lope de Vega*. Salamanca: Anaya, 1968.

Corominas, Juan M. "Las fuentes literarias del *Arauco domado*." *Lope de Vega y los orígenes del teatro español: Actas del I Congreso Internacional sobre Lope de Vega*. Madrid: Edi-6, (1981): 161–170.

Crawford, J.P. Wickersham. *Vida y obras de Cristóbal Suárez de Figueroa*. Trans. Narciso Alonso Cortés. Valladolid: Colegio de Santiago, 1911.

Cueva, Juan de la. *El infamador*. Ed. Francisco de Icaza. Madrid: Clásicos Castellanos, 1941.

Diez del Corral y Pedruzo, Luis. *Velázquez, la monarquía e Italia*. Madrid: Espasa-Calpe, 1979.

Dille, Glen F. "El descubrimiento y la conquista de América en la *comedia*." *Hispania* 71 (1988): 492–502.

Dinamarca, Salvador. *Estudio de "Arauco domado" de Pedro de Oña*. New York: Hispanic Institute in the United States, 1952.

Elliott, John Huxtable. *Imperial Spain: 1469–1716*. New York: Saint Martin's P, 1967.

Elliott, John Huxtable and Jonathan Brown. *A Palace for a King: The Buen Retiro and the Court of Philip IV*. New Haven: Yale U P, 1980.

Enciclopedia Universal Ilustrada Vol. 9. "Brasil."

Entrambasaguas, Joaquín. *Estudios sobre Lope de Vega*. 3 vols. Madrid: CSIC, 1946.

—. *Vida de Lope de Vega*. Barcelona: Labor, 1936.

Fernández-Shaw, C.M. "América en Lope de Vega." *Cuadernos hispanoamericanos* 54 (1963): 675–697.

Fite, Emerson David and A. Freeman, Eds. *A Book of Old Maps*. Cambridge: Harvard UP, 1926.

Gibson, Charles. *Spain in America*. New York: Harper Torch, 1966.

Gilman, Stephen, "Lope de Vega and the 'Indias en su ingenio.'" *Spanische Literatur im Goldenen Zeitalter*. Ed. H. Baader and E. Laos. Frankfort: Klosterman (1973): 102–116.

Hanke, Lewis. *The Spanish Struggle for Justice in the Conquest of America*. Boston: Little, Brown, 1965.

—, Ed. *A History of Latin American Civilization: Sources and Interpretations*. Boston: Little, Brown, 1967.

Jackson, Gabriel. *The Making of Medieval Spain*. London: Thames and Hudson, 1972.

Jiménez Rueda, Julio. *Juan Ruiz de Alarcón y su tiempo*. Mexico: José Porrua e Hijos, 1939.

Justi, Karl. *Velázquez y su siglo*. Trans. Pedro Marrades. Madrid: Espasa-Calpe, 1953.

King, Willard F. "Cervantes' *Numancia* and Imperial Spain." *MLN* 94 (1979): 200–221.

Lomax, Derek W. *The Reconquest of Spain*. New York: Longmans, 1978.

Martínez Torrón, Diego. "Valores informativos en el teatro de Lope de Vega: La fuente de *El Brasil restituido*." *Lope de Vega y los orígenes del teatro español: Actas del I Congreso Internacional sobre Lope de Vega*. Madrid: Edi-6 (1981): 151–160.

Menéndez Pelayo, Marcelino, Ed. *Antología de poetas hispano-americanos*. 4 Vols. Madrid: Sucesores de Rivadeneyra, 1895.

—. "Arauco domado." Vol. 34. *Obras completas: Estudios sobre el teatro de Lope de Vega*. Ed. Enrique Sánchez Reyes. 65 vols. Santander: Aldus, 1949. 193–209.

—. "El Brasil restituido." Vol. 34. *Obras completas: Estudios sobre el teatro de Lope de Vega*. Ed. Enrique Sánchez Reyes. 65 Vols. Santander: Aldus, 1949. 228–242.

—. "El nuevo mundo descubierto por Cristóbal Colón." Vol. 33. *Obras completas: Estudios sobre el teatro de Lope de Vega*. Ed. Enrique Sánchez Reyes. 65 Vols. Santander: Aldus, 1949. 306–325.

Menéndez Pidal, Ramón. *El Padre Las Casas: Su doble personalidad*. Madrid: Espasa-Calpe, 1963.

Mesonero Romanos, Ramón de, Ed. *BAE, Dramáticos contemporáneos a Lope de Vega*. Madrid: Atlas, 1951.

Miró Quesada, Aurelio. *América en el teatro de Lope de Vega*. Lima: n.p., 1935.

Morínigo, Marcos A. *América en el teatro de Lope de Vega*. Buenos Aires: Instituto de Filología, 1946.

Morley, S. Griswold and Courtney Bruerton. *Cronología de las comedias de Lope de Vega.* Madrid: Gredos, S.A., 1968.
—. *The Chronology of the Plays of Lope de Vega.* New York: MLA, 1940.
Nolasco Pérez, Pedro. "Tirso de Molina: Pasajero a Indias." *Estudios: Tirso de Molina: Ensayos sobre la biografía y la obra del padre maestro Gabriel Téllez* (1949): 185–197.
Noreña, Carlos. "Francisco de Vitoria, America and the Empire." *Revista de Estudios Hispánicos* 12 (1978): 71–89.
Rennert, H.A. "Notes on Some *Comedias* of Lope de Vega." *MLN* 1 (1905–6): 96–110.
—. *The Life of Lope de Vega.* Glasgow: Gowans and Gray, 1904.
—. *The Spanish Stage in the Time of Lope de Vega.* New York: The Hispanic Society of America, 1909.
Scott, James Brown. *The Spanish Origin of International Law.* Washington, D.C.: School of Foreign Service at Georgetown U P, 1928.
Seneca. *Thystes. Four Tragedies and Octavia.* Trans. E.F. Watling. Baltimore: Penguin, 1966.
Shergold, N.D. *A History of the Spanish Stage From Medieval Times Until the End of the Seventeenth Century.* Oxford: Clarendon, 1967.
Shergold, N.D. and J.E. Varey. "Some Palace Performances of Seventeenth-Century Plays." *Bulletin of Hispanic Studies* 40 (1963): 212–244.
Solenni, Gino de. "On the Source of *El Brasil restituido.*" *Revista de Estudios Hispánicos* 1 (1928): 168–169.
Spencer, Forest Eugene and Randolph Schevill. *The Dramatic Works of Luis Vélez de Guevara: Their Plots, Sources, and Bibliography.* Berkeley: University of California P, 1937.
Turner, Daymond. *Gonzalo Fernández de Oviedo y Valdés: An Annotated Bibliography.* Chapel Hill: University of North Carolina P, 1967.
Umpierre, Gustavo. *Songs in the Plays of Lope de Vega.* London: Tamesis, 1965.
Uslar, Pietri, Arturo. "Eso que los europeos llamaron nuevo mundo." *Americas* 28 (1976): 9–16.
Valbuena Briones, Angel. *Perspectiva crítica de los dramas de Calderón.* Madrid: Rialpa, 1965.
Vega Carpio, Lope Félix de. *Adonis y Venus.* RAE 6. Ed. Marcelino Menéndez Pelayo. *Obras de Lope de Vega Carpio.* 15 Vols. Madrid: Sucesores de Rivadeneyra, 1913.
—. *Fuenteovejuna. Diez comedias del Siglo de Oro.* Eds. J. Martel and H. Alpern. 2nd ed. New York: Harper and Row, 1969. 71–142.
—. *La Dragontea.* Ed. Gregorio Marañón. Burgos: Aldecoa, 1935.
—. *La Dragontea.* Vol. 2. *Lope de Vega: Obras escogidas: Poesía y Prosa.* Ed. Federico Carlos Sainz de Robles. 3 Vols. Madrid: Aguilar, 1964.
—. *Laurel de Apolo.* Vol. 2. *Lope de Vega: Obras escogidas: Poesía y Prosa.* Ed. Federico Carlos Sainz de Robles. 3 Vols. Madrid: Aguilar, 1964.
Whitaker, Shirley B. "The First Performance of Calderón's *El sitio de Bredá.*" *Renaissance Quarterly* 31 (1978): 515–531.
Zavala, Silvio. "New Viewpoints on the Spanish Colonization of America." *History of Latin American Civilization: Sources and Interpretations.* Ed. L. Hanke. Boston: Little, Brown (1967): 126–154.

Index